THE EU & UKRAINE

Neighbours, Friends, Partners?

edited by
Ann Lewis

THE FEDERAL TRUST
europe's eastern borders

This book is published by the Federal Trust, whose aim is to enlighten public debate on federal issues of national, continental and global government. It does this in the light of its statutes which state that it shall promote 'studies in the principles of international relations, international justice and supranational government.'

The Trust conducts enquiries, promotes seminars and conferences and publishes reports and teaching materials. The Federal Trust is the UK member of the Trans-European Policy Studies Association (TEPSA), a grouping of fifteen think-tanks from Member States of the European Union.

Up-to-date information about the Federal Trust can be found on the internet at www.fedtrust.co.uk

ISBN 1 903403 18 9

NOTE: All contributors to this volume are writing in a personal capacity. Views expressed should not be taken as those of their government or institution.

The publishers acknowledge with thanks the helpful support of Weber Shandwick Public Affairs, Brussels, and White's Creative Solutions, Kiev, whose financial contribution has made this publication possible.

The Federal Trust is a Registered Charity No. 272241

Dean Bradley House, 52 Horseferry Road,

London SW1P 2AF

Company Limited by Guarantee No.1269848

Marketing and Distribution by Kogan Page Ltd

Printed by JW Arrowsmith

Contents

Introduction by the Editor 7

Ukraine: A Brief History 13
Elizabeth Teague

Part 1
Overviews from Three Perspectives

Ukraine and the EU: It Takes Two to Tango 21
Anatoliy Zlenko

The EU and Ukraine: Ten Years After Independence 27
Javier Solana

The EU and Ukraine: A Transatlantic View 31
John Tedstrom

Part 2
Ukraine: Political Progress and Prospects

The Political Process in Ukraine: Democratisation or Virtualisation? ... 39
Andrew Wilson

Local Democracy: Unfinished Business 55
Serhiy Maksymenko

Between a (Russian) Rock and a (Crimean Tatar) Hard Place?
Ethnic, Linguistic and Minority Issues 61
Bill Bowring

Unleashed, but Still Muzzled: The Media in Ukraine 71
Olexiy Solohubenko

NGO Development in Ukraine: The Beginnings of Civil Society 81
Vira Nanivska

Part 3
Ukraine: Economic Progress and Prospects

Ukraine: The Evolution of its Economy Since Independence 93
Edilberto Segura

Energy: Current Problems and Long-Term Strategy 103
Volodymyr L. Saprykin

Gas Transit: A Critical Strategic Issue for Ukraine 117
Frank Duffield

Beyond Chernobyl: A Way Forward? 123
Michael McCulloch

Part 4
Foreign Policy, Defence and Regional Relations

Ten Years On: Ukraine's Foreign Policy Priorities 133
Anatoliy Orel

Ukraine and Nato: A Reviving Partnership? 139
James Sherr

Two Eagles: Story of the Polish-Ukrainian Battalion 153
Robert Pszczel

Ukraine and Russia: A Geopolitical Turn? 157
James Sherr

Ukraine: Poland's Failing Project 171
Roman Wolczuk

Part 5
The EU and Ukraine

Ukraine and the EU: What Prospects for Integration 183
Inna Pidluska

Ukraine's Relations with Europe: A British Perspective 199
Roger Liddle

EU-Ukraine Relations: A View from the European Parliament .. 207
Christopher Beazley

The EU Common Strategy on Ukraine:
A Response to Ukraine's 'pro-European Choice'? 213
Gwendolyn Sasse

Ukraine-EU Economic Co-operation: The Soviet Legacy Strikes Back . 221
Igor V. Burakovsky

Barriers to European Investment in Ukraine 233
Yuriy Petrus

A Success Story: Ukraine International Airlines 237
Richard Creagh

Justice and Home Affairs Beyond Enlargement
What Kind of Border? 241
Inna Pidluska

EU Aid Policy: More Commitment Required 253
Andre Vanhaeverbeke

Ukraine: Where Next? 259
Ann Lewis

APPENDICES

Appendix 1 269
Appendix 2 285
Appendix 3 293

Abbrevations 309
Notes on Contributors 313

Notes on TEPSA and the British Embassy Seminar Series 319

UKRAINE AND ITS NEIGHBOURS
POLAND
BELARUS
RUSSIAN FEDERATION
SLOVAKIA
HUNGARY
ROMANIA
MOLDOVA
CHISNAU
BLACK SEA
CRIMEA
Lutsk
Rivno
Lviv
Zhytomyr
KIEV
Chernihiv
Sumy
Ternopil
Khmelnytsky
Uzhhorod
Ivano-Frankivsk
Chernivtsi
Vinnytsya
Cherkasy
Poltava
Kharkiv
Luhansk
Kirovohrad
Dnipropetrovsk
Donetsk
Zaporizhya
Mykolayiv
Odessa
Kherson
Simferopol
Sevastopol
International Boundary
Republic or Oblast Boundary
National Capital
Republic or Oblast Centre
0 50 100 miles
0 50 100 150 kms

INTRODUCTION

Ukraine is the second largest country in Europe and has a population of some 50 million. It occupies a strategic position between Central Europe and Russia, sits astride the major energy routes into Western Europe and is an important channel for westward migration. Following EU enlargement, Ukraine will be on our new frontier. Yet Ukraine is comparatively little known in much of Western Europe: there are few tourists, little trade, and scant coverage in the press, bar the occasional scandal.

Now seems a good moment to take stock: 10 years since independence, parliamentary elections due in March 2002 and a crucial presidential election looming in 2004. This book aims to provide the general reader with a multifaceted view of the country at this time: how it has fared since independence, its prospects for the future, and the development of its relations with the EU.

Ukraine embarked on independence in 1991, following the collapse of the Soviet Union, with a peculiarly difficult inheritance. There had never before been an independent Ukraine within the current borders. It had a chequered history, constantly split and re-formed. It had distinct regions with their own cultural identity and plenty of scope for friction. The administrative machinery had hitherto been run by the one-party state ruled from Moscow. Industry and most of the economy was run as part of a larger Soviet-wide enterprise which made few concessions to local autonomy. Ukraine was a supplier of parts to the great Soviet machine.

Independent Ukraine had to establish itself quickly as a self-sustaining entity, with precious few examples to follow. It is scarcely surprising that the process was fraught with difficulty.

Ukraine is a palpably different place now from what it was 10 years ago. It has a full array of democratic structures, information is available to those who look for it, people can travel and express their views. Furthermore, it has remained calm and stable through very difficult times. And yet there is a long way to go before Ukraine becomes a fully-fledged democracy. One of the recurring themes of this book is that of work in progress.

Ukraine's first President, Leonid Kravchuk, oversaw the establishment of a first parliamentary framework and fended off attempts to reabsorb Ukraine completely into a Russia-dominated Commonwealth of Independent States (CIS), but his term of office (1991-94) was marked by a failure to reform the command economy, hyper-inflation, and a catastrophic decline in the standard of living. GDP was halved. He made overtures to the EU and forged good relations with Nato, including membership of the Partnership for Peace. To the EU, preoccupied with its crucial relationship with Russia, with the Central European countries embarking on radical reform and with crises in the Balkans, Ukraine was of secondary interest. For the West in general the main concerns relating to Ukraine were the aftermath of Chernobyl and the removal of nuclear weapons. Nevertheless work began on a new framework for relations with the EU, and substantial aid programmes were established.

President Kuchma was elected in 1994 on a platform of reform, opening to the EU and other Western institutions, and improved relations with Russia. His first couple of years saw a new post-Soviet Constitution adopted, a new currency introduced, and the economy stabilised with Western help.

A Partnership and Co-operation Agreement (PCA) with the EU, the first with a post-Soviet state, was signed in 1994 though not ratified until 1998. The PCA provided a blueprint for a closer relationship, including political dialogue and co-operation over a broad field, especially trade and investment. (See the 'brief guide' in Appendix 1.) But its commitments fell short of those in the 'Europe Agreements' with Central European countries which were seen as stepping-stones to EU membership.

The PCA was scarcely ratified when President Kuchma approved a much more ambitious 'Strategy of Ukraine's Integration to the EU' (Appendix 2).

This defined associate membership of the EU as Ukraine's top medium-term goal, and set out a programme of internal change designed to enable it to gain full membership by 2007.

The EU adopted its own 'Common Strategy on Ukraine' in late 1999 (Appendix 3). This acknowledged Ukraine's European aspirations, but made no further commitments as regards Ukraine's future membership. Since then there has been something of a stand-off, with Ukraine pressing for a 'positive signal' that its efforts will be rewarded with at least associate membership once it meets the requirements, and the EU merely indicating that Ukraine should concentrate on meeting its existing commitments before any change is considered.

On the ground, meanwhile, progress in building a mature democracy and market economy was slow, and GDP continued to decline until 2000, when, following President Kuchma's reelection and the appointment of a reformist Prime Minister, Viktor Yushchenko, Ukraine enjoyed its first economic growth since independence. The Prime Minister succumbed to a vote of no confidence in Parliament in May 2001, when his reforms ran into strong opposition from Communist deputies – still the largest faction in Parliament – and from influential tycoons. But so far the reforms have been maintained. Ukraine's economy has continued to show healthy growth in 2001, leading the IMF and World Bank to resume lending in September.

Ukraine seems to have risen somewhat on the EU's agenda in 2000-2001 thanks to these signs of reform and economic recovery, Ukraine's generally constructive approach to foreign policy issues especially in the Balkans, and, above all, the prospect of enlargement, the first wave of which will give Ukraine a direct frontier with the EU with considerable potential for instability. Ukraine, for its part, is keen that the EU's new Eastern border should not become a new iron (or paper) curtain isolating Ukraine from the European heartland.

This book looks at various aspects of Ukraine's internal and external development of relevance to its European aspirations, and at various facets of EU/Ukraine relations. It does not claim to be comprehensive – impossible in one short volume. But it does look at issues from a wide variety of perspectives, with contributions from policy-makers and analysts, professionals and practitioners, from Ukraine, the EU and beyond. It presents a kaleidoscopic picture, but hopefully one the reader will find illuminating and thought-provoking.

The book is divided into 5 sections, following a brief history which casts useful light on the background to various issues of current relevance. Part I presents 3 overviews of EU/Ukraine relations, from senior figures from Ukraine, the EU and, for an outside view, the USA. Part II looks at political issues, Part III at economic issues, Part IV at foreign policy, defence and regional relations, and Part V at EU/Ukraine relations. Each section opens with one or more broad surveys of the subject, followed by several articles covering specific issues or case studies. Each section contains contributions from both Ukrainian and Western authors. The book ends with some personal observations by way of conclusions.

All contributors to this volume are writing in a personal capacity. Views expressed should not be taken as those of their government or institution. Short biographical notes on authors can be found at the end of the book.

In this book Ukrainian names have mostly been transliterated directly from the cyrillic original into English. The exceptions are names which have familiar English equivalents, including Kiev, Odessa, Crimea and Chernobyl.

This book, like its predecessor on Kaliningrad, had its origins in a conference organised by TEPSA (the Trans European Policy Studies Association) and the British Embassy in Brussels. The conference on Ukraine, held on 24 April 2001, coincided with a vote of no-confidence in the Prime Minister in the Ukrainian Parliament and a vote in the Council of Europe to expel Ukraine. Neither issue was resolved that day (the former subsequently went through, the latter was rejected) but the crisis made the conference particularly lively, relevant and timely. A few of the articles in this volume, including the overviews, are based on presentations at that conference.

I am grateful to the organisers of the Brussels Conference, especially Margareta Theelen and James Baxendale; to the many people who helped with suggestions for additional contributors; and above all to the authors themselves, with whom I have enjoyed a sometimes lengthy but always interesting dialogue during the course of editing this book.

Ann Lewis
London
November 2001

UKRAINE
A BRIEF HISTORY

Elizabeth Teague

The name Ukraine comes from the Russian *okraina*, meaning outskirts, or borderland. The territory has experienced centuries of invasion and domination by foreign rulers – the Polish-Lithuanian Commonwealth, the Ottoman Empire, the Crimean Khanate, the Russian and Hapsburg Empires, and the Germans. For much of its recent history, Ukraine has been divided between the Ukrainian-speaking West, which belonged to Poland until 1939, and the Russian-speaking East, which became part of Russia in 1654. A Ukrainian national movement can be traced to the seventeenth century but, until the country became fully independent in 1991, Ukraine had known independence and national unity only for brief periods in the seventeenth century and in 1918-21.

The Ukrainians are descended from the Southern branch of the Eastern Slavs. In the ninth century AD, the Eastern Slavs united in the feudal state of Kievan Rus – the first Russian polity. This was a loosely organised group of city-states. Its capital, Kiev, grew rich on trade in amber, furs and slaves from the North which it exchanged for silks and spices from the South. In 988, having researched the major alternative religions, Prince Vladimir of Kiev converted his people to Orthodox Christianity.

Kievan Rus was the dominant force in Eastern Europe until its conquest by the Mongols in 1240. That conquest precipitated the separate development of the major Eastern Slav nations. When the Mongols were finally repulsed from the Slav lands in the sixteenth century, a new Russian state came into being not around Kiev but around Moscow.

In 1349, Western Ukraine (Eastern Galicia) was annexed by the Polish-Lithuanian Commonwealth. The local boyars were forced to adopt the Catholic faith and the rule of the Polish and Lithuanian nobility was established in Western Ukraine. Western and Eastern Ukrainians became divided not only by territory but also by culture. The divisions deepened over the centuries and, under various foreign influences (mainly those of Austria-Hungary and the Russian Empire), two Ukrainian identities evolved.

In 1647, the Cossack hetman (military leader) Bohdan Khmelnytsky led a rebellion and freed Kiev and other parts of today's Ukraine from Polish rule. The following year, he established an independent Ukrainian Cossack state. This lasted only until 1654 when, threatened by the Poles, Khmelnytsky turned to Russia for help. In January of that year, Khmelnytsky signed the Treaty of Pereyaslav with the Russian Tsar. Under its terms, Ukraine was united with Russia. So ended Ukraine's first brief experience of independence and three centuries of Russian domination began.

The act of union has been the subject of bitter debate. Russian historians tend to celebrate it as the reunion of two fraternal nations, while Ukrainian historians have tended to depict it as a retrograde step. Russian rule was repressive and before long the Ukrainian Cossacks rebelled against it. In 1659, they appealed to Poland for support and reasserted their independence from Russia. In 1667, Russia and Poland partitioned Ukrainian territory along the River Dnepr. Eastern Ukraine remained under Russian control while Western Ukraine, including the city of Kiev, returned to Polish control. But Poland had entered a period of decline. Under the first partition of Poland (1772), Western Ukraine was annexed by the Austro-Hungarian Empire, of which it remained a part until the end of the First World War. Eastern Ukraine remained under the influence of Orthodoxy and the Russian Empire.

Ukrainian intellectuals responded to the Tsarist yoke in the nineteenth century by founding a strong nationalist movement, based largely on a reinvention of Ukrainian history that depicted the Khmelnytsky era as an ideal age and seventeenth-century Ukrainian Cossackdom as the first Ukrainian nation-state. The rise of Ukrainian national consciousness provoked a tough response from the Russian authorities. In the 1860s, the Russian Interior

Ministry banned the use of the Ukrainian language in public places; by the 1880s, the language was outlawed entirely.

A movement for Ukrainian independence emerged in response to Russia's defeat in the First World War, and the Ukrainian People's Republic was established. In January 1918, its Rada (Parliament) formally proclaimed Ukrainian independence. By 1919, Ukraine was engulfed by civil war. Six mutually hostile armies occupied the country: those of Ukrainian nationalists, Bolsheviks, Russian Whites, the Entente, Poles and peasant anarchists. The Kiev-based Ukrainian National Republic, led by Semyon Petlyura, formally united with the West Ukrainian National Republic based in Lviv, while a Soviet Ukrainian regime was established in Kharkiv in the Eastern part of the country. In the summer of 1920 the Poles, under General Pilsudski, advanced as far as Kiev. Their purpose was to capture Ukraine's fertile grainlands and prevent the establishment of communism in Eastern Europe. The Red Army counterattacked, drove the Kiev-based Ukrainian army out of Ukraine and reached almost as far as Warsaw. The confrontation ended in the Treaty of Riga in 1921, which brought Ukraine's brief experience of independence to an end and fixed the Russo-Polish frontiers. Ukraine was repartitioned. Eastern Ukraine was incorporated into the USSR, while Western and Eastern Galicia returned to Poland.

In December 1922, Ukraine was declared a Union republic within the USSR. The articles of Union were signed by representatives of the Communist Parties of the four republics concerned – the RSFSR, Ukraine, Belorussia and Transcaucasia. The Ukrainian language was briefly revived in the early Soviet period, only to be suppressed again under Stalin. Three million Ukrainians had died during the civil war of 1918-20, and an estimated seven to ten million more perished as a result of the Great Famine of 1931-32. Historians believe the famine was deliberately created by Stalin in order, first, to gain control of the countryside by replacing private, peasant farmsteads with large, state-owned collective farms and, second, to destroy Ukraine's national identity by undermining its agrarian-based social structure.

Soviet rule brought Ukraine rapid industrialisation, urbanisation and mass education, but the Ukrainian intelligentsia was ruthlessly persecuted and the Ukrainian language and culture suffered serious setbacks as a result of policies of Sovietisation and Russification.

In September 1939, the USSR invaded Eastern Galicia (then Eastern Poland) in accordance with the secret protocols to the Molotov-Ribbentrop Pact. Stalin turned the territory into Ukraine's Ternopil, Lviv, and Ivano-Frankivsk Regions. In June 1940, the USSR annexed Northern Bukovina and Bessarabia from Romania. Stalin created Ukraine's Chernivtsi Region out of Northern Bukovina, the North Bessarabian district of Khotyn and the Romanian area around Hertsa. Southern Bessarabia was turned into the Southern extension of Ukraine's Odessa Oblast.

Germany invaded the Soviet Union in June 1941 and Kiev was taken by Nazi troops in September 1941. A few thousand Ukrainians collaborated with the Nazis, and thousands of others later fought as guerrillas against the Red Army, but millions joined Russians and others in fighting against the Nazis.

After the war, Eastern Galicia remained within the USSR, while Polish-settled Western Galicia was returned to Poland. The Soviet authorities took care to keep Ukraine under tight control. The leaders of Ukraine's Communist Party and secret police were among the toughest in the USSR, and a policy of Russification was implemented throughout the country. Use of the Ukrainian language was banned from government and education. Western Ukraine was regarded with particular suspicion.

A critical role in Ukraine's path to independence and democracy was played by Rukh — the country's main independence movement which emerged in the late 1980s, under the impact of Gorbachev's *glasnost* and *perestroika*. On 16 July 1990, Ukraine's Parliament adopted a Rukh-inspired 'Declaration of State Sovereignty of Ukraine' that not only proclaimed Ukraine's sovereignty vis-à-vis Moscow but included assurances regarding the protection of individual rights and freedoms.

On 24 August 1991, following the failed coup in Moscow, the Ukrainian Parliament issued a Declaration of Independence. This was confirmed in a national referendum held on 1 December 1991, when over 90 per cent of those who voted cast their ballots in favour of Ukrainian independence. Former Communist official Leonid Kravchuk was elected President at the same time. The outcome dealt a fatal blow to Gorbachev's attempts to hold the USSR together and was followed within a week by the formal collapse of the USSR. On 7 December 1991, Kravchuk met Russian President Yeltsin and Belarusian President Shushkevich at a forest retreat outside Brest and announced to a startled world that they were disbanding the USSR and creating a new association, the Commonwealth of Independent States. Ukraine and the other former Soviet republics became independent countries. Gorbachev resigned and the USSR ceased to exist.

The population of Ukraine is ethnically diverse, with people of non-Ukrainian nationality making up over a quarter of the total. Of Ukraine's 51 million inhabitants at the time of the 1989 population census, 73 per cent identified themselves as ethnic Ukrainians and 22 per cent as ethnic Russians. As one travels East from the Polish border in the foothills of the Carpathian Mountains, through Kiev and on to the city of Luhansk on the Russian border, the internal variation is clearly apparent. In the West, the population is predominantly ethnic Ukrainian and Catholic (Uniate). As one moves eastward, Ukrainian language gradually gives way to Russian, and Catholicism (Roman and Greek) to Orthodoxy.

While Western Ukraine tends to look toward Western Europe, the heavily industrialised Eastern regions tend to look toward Russia, as does the Crimean Autonomous Republic. The only administrative region in Ukraine with an ethnic Russian majority, Crimea was part of Russia until 1954, when it was transferred to Ukraine by Soviet leader Nikita Khrushchev. Special problems are faced by the indigenous population of the peninsula, the Crimean Tatars. A Turkic people, the Tatars were deported to Central Asia by Stalin in 1944. Only in 1990 did the Soviet authorities permit them to return to their homeland. About half of them – some quarter of a million people – have since returned to Crimea, where they now make up about 10 per cent of the population. An approximately equal number remain in Central Asia. Those in Crimea are living in difficult circumstances; many are unable to find work and large numbers have inadequate housing.

Commentators speak of Ukraine's Janus-like character – looking both East and West. Telling in this respect was the fate of efforts made in the early 1930s to modernise the capital, Kiev. At that time, plans were drawn up for a new Soviet administrative centre on the site of the old city – the area between St Sophia's Cathedral and St Michael's monastery. Plans called for a massive boulevard leading along the hilltop and rounded off at the river end by two huge, semicircular buildings. One of these was built and now houses the Ministry of Foreign Affairs while, on the adjoining corner, the old monastery was demolished in order to make place for what was to be another huge government building. Before the plans could be executed, however, they ran into dissent. A large statue of Lenin was to be erected at the central point where the two semicircular buildings met. But should the leader of the October Revolution look westward, down the boulevard, as common sense and architectural convention would suggest, or should he turn his back on passers-by and gaze, as ideology would dictate, eastward toward Moscow? Neither solution seemed right. In the end, the plans were abandoned – chiefly because of the onset of World War Two – and only the Foreign Ministry was completed. To this day, however, the episode seems to symbolise Ukraine's situation, poised between East and West.

FURTHER READING

Anna Reid, *Borderland: A Journey through the History of Ukraine*, London: Phoenix, 1998.

Orest Subtelny, *Ukraine: A History*, second edition, Toronto: University of Toronto Press, 1994.

1
Overviews from Three Perspectives

UKRAINE AND THE EU
IT TAKES TWO TO TANGO

Anatoliy Zlenko

2001 is a special year in modern European history. Many countries, including Ukraine, are marking the tenth anniversary of their independent existence and the collapse of totalitarianism. In my view this is a proper occasion to take a distant look at the events that shook the world ten years ago and to analyse their impact on today's Europe.

The dissolution of the Soviet Union and the Warsaw Pact, rapid economic changes in the countries of the former socialist camp, and the reunification of Germany have added unforgettable pages to the history of Europe. The restoration of Ukrainian independence is not the least significant item on this list. Moreover, it can rightly be said that the Ukrainian referendum of 1 December 1991 put an effective end to the 70-year history of the Soviet Empire. In some 18 months the face of Europe became almost unrecognisable.

I might be wrong, but I have the impression those events took the Europeans by surprise. And, although they managed quickly to overcome their initial confusion towards the countries of Central Europe, not everyone could immediately believe that Ukraine's independence was here to stay.

At that point no-one in the European Union was willing to discuss – even in theory – the possibility that Ukraine might join the EU. Ukraine just did not fit the vision of the future configuration of the Union which was in place at that time. There were and probably remain some stereotypes:

- The Ukrainians had lived under a communist regime for too long to be able to associate themselves with European democratic values;
- Ukraine was a zone of special vital interests to Russia, so attempts to break this connection would ultimately infuriate Moscow;
- Ukraine was too bulky to integrate painlessly into the EU. Some people placed Ukraine in another civilization altogether, arguing that Ukrainian culture was incompatible with Western European traditions.

I could subscribe to all those statements had I not myself seen the destruction of even more viable stereotypes during the last decade.

I sincerely rejoice over our friends and partners in Central Europe who have managed to make a powerful economic breakthrough and get really close to EU accession. However we should not ignore the fact that this success was achieved against the background of a clear signal from the EU. The signal read that the people of those countries could count on their prospective place in the common European house.

Almost all Europe's borders were quite soon open to the residents of Central Europe. Many of those who were brought up under communist dogma could see for themselves the goals worth striving for. A trip to Vienna for an ordinary Czech or to Germany for an ordinary Pole became commonplace.

Central Europe was being filled with the spirit of European integration, which was gradually absorbed into the national psyche.

And what about Ukraine? Having proclaimed European integration a priority in our foreign policy, Ukraine received quite a different response. While the countries of Eastern Europe were told 'We will admit you to the EU, but only after you have carried out reforms and met certain criteria', Ukraine was told 'First you must carry out reforms and meet certain criteria and only after will we discuss the possibility of membership'.

In fact, things have changed little for Ukrainians who want to visit EU countries. Before, they had to pass through painstaking checks by their own security services to obtain permission to travel abroad; now this function is performed by the strict Schengen rules. In addition, not every Ukrainian citizen can afford to pay the substantial sum required for a visa. Back in 1991 it would have been hard to believe that we would meet the new Millennium fenced off from Europe by a new wall, made of paper this time.

I feel that many would like to ask – has Ukraine done everything possible to get closer to Europe? My answer is unambiguous – no. We have by no means done everything we could.

Moreover, we have made a number of mistakes even in what we have done. We have not always been consistent. Often we have been hasty. Even more often – indecisive. However, from another point of view we have made quite a lot of progress, taking into account our starting conditions. We have built our state infrastructure almost from the ground up. We have established financial and legislative systems. We have preserved inter-ethnic peace and stability. We have managed to rescue our economy, more than half of which used to be oriented towards the interests of the military industries of the former USSR, from what looked like imminent collapse. As a result, in 2000 the economic reforms in Ukraine started to yield their first and quite real fruits.

Nowadays European integration is not only our strategic goal, for which we carry out our economic and political reforms. For us it has become an inalienable component of our long-term national development strategy, a factor which at the same time gives meaning, purpose and direction to the reforms. We may even think of it as a means of achieving our domestic development goals.

I think that favourable conditions are gradually emerging in Ukraine to start the engine of European integration at full power. I would say that now our country has an opportunity which it has probably not had since 1991.

At that time the European express passed through the Ukrainian station without even slowing down. We hope that this time it will be hard for the passengers on the Eurotrain to overlook a modern terminal which, though still incomplete, is being built to entirely European standards.

An active dialogue between Ukraine and the European Union is under way. A Ukrainian co-ordinating executive authority on European integration is being set up under a special Order of the President of Ukraine.

We are moving actively towards accession to the WTO. In particular, our representatives recently signed with WTO member states a range of important bilateral protocols on mutual access to markets.

Some say Ukraine is making excessive and inappropriate work by flooding the European Commission with unrealistic proposals for broadening co-operation with the EU in this or that sphere.

I recall that earlier we were criticised for quite the opposite – for insufficient activity and lack of initiative. I do not intend to go into these proposals. The European Commission knows them very well.

I want to stress only one thing: we are now both willing and able to develop mutually beneficial co-operation with the EU in certain fields, including security, home affairs, and transportation of energy resources. We already have some positive experience, for example our successful co-operation in dealing with the crisis on the Macedonian-Yugoslav border.

Ukraine is in a position to be a fully-fledged participant in the realisation of a new energy strategy for the European Union. We have suggested the establishment of an international mechanism for managing the Ukrainian gas transportation system and would welcome the participation of strategic investors in this. One should not forget that Ukraine has exceptional transit and transport potential. In my opinion, it would be a big mistake for the European countries not to take up this opportunity.

However, it is impossible for Ukraine to take part in relevant European programmes and strategies without some forthcoming gesture from the EU. For example, in our view the European Union could consider the possibility of extending to Ukraine some elements of the pre-accession strategy developed for candidate countries.

When I hear about discussions within the EU regarding the future model of the Union I cannot but worry about proposals aimed at sealing the doors of the EU to certain countries a priori. Though the criteria for designating countries to be excluded are unclear, the approach is quite familiar. After the trials of the last decade in Europe, there are still some people who believe that the stability and security of EU countries can be ensured only by denying access to the Union to what they consider to be potential sources of tension.

I think the reverse: that we can eliminate sources of tension only by bringing the relevant countries into the sphere of European co-operation and integration. The beginning of the twenty-first century has brought us the chance to rid ourselves of boundary lines within our continent and to build a truly united Europe.

Charles de Gaulle once said jokingly: 'It will not be any European statesman who will unite Europe: Europe will be united by the Chinese'. I think that the deep meaning of these words is that the Europeans must finally realise that the destiny of Europe depends only on themselves. It depends not only on current EU Member States, but also to a great extent on those at present beyond its borders.

Now is the time for us to think about our vision of the continent in, say, fifteen years. At the same time, when making any decision we should assess its necessity from not just yesterday's or even today's positions – we should try to look a little bit ahead.

Nevertheless I remain optimistic. So I allow myself to disagree with Charles de Gaulle, whom I respect very much: the Europeans will unite Europe.

THE EU AND UKRAINE
TEN YEARS AFTER INDEPENDENCE

Javier Solana

The period since Ukraine gained independence has brought with it immense changes, with Ukraine and the rest of Europe having to adjust to a new environment. Ukraine has had both to come to terms with the privileges and responsibilities which come with independence and to embark on a process of substantial political and economic reform. But it has not been alone in these endeavours. The European Union in particular has supported and will continue to support that reform process.

The past ten years have brought about profound and welcome change to the political landscape of Europe. For decades the Eastern limits of the EU were set by the political split which ran through the heart of Europe. That has gone, and the EU has taken the initiative in embarking on an ambitious process of enlargement. It has had to undergo internal reform to make that process possible, and it has provided substantial support to enable the candidate countries to make the political and economic reforms necessary to meet the obligations of EU membership.

At the same time, and also as a response to the end of the Cold War, the EU is changing in other ways. It now not only brings its influence to bear in the world in the economic and trade system, but increasingly also in the political arena. We have had to take responsibility for issues which have a direct impact on our security, such as the Balkans, and we are widening the scope of instruments at our disposal by establishing a European Security and

Defence Policy, which will enable us to become a more effective player in crisis management.

How do these changes – those in Ukraine and those in the EU – affect each other? I start with the premise that we share a number of key interests. The EU is important to Ukraine, and Ukraine is also important to the EU. We share a vital interest in the maintenance of stability and prosperity in Europe. This ultimately depends on some key values which are important to us all.

Stability is linked to security. It begins with the absence of conflict. It lies at the heart of the EU, whose original purpose was to bring to an end the terrible wars which had ravaged Europe for centuries. Its success is founded on co-operation and engagement with its neighbours. In an increasingly globalised world, we have more reasons than ever to co-operate with others, in particular our neighbours. That is why the EU itself has a world-wide network of relationships both with individual countries and with regional groupings. Many of these relationships are underpinned by formal agreements, as in the case of Ukraine. Our Partnership and Co-operation Agreement provides a framework within which we can work together to tackle many of the problems of today's world. Many of these do not respect national boundaries – for example the environment, security, drug trafficking and terrorism. None of us is immune from them. Only by working together can we be effective in combating them. This is why the EU has recognised Ukraine as a future partner in crisis management.

No less important is the issue of internal stability. The EU can only function if its members are democratic, open and based on the rule of law. In this way the EU has proved a catalyst for individual countries to move from totalitarian regimes to democracies. The end of the Cold War demonstrated that closed societies cannot survive indefinitely. Ukraine has made the transition over the last ten years to an independent democratic nation state. This process still requires careful nurturing. The more open a country is, and the more ready it is to accept and respond to criticism, the stronger it will be. That means continuing to encourage an open and independent media. It means accepting the need for dialogue within the political system, even across party lines. Sometimes it means agreeing to disagree. That is the true mark of maturity.

Stability is of course closely linked to economic growth and prosperity. Each encourages the other. The level of foreign direct investment is key to stability. Business puts its money where it can be confident of the future. Ukraine has undertaken major economic reforms over the last ten years. These have gone a long way to opening up the economy and encouraging inward investment. I believe that Ukraine is now at a point where the reform process must be clearly demonstrated to be irreversible. The EU supports an open trade agenda. We would like to see Ukraine a member of the World Trade Organisation, but that means delivering on key reforms in order to meet the requirements of membership.

The enlargement of the EU will provide Ukraine with an immense new opportunity to expand trade and encourage inward investment. The enlarged EU will provide a single market of over 300 million people with the same standards and rules and offer the potential for increased trade, economic growth and prosperity. The EU also stands to benefit from a more prosperous Ukraine.

But the EU is more than just a single market. Ukraine will also benefit from having on its doorstep an area of proven stability and security, which can only lead to a closer relationship between the EU and Ukraine. I know of course that there are concerns in Ukraine over specific problems related to enlargement, not least over the movement of people. It is not always easy to reconcile our objective of openness to our neighbours with the legal requirements which flow from the EU's institutional arrangements. But we are ready to discuss Ukraine's concerns so that we can resolve them together wherever possible.

We all have good reason to welcome much of what has happened in Europe over the last ten years. There have of course been difficulties too, particularly in relation to the Balkans. These are beginning to be resolved, and I welcome the good spirit in which the EU and Ukraine have co-operated within KFOR in Kosovo. But these darker events are a warning to us. They serve to underline the obligation which we all have to preserve the values of democracy, freedom and tolerance, the values which guarantee the future stability of Europe. The greatest encouragement any country can have in this is the support of others. On this basis I look forward to a closer relationship between the European Union and Ukraine.

THE EU AND UKRAINE
A TRANSATLANTIC VIEW

John Tedstrom

Resolving the 'dialogue of the deaf' between Ukraine and the EU is an issue of crucial strategic importance to the continent of Europe and to the Trans-Atlantic relationship. I shall focus here on three main areas. First, I shall try to put Ukraine in its geopolitical context. Next, I shall look at recent political and economic developments in Ukraine and ask: can Ukraine be a success in the European context? Third, I will sketch out some ideas about what Ukraine and the West can do to improve their relationship and to accelerate Ukraine's transformation into a fully European country – not just a country that is located in Europe.

First, Ukraine in its geopolitical context. It is a sad fact that many of us have become quite used to, if not comfortable with, President Lukashenka and the situation in Belarus. None of us in the West devotes nearly enough attention to that country and we have as a result become somewhat blasé about its problems. Moldova, which is also in Ukraine's immediate neighbourhood, has recently seen deterioration in terms of political and economic development. However, Moldova is a small country and most Western countries do not have enough resources to allow them to devote adequate attention to it, either. But if the situation in Ukraine deteriorates, we'll all notice and we'll all care. Both Belarus and Moldova are important in their own right. But in geostrategic terms Ukraine is a country of qualitatively different importance to Europe and the US.

Just look at the region more broadly, and we see a range of countries that are struggling with the transition, including Georgia, Azerbaijan, Armenia or other countries still further away. Ukraine's failure would have a tremendous negative impact on those countries. Leaders from Tallinn to Tbilisi argue that Ukraine is the linchpin in the region. Looked at from this perspective, Ukraine becomes one of the most important countries in Europe.

It is also important to remind ourselves that what happens in Ukraine is important for Russia. Ukraine's success, its integration into Euro-Atlantic institutions, can have a positive effect on the transition in Russia. We need to be aware of this and to tailor our policies in order to foster such a positive dynamic.

Next, let us turn to recent political and economic developments and ask: can Ukraine be a success in the European context? If we look at political and economic progress in 2000-2001, the answer has to be yes. Ukraine has achieved a tremendous amount since December 1999 when President Kuchma was elected to his second term and appointed Viktor Yushchenko as Prime Minister. In late 1999/early 2000, President Kuchma laid out a reform agenda that was realistic and promising. Prime Minister Yushchenko worked with colleagues to fulfil the main directions of that reform agenda. In early 2000, they restructured their Eurobond debt. They paid off over $400 million in international debt without the support of an IMF programme. Industrial production grew in 2000 for the first time since independence. Agricultural production also grew for the first time since independence, and in 2001 grew even more strongly thanks to the introduction of a real credit financing mechanism for farmers. Arrears of wages and pensions have been paid off. Barterisation of the economy has been dramatically reduced. Monetarisation has increased and has provided a dynamic to economic life in Ukraine.

All this has had an important impact on the way Ukrainians see themselves in the European context. During the previous ten years, public opinion polls had revealed the extent to which the population were split on the issue of Ukraine's European identity. Despite the efforts of former Foreign Minister Borys Tarasyuk and others to promote Ukraine's European choice, at the grassroots level European identity was weak. From 2000, however, opinion polls have started to show an encouraging increase in the number of people at grassroots level who identify themselves and their country with Europe.

Third, a look at what Ukraine and the West can do to improve their relationship and to accelerate Ukraine's transformation into a fully European country – not just a country that is located in Europe.

Ukraine's recent successes create a strategic opportunity for Ukraine and the West to deepen their partnership and to move forward. What might Ukraine do here? Ukraine needs, first and foremost, to resolve its political crisis. This is not just a matter of choosing a new Prime Minister. President Kuchma needs to exert his leadership to ensure that the reformist agenda is continued and strengthened, and that the partnership between the President, Prime Minister and Parliament that brought successes in 2000 continues in 2001 and beyond. There is no other way to develop the political consensus that will allow the reforms to move forward. Second, President Kuchma has to isolate the bad guys. The single largest impediment to good relations between Ukraine and the US – and I would venture to say between Ukraine and its European partners – is the high level of corruption in Ukraine. Unless President Kuchma takes decisive measures to isolate corrupt officials and to distance them from political life in Ukraine, Ukraine's opportunities to integrate with the West will be limited.

Ukraine's leaders have taken some promising concrete steps to promote their country's integration with Europe. Recently, they established a new Ministry to oversee and take forward the process of European integration, adopting the practice that proved successful in Hungary, Poland and the Baltic States. Going forward, Ukraine needs to commit to completing, within the next two years, the terms of the Partnership and Co-operation Agreement it signed with the EU. The EU's frustration with Ukraine is not unjustified in this respect. With hard work, with vision, and with leadership from the President, the Prime Minister and the Speaker, Ukraine can meet its commitments under the Partnership and Co-operation Agreement and it needs to do so.

What can the West do? First, I believe we should avoid drawing new lines in Europe. There is much talk of building new institutions and forging new kinds of relationships for those counties that won't immediately join the EU, but there is a danger here that all that will be created will be new divisions. The Ukrainians have a valid point when they talk about associate membership status in the EU: is Ukraine really making any less or any slower progress than countries such as Romania, Bulgaria or Albania? I think a sober, dispassionate analysis would find that in some respects Ukraine is making just as much progress as those countries. I welcome the position taken buy the European Parliament, which believes the EU should be open to Ukraine's membership of the EU at an appropriate time in the future. This is an important example of strategic thinking.

Second, I would encourage the US, the EU and the G7 jointly to commit to a new ten-year programme of engagement with Ukraine, consisting of the following measures:

a) the West should commit to a symbolic increase in the value of its engagement, technical assistance and partnership programmes by ten percent over the life of this new ten-year programme.

b) the West should initiate an immediate review of what has and what has not worked in terms of technical assistance; this should be undertaken together with Ukraine, including both the governmental and the non-governmental sectors. We should look hard at shifting our technical assistance to Ukraine from the Tacis model to the Phare model. We should use the technical assistance models that worked in Poland, Hungary and the other countries of Central Europe. These focused on institution building and infrastructure development and used methods such as twinning. None of that has been done in Ukraine. Part of the difference in terms of pace of reform is the result of that.

c) the West needs to invest in Ukraine's grassroots. The increase in European identity is promising and we need to seize that opportunity in order to strengthen Ukraine's reforms and its civil society. This means increasing our investment in exchanges, in the Internet, mass media, NGOs, and also in education reform, an area that is especially weak as far as US involvement is concerned.

If the EU, and the West in general, can adopt this more positive approach, and if the Ukrainian leadership can take further steps to deepen democracy, strengthen civil society and build people's confidence in their institutions, I believe that Ukraine will become more fully engaged in Europe and able to contribute better to its important role in the wider world as we face our global problems and challenges.

2

Ukraine: Political Progress and Prospects

THE POLITICAL PROCESS IN UKRAINE

DEMOCRATISATION OR VIRTUALISATION?

Andrew Wilson

Given that it had to begin the construction of a democratic polity virtually from scratch after independence in 1991, Ukraine deserves credit for the progress that it has made to date. In contrast to some of its neighbours, elections have never been cancelled or delayed or blatantly rigged. Contested multi-party voting has become the norm: elections were held for Parliament in 1994 and 1998, with the next vote scheduled for March 2002; and for President in December 1991, 1994 and 1999, the next poll being due in November 2004. The 1994 presidential election resulted in a peaceful handover of power from first President Leonid Kravchuk to his successor Leonid Kuchma, who was re-elected in 1999. Despite long and seemingly intractable dispute, sufficient consensus was found to pass a post-communist Constitution in 1996. Ukraine has an apparently excellent record in accommodating national minorities. There is little evidence of widespread human rights abuse.

Ukraine therefore seems to meet many of the *political* elements in the 'Copenhagen criteria' for eventual EU membership agreed in 1993. Its progress towards establishing a market economy capable of coping with the competitive pressures and meeting the dynamic opportunities of membership is assessed elsewhere in this book. On the other hand, the 'Gongadze scandal' that erupted in November 2000 (the disappearance and presumed death of an opposition journalist, the dramatic revelations of the 'Melnychenko tapes' that supposedly implicated the President and his entourage in the affair) has cast doubt on Ukraine's progress in other key Copenhagen areas, most notably the rule of law and the extent of media and civic freedom. The affair has also placed in doubt the stability and good intent of the institutions and persons supposedly guaranteeing democracy, and led to accusations of 'creeping authoritarianism' since 1994.

This chapter is in five main parts. First, the extent to which a true *political society* – a system of effective constitutional checks and balances grounded in a liberal and legalistic culture – has emerged in Ukraine is briefly assessed. Second, Ukraine's record in providing individual and group rights is scrutinised. Third, it is argued that the key problem with establishing a functioning democracy in Ukraine is not the Gongadze scandal itself, but the increasing tendency towards the *virtualisation* of politics that lies behind it. Fourth, some underlying problems are briefly outlined; and finally some possible future changes discussed.

Political institutions

On paper, the new Ukrainian state has established a political system that is technically described as semi-presidential, or more accurately, president-parliamentary. It did so not immediately after independence – in 1991 or 1992 – but in the constitutional settlement that followed President Kuchma's election – the 'Constitutional Agreement' of 1995 and the Constitution proper of 1996. The President is directly elected, but elections are not synchronised with those for Parliament. Competition over who has the more recent or more real mandate has therefore been rife. There is also 'dual control' of the executive. The Prime Minister heads the Cabinet of Ministers and is appointed by the President. Parliament must confirm, but dismissal powers are lopsided. The President can dismiss with ease, Parliament can only discuss no-confidence motions once a year – and not within one year after it has first approved a government's programme. The President has wide appointment powers and some powers to rule by decree, and special powers over the 'Autonomous Republic of Crimea'.

Parliament (in Ukrainian the *Verkhovna Rada* or 'Supreme Council') on the other hand has had to accept reduced powers since 1995-6. Its practical control over the government is minimal. Budgets are largely determined by executive structures. The Rada's scrutiny powers and committee structure are as yet undeveloped. Parliament's basic problem, however, has always been its lack of a coherent majority, given that it has never been clearly structured on party lines. The 1994 election law discriminated against parties. Some progress was initially made after the 1998 elections, with Parliament initially dominated by the eight parties which had led in the elections. In December 1998, however, the Constitutional Court effectively tore up the original result by granting permission to deputies elected on party lists to swap sides or create new factions (225 deputies were elected from national lists, 225 from territorial constituencies). The minimum number to create a faction was set at a ludicrously low fourteen. As a result, there were fourteen factions as of March 2001, and only four of the original eight had survived (see Table 1 on page 43). A 'New Majority' was temporarily stitched together out of this diversity in January 2000, but the strains of the Gongadze scandal tore it apart within a year. No real majority therefore exists to overcome a presidential veto (two-thirds), enact constitutional change (two-thirds) or attempt impeachment (three quarters), or even, all too often, legislate (simple majority). Nevertheless, the Rada retains a certain passive power. The President does not enjoy the crucial power of dissolution. Legislation proposed by the President requires the Rada's consent.

In practice, however, the Ukrainian system is more strongly presidential than it appears. Old informal habits die hard, and the presidential administration functions as a parallel government, with the same reserved powers over the 'power vertical' and 'cadre policy' as the Communist Party Central Committee of old. Significantly, it is housed in the same building. Some have even argued that clan politics and presidential para-structures have helped create a 'super-presidential' system, especially after a system of 'State Secretaries' was introduced in May 2001. Totally unknown to the Constitution, they are designed to act as the President's plenipotentiaries in every government department, 'organising' the work of the executive and controlling the distribution of all state funds. They are even designed to outlive Kuchma, as appointments were made for five years.

As concerns the other main branch of state, legal reform is a work in progress. Fifteen 'Transitional Provisions' were attached to the 1996 Constitution. Three are worth quoting in detail. Provision 13 declares that 'the current procedure for arrest, holding in custody and detention of persons suspected of committing a crime, and also for the examination and search of a dwelling place or other possessions of a person is preserved for five years after this Constitution comes into force'. In other words, draconian post-Soviet practices were retained, but only till 2001. More seriously, Provision 12 accepts that the current legal system is inadequate, but again promises that it will survive 'for no more than five years' (1996-2001). Reform is now due – but seems unlikely. Judges, who were nearly all appointed in Soviet times and are therefore used to the system of 'telephone justice' (taking order from political masters) are allowed to remain in office 'until the expiration of the term for which they were elected or appointed' (if before 1996). Ukraine's most famous 'independent' judge, Mykola Zamkovenko, whose jurisdiction (because it includes the Rada and many government buildings) has often required him to judge appeals against state authorities, was harassed and threatened with dismissal in May 2001.

Perhaps most seriously of all, the apex of the whole judicial system, the State Procuracy with its vast concentration of powers, is allowed indefinite after-life 'until laws regulating the activity of state bodies in regard to control over the observance of laws are put into force, and until a system of pre-trial investigation is formed and the laws regulating its operation are put into effect' (Provision 9). The President appoints the Procurator, and the politicisation of the system has become increasingly apparent during the Gongadze scandal, with proper investigation of the case woefully inadequate and serious question marks developing over the system's ability to bring accused politicians (one of whom was the Procurator himself) to account. Besides the President and Procurator, the Interior Minister and heads of the security and tax collection services were all allegedly revealed on the Melnychenko tapes acting and thinking *ultra vires*, or perhaps more precisely revealing the *ad hoc* and *ad hominem* nature of what passes for law in Ukraine. Leonid Derkach, then head of the security service, for example, is reported saying of the Procuracy, 'if we are the power, that is an instrument of our power.'

In short, none of three key aspects of the rule of law – due process, no individual or group above the law, and an independent judiciary to ensure an absence of arbitrary power – is yet well established in Ukraine. Nor is a further aspect, namely constitutional*ism* – the willingness to abide by the existing system and the rules of the game it lays down. Although the Constitution is only five years old, President Kuchma has repeatedly sought to change it. The most serious threat to the existing order came from the highly controversial referendum forced through after Kuchma's re-election in April 2000. Even after two of six questions were struck out by the Constitutional Court, the referendum proposed to give the President the long-sought dissolution power (albeit only in specific circumstances, if the Rada 'fails to establish a majority' within one month of assembly or pass a proposed budget within three), abolish deputy immunity, reduce the number of Rada deputies from 450 to 300 and establish a bicameral assembly 'with one chamber representing the interests of the regions of Ukraine'. No mention was made as to whether the new upper house would be elected, or, if so, how. Amidst widespread accusations of fraud and intimidation, the administration claimed the proposals had been backed by an implausible 82 per cent to 90 per cent of voters – turnout figures remained imprecise.

If enacted, the proposals would dramatically tip the constitutional balance in the President's favour; but, with his position weakened by the Gongadze affair, Kuchma has been forced to place them on the backburner. On the other hand, stalemate does not mean consensus. The President's opponents have also constantly sought to redefine the constitutional map. The Communist Party openly advocates the abolition of the presidency; as of Summer 2001 the disparate opposition was planning a referendum aiming at either impeachment (constitutionally, a matter for the Rada) or reduced presidential power. Political stability still seems a long way off.

The Constitutional Court belatedly established after 1996 has failed to establish a reputation as the defender of constitutionalism. One third of its eighteen judges are appointed directly by the President, one third by the Rada (Main Constitution – Article 148). But because the remainder are appointed by a 'Congress of [existing] Judges', the President has the edge in influence – most existing judges being politically loyal. Most of the Court's more controversial decisions have reflected this basic fact. Under the existing Constitution, it is unlikely to be truly independent until the same can be said of the judiciary as a whole. The Court's judgement on the constitutionality of the State Secretary system would be a key test.

Rights, minority and general

Ukraine has a much better record in the field of rights (this section will be necessarily brief, as many of the topics – especially civil society, media freedom and minority rights – are dealt with elsewhere). Ukraine is a multi-ethnic, multi-linguistic and multi-cultural society, but this reality has been well-reflected in law and practice. Unlike Estonia or Latvia, a generous 'zero option' citizenship law was passed in year zero (October 1991), granting citizenship to anyone then resident on Ukrainian territory. The only problem encountered has been with Crimean Tatars who have returned to the peninsula since that date – perhaps 40,000 of whom were still non-citizens at the time of writing.[1] As well as the citizenship issue, there remains the problem of establishing political mechanisms to represent the Crimean Tatars' voice and interests. The historical majority on the peninsula, they currently make up only 12 per cent of the local population. One experiment, granting the Tatars fourteen reserved seats in the local assembly (out of 98), was begun in 1994, but abandoned in 1998. An alternative scheme – a 'Council of Representatives of the Crimean Tatar People Attached to the President of Ukraine' – has been in hesitant operation since 1999.

Other minorities (Romanians, Jews, Hungarians, etc.) have an active civic life and there are few grievances expressed over minority education or language use. Kiev, however, refuses to admit that the self-proclaimed 'Rusyn' or 'Ruthenian' minority in Transcarpathia actually exists, arguing that the locals are ethnically and linguistically part of a greater Ukrainian whole. The real 'minority' problem in Ukraine, however, is with the Russians and with the Russian language. According to the outdated 1989 census (a successor was finally to be undertaken in 2001) 22 per cent of the population are ethnically Russian. According to polling data, almost half, including many Ukrainians, are Russian-speaking. No one can dispute that provision for the

Russian language and for Russian schooling remains extremely generous in Ukraine – 34 per cent of children were still in Russian-language schools in the 1998-99 school year. The real question is *how* generous it should be. Many Ukrainians continue to feel aggrieved at the inroads made by Russian into their own language and culture, and seek to reduce its sphere of influence to that of the *Russian ethnic minority* (the 'national minority'). Many Russian and/or Russophone activists refuse to accept 'minority' status, and argue for the preservation of what they claim to be a specific Ukrainian Russian culture. One side argues that the latter is a 'colonial' relic, the other that Russian remains a 'voluntary' *lingua franca*. To the former, the need for the 'Programme on Strengthening the Position of the Ukrainian Language as the State Language' introduced in February 2000 was self-evident, given that the language's position is so precarious; to the Russian Foreign Ministry it was an assault on the rights of 'Russian-speakers' – not just ethnic Russians alone.

In the sphere of religion, the 1996 Constitution (Article 35) declares rather more clearly than its Russian equivalent that 'everyone has the right to freedom of personal philosophy or religion', and that 'the Church and religious organisations in Ukraine are separated from the state, and the school from the Church. No religion shall be recognised by the state as mandatory'. There is no Ukrainian equivalent of Russia's 1997 Law on Religion, which privileges 'traditional' faiths. Unlike the Russian Orthodox Church, Ukraine has four rival would-be 'state' Churches. Unity between two is possible (the Ukrainian Orthodox Church-Kievan Patriarchate and the Ukrainian Autocephalous Orthodox Church), but between their combined forces and the Moscow Patriarchate unlikely. Ukraine is therefore unlikely to gain a 'united' Church, still less one with state support, capable of threatening the rights of its rivals. One or two 'fringe' religions, evangelical Protestants in particular, have however argued that conditions have become less free in recent years.

The extent of civic freedoms promised in Chapter II of the 1996 Constitution is impressive, although too many exceptions are listed. According to Article 39 for example, 'citizens have the right to assemble peacefully [...]. Restrictions on the exercise of this right may be established by a court in accordance with the law and only in the interests of national security and public order'. In practice, the two cancel each other out and give the authorities *carte blanche* (a 'tent city' set up by protestors in Kiev during the Gongadze affair was removed when ruled a small construction without adequate 'planning permission'). The protection of civic rights, moreover, requires adequate judicial reform (see above). Political reform is also necessary to protect the citizen from the arbitrary power of many elements in the state: particularly the tax administration and Interior Ministry. A situation where the head of the State Tax Inspectorate emerged as the leader of one of Ukraine's newest political parties in 2001 is bizarre to say the least.

Readers interested in the issues of civil society and media freedom are referred to the relevant chapters elsewhere in this volume. Suffice it to say, that it is in these areas that the Parliamentary Assembly of the Council of Europe based its criticism of Ukraine (up to and including the threat of suspension of membership) in 2001.

Virtual politics

The most serious criticism of Ukraine's mixed record in democratisation, however, is that so many aspects exist only on paper. The main actors in the political process, politicians and political parties, are indeed actors, whose public mask may provide little guide to their private purpose. Some commentators have referred to the 'oligarchisation' of Ukrainian politics, and the vast riches of Ukraine's new politico-economic class; but less attention has been paid to their consequent need to disguise their true interests and the manner in which this has distorted open and accountable politics. To explain this point, it is worth looking at the real identities of the key players in the current Parliament (see Table 1 opposite). Because so many political actors are 'virtual', it makes little sense to attempt a conventional classification of 'left', 'right' and 'centre'. For example, the Communists, Socialists and Labour Ukraine are all left-wing in terms of their public rhetoric – but it would be highly misleading to group them together. The Communists oppose reform but are currently in secret accord with the President, Labour Ukraine is a front organisation for the Interior Ministry and security services, while the Socialists have leap-frogged into real opposition in uneasy partnership with the nationalist right. This can be confusing for the reader – but, rest assured, it is equally confusing for Ukrainian voters – which is unfortunately how many politicians prefer it.

Table 1: Factions in the Ukrainian Parliament, as of March 2001.[2]

Left	
Communists	112
Centre-Oligarchs	
Solidarity	24
Labour Ukraine	46
Social Democrats	34
Yabluko	14
Revival of the Regions	30
Regions of Ukraine	16
Greens	17
National-Democratic Party	18
The disparate 'opposition' after the Gongadze affair	
Socialists	16
Fatherland	31
Reforms-Congress	15
Rukh (Udovenko)	16
Rukh (Kostenko)	23

The core of the current power system in Ukraine is the troika that emerged to defend and finance Kuchma's re-election in 1999. Currently most powerful of the three is Labour Ukraine, which, as mentioned above, is in fact a vehicle for the Interior and Security Ministries and their allies. The Social Democratic Party also apes the left-centre slogans its PR-men have provided, but is in fact a front for Kiev businessmen, some with alleged mafia links. Yabluko has nothing to do with its Russian equivalent (the reform party led by Grigorii Yavlinskii), but is (in origin at least) a satellite party of the same group – a second bet if the Social Democrats fail at the polls. Third is the group Revival of the Regions, led by leading presidential confidante Oleksandr Volkov. Something of its nature can be gleaned from the fact that in the mid-2001 street demonstrations, protesters referred to it as 'Revival of the Belgian Regions', given that Volkov is under investigation for alleged money laundering in Belgium. Then there are the Greens, who were a genuine environmental party when originally established back in 1990, but who sold their good name to business interests in 1998 – mainly high polluting oil and gas traders. Four Green deputies are currently under investigation for corruption. Most worryingly again, the newest Ukrainian party, Ukrainian Regions, is headed by Mykola Azarov, head of the State Tax Inspectorate. The impropriety is obvious: weary Ukrainians simply expect it to be one of the best-financed parties in the upcoming 2002 elections.

Ukraine therefore has at least two types of virtual parties, fronts for 'new business' *and* for state structures. The two are increasingly symbiotic. As former Prime Minister Yushchenko remarked just before his downfall, the oligarchs' next goal is likely to be the 'privatisation of the state' itself. Virtuality, however, also affects and corrupts the opposition, those apparently standing outside the charmed circle of power.

Aspects of real opposition exist. In recent months, thousands have been able to demonstrate. The re-emergence of a proper student movement for the first time since 1990 is a notable phenomenon. At least three anti-Kuchma groups have emerged (which of course creates a problem in combining their forces), Ukraine without Kuchma, The National Salvation Forum and For Truth. But the opposition is also artificially divided. *Agents provocateurs* are doing their work. The administration has a long history of creating (or at least helping develop) 'phantom' or 'spoiler' opposition parties – to create the illusion of pluralism or to siphon away opposition votes. The so-called Progressive Socialist Party of Nataliya Vitrenko in the 1999 election is but the most notorious example – the allotted function of her radical rhetoric (repudiation of all debts, reformers 'to Siberia', the closure of all borders and accounts on the day of her election) being to convince the West, its lending institutions in particular, that there was someone worse than Kuchma around.

A new phenomenon is the emergence of the Communist Party as an increasingly virtual opposition. The Party has privately supported the administration in the recent political crisis, and will probably continue to do so. The Party and the President have a common interest in maintaining the

Communists' status as the 'official opposition'. The Party also has nascent business interests to protect. The Party leadership calculate, probably correctly, that their 'captive electorate' will still vote for them anyway (especially if they are not exposed in the state-controlled media); even, to be brutally honest, that the state's 'administrative resources' can be used to see off the challenge of the 'true left' Communist Party of Workers and Peasants that split from its ranks in April 2001.

Underlying problems

Many of these problems can be identified in other post-Communist states, but Ukraine also suffers from a particular bind making the problem of virtuality even worse, namely the *static political arithmetic* in which it has been trapped more or less since independence in 1991 (and even before). Roughly speaking, Ukraine can be classed as a '20-40-40' society. To date, the right wing has had the minority support of about 20 per cent, the left a somewhat larger 40 per cent, with the remainder being classed as 'centre' by default. Each camp has had roughly fixed support – in their own regional redoubts – which brings other sub-problems in its wake. Neither the right nor the left has seemed capable of breaking its particular bonds, and the long free ride for the centre has not been good for Ukraine – allowing the oligarchs to flourish and develop the type of virtual politics briefly described above.

There are also specific dilemmas facing the right, left and centre. Unlike many other East and Central European states, Ukraine has never been able to build a broad anti-Communist reform coalition like Solidarity, Civic Forum or *Sajudis*. The forces of the right have therefore narrowed to a basically nationalist movement, which for historical reasons has confined its support to Western Ukraine and the central Ukrainian intelligentsia – with some pockets of relatively passive support in the countryside. The right therefore cannot govern alone. It has been forced to support successive administrations from the outside, so long as their cultural and foreign policies were sufficiently 'Ukrainian', largely accepting the argument of 'lesser evil' in the face of the supposed left-wing threat. The 1999 election was particularly illustrative of this problem. No really strong candidate stood for the right, gifting Kuchma its electorate (some 20-25 per cent) for very little return. On the Melnychenko tapes, Kuchma is apparently recorded threatening local leaders elsewhere to maximise his vote, but he tells his underlings not to bother with Galicia, where his vote is already assured. 'We don't need the West (of Ukraine)', he allegedly says, 'there are no questions there'.

The problem on the left is the predominance of the almost completely unreconstructed Communist Party. So long as it remains the dominant force, Ukraine suffers the worst of both worlds. The left as a whole cannot govern, *and* Ukraine remains a 'blocked society', with reform always difficult. In all three post-Soviet Ukrainian Parliaments, the left have controlled a block of seats large enough to hinder the passage of legislation and budgets of which they disapproved – though never, it should perhaps be stressed, the 'red majority' often reported in the West. There are three possible ways out of this particular bind. One, the Socialists might eventually displace the Communists as the main partner in the left alliance, allowing the left as a whole to become electable, as in François Mitterand's 'Long March of the French Left' to power in 1981. This is highly unlikely – the Communists remain an immovable force, tacitly supported by the existing regime. The second option is that the Communists reform themselves. Unfortunately, there is no indication that the Party has even learnt from the limited evolution of its Russian equivalent. Despite the relaunch of the party journal *Communist of Ukraine* with great fanfare in 1999, it contains no new ideas, no real discussion of the Party's future role. The third alternative – for the Socialists to strike out on their own – is discussed below.

That leaves the so-called 'centre', where the problem is simple – Ukraine has long suffered from what might be called a 'missing liberal' problem. There is no powerful reform party, let alone a liberal government of the like of Balcerowicz or even Gaidar. Instead the so-called centre is dominated by the oligarchs. There has therefore never been a sufficiently powerful *domestic* lobby for reform. External pressure can achieve results, but it is no substitute for real home-grown impetus. Unfortunately, public opinion is also divided '20-40-40'. No natural majority exists. Even when support for reform is apparent or latent, it has failed to coalesce because of divisions on other subjects (the divisive language/culture question, the choice between Russia and the

West). A potential reform block led by Yushchenko will not be looking for a majority in 2002, just to punch at a slightly higher weight.

Factors for change

There is no space here to discuss the details of current political controversy, but arguably some of its effects have been positive, in that as of 2001 some of the ice that has encased the Ukrainian political scene for so long may be breaking up. Paradoxically or not, in some respects things were actually worse before the Gongadze scandal broke, in 1999 and the first half of 2000, in that the political agenda was then more closely under the oligarchs' control.

Amongst the more important recent changes are:

- The emergence of a real, not a virtual centre, loyal to, if not necessarily organised by, former Prime Minister Viktor Yushchenko. Even with Yushchenko, however, things have been somewhat back to front. He was appointed as Ukraine's first real liberal Prime Minister in 1999, largely as a result of external pressure, in the hope that a reform party would then *subsequently* coalesce around him. Since his dismissal in April 2001, the attempt will have to be made with Yushchenko out of office, deprived of the 'administrative resources' others are prepared to use without compunction against him. He will also have to lead an awkward alliance of reform-liberal and right-nationalist forces.

- The emergence of an alternative opposition led by former Deputy Prime Minister Yuliya Tymoshenko and her Fatherland Party. During her brief period in government (December 1999 to January 2001), she led a successful campaign to re-monitise the economy, largely by squeezing energy 'oligarchs' to pay arrears in wages and pensions. Her success was arguably due to her former role as an energy oligarch herself, and her intimate knowledge of her former colleagues' schemes and scams. Hence their furious reaction. Unfortunately, they were also able to use allegations about her past to force her resignation and temporary arrest under charges of money laundering until freed by Judge Zamkovenko in February. Tymoshenko may continue to be in and out of prison. But the logic of 'oligarchical patriotism' – wealth of questionable origin seeking to go legitimate and defend itself with retrospective legal order – may eventually tempt others in her stead.

- Other upheavals are possible in the so-called centre. Ukrainian oligarchs have always been greedy and short-sighted, but the ongoing struggle over the division of the spoils is now threatening the stability of the centre 'troika' that emerged in 1999 (Labour Ukraine, Revival of the Regions, the Social Democrats). The emergence of the Ukrainian Regions Party (its very name being a direct challenge to Revival of the Regions) is a potential threat to the previous centre tradition of consensus, if not honour amongst thieves, especially as it has poached members from across the board and also enjoys de facto control of another virtual faction (Solidarity) in Parliament. If the oligarchs were to break ranks, a Kuchma succession might be brought forward and could be contested in the open.

- On the right, increasing divisions have become apparent between supporters of Kuchma and Yushchenko. Kuchma's own past statements of commitment to reform now seem mere lip-service. He has kept some of his nationalist support through his efforts to deliver on the language issue in 2000, but the more honest right is now more likely to back the 'new centre' (Yushchenko and/or Tymoshenko). The right has no objective need to sell its support as cheaply as in the past, and is no longer in the ghetto in which it found itself at its lowest moments. Significantly, in the current crisis West Ukraine has begun to re-emerge as the leading centre of protest. Without the right, the oligarchs are likely to try and solidify their pact with the Communists, but as a governing formula this may prove unstable and, of course, impossible to defend in public.

- The divorce of the Socialist and Communist parties.

The Socialist leader Oleksandr Moroz was involved in exposing the tapes allegedly incriminating Kuchma, while the Communists by contrast have backed the President in Parliament. This end of the old 'left block' that (de facto) contested the 1994 and 1998 elections is an extremely important factor. On their own, the Communists may continue to poll 25 per cent or so; but not the 40 per cent that the left as a whole was formerly able to command. 40 per cent was a potential majority, a threat to Ukraine's fundamental direction; 25 per cent is not. The Communist Party may keep its electorate, but it is now revealed as a 'virtual opposition'. The West should no longer take seriously the idea of a 'red threat' to Ukraine, and certainly should not see this as a reason to back tainted politicians as a 'lesser evil'. Kuchma is not restrained from choosing the path of reform by a 'red parliament', only by his cosy relations with the oligarchs who surround him.

The Socialists, on the other hand, have finally found a way out of the left-wing ghetto. They may even leap-frog into alliance with the centre, even the centre-right. This is a healthy development. The party's recent statements show that it is now firmly committed to Ukrainian statehood, while the Communists dream of a Soviet Restoration or 'Slavic Union'. Arguably in fact, the Socialists are one of Ukraine's most patriotic parties. Between the Soviet nationalism of the Communists, the corrupt and opportunistic centre and the hyper-nationalism of many on the right, they have added considerable stability to the state-building process. But, and this is a big but, despite much discussion of the 'social-democratisation' of the party's domestic programme, since 1998 in particular, this has yet to happen. Although they have played an important role in advocating 'real reform' and posing as the friend of the 'honest businessman', by West European standards the Party is still a left socialist one. Significantly, even somewhat bizarrely, its leader Moroz considers that the Party's nearest equivalent is the 'modernising' *Parti Communiste Français*. Moroz is clearly worried that his new course will leave his party behind. Certainly, if he moves too far too quickly, its place may well be taken by the 'virtual left': Parties such as Labour Ukraine and the Social Democrats, possibly a new Communist Party, were one to emerge, in a new anti-reform alliance.

- Whether or not the accumulation of these changes leads to a less 'virtual' style of politics is hard to say, but change is at least on the agenda. A potential 'anti-Kuchma' majority is not yet in existence, still less an 'anti-oligarchic' majority. Any successor to Kuchma is still more likely to come from within the oligarchs' ranks. But the next elections promise to be a more interesting affair.

Against this has to be set the very real possibility of a sharp turn towards authoritarian rule in Ukraine. A full Belarusian scenario is unlikely. Ukraine has much more invested in its linkage with the West. It is still a relatively open society. And, frankly, Kuchma is not popular enough to pursue the option of charismatic dictatorship. Hence, the West can exercise considerable influence by monitoring the next elections much more effectively (and at *an earlier stage*) than in the past. As well as its inherent virtue, this will have a vital indirect effect. In so far as the circles around Kuchma are forced to calculate whether current practices will do them more harm than good in 2002 and 2004, they will also need to rethink their practice in the present. Conditional engagement with the existing regime remains a necessity, but the West should make it crystal-clear what standards are and are not compatible with any type of relationship with the EU. The West should also encourage *all* six of the positive trends mentioned above. Our interest in a stable and prosperous Ukraine is served just as much by a 'patriotic' Socialist Party (or even by a reformed Communist Party) as it is by Mr. Yushchenko. We can also learn from the positive results of Western engagement in Belgrade: put pressure on the corrupt, encourage the opposition to unite and help them to develop ways of puncturing the virtual vainglory of the oligarchs.

NOTES

1 See Bill Bowring, 'New Nations and National Minorities: Ukraine and the Question of Citizenship', in P. Cumper and S. Wheatley (eds.), *Minority Rights in the 'New' Europe* , (London: Kluwer Law International, 1999), pp. 233-50. At p. 242 Bowring cites a figure of 93,600; but the Ukraine-Uzbekistan agreement of August 1998 has eased procedures (Uzbekistan being the main Soviet Republic in which deported Crimean Tatars settled after 1944). As a result, 53,338 reportedly acquired citizenship by the beginning of 2001. See the report at www.uncpd.kiev.ua.update volume 7, number 3, 15 January 2001.

2 Source: *Interfax* , 21 March 2001. 'Solidarity' is largely made up of former leftists who took the oligarchs' shillings. The Socialists may have moved from the left to the opposition, but surprised many by voting for Anatoliy Kinakh as Yushchenko's successor in May 2001. Rukh split in 1999, and does not always behave like an opposition.

LOCAL DEMOCRACY
UNFINISHED BUSINESS

Serhiy Maksymenko

When Ukraine took the strategic decision to seek integration into the EU it accepted the need for the development of democratic institutions, including the establishment of devolved local government for self-sustaining communities as an essential component of a civil society. This required radical transformation from the Communist system of local government, which had been a Party-controlled vehicle for the transmission of instructions from the centre. This paper examines the progress made in establishing an appropriate legal framework and creating the practical conditions for a flourishing local democracy.

The formal framework

The 1996 Constitution and the 1997 Law on Local Self-Government set out a constitutional and legal framework for local self-government. In July 1997 the Ukrainian Parliament ratified the European Charter for Local Self-Government, which states that 'municipalities' (i.e. local government bodies at all levels) should have not only the theoretical but also the real capacity to carry out the tasks of local government (in practice mainly the provision of basic services). Ukraine's EU Integration Strategy of 1998 also encouraged the idea and use of direct contacts between local authorities in Ukraine and in EU member and candidate countries in order to strengthen local government by sharing experience.

Back in 1998 many regarded the emerging prospects as very promising. Three years later, on the tenth anniversary of Ukraine's independence, many former optimists, strong advocates of the principles and values of the European Charter for Local Self-Government, are close to becoming incorrigible pessimists.

The Council of Europe bodies in charge of monitoring democracy and local self-government building have expressed concern about certain developments in Ukraine and the lack of a receptive approach on the part of the Ukrainian authorities. In December 1998 the relevant committee of the Congress of Local and Regional Authorities of Europe (CLRAE) reported:

> 'Legislation on local self-government should be passed without further delay in conformity with the principles of the European Charter of Local Self-Government, including a clear distinction between the state administration and elected municipal councils. A new status for Kiev and Sevastopol should be adopted in conformity with the Constitution and the European Charter of Local Self-Government'.

Following visits in 1997 and 1998 a CLRAE team pointed to legislative deficits in different aspects of local self-government in Ukraine. In its recommendations to the Ukrainian authorities, they suggested that the 1997 outline Law on Local Self-Government in Ukraine should be completed with additional legislation conforming to the provisions of the European Charter of Local Self-Government, including:

- A new status for Kiev and Sevastopol
- New legislation on territorial administration
- Provisions on local finance, tax, and local authority budgets
- Local authority land and property ownership
- The status of elected representatives and officials
- The role of the mass media in local life.

We deliberately refer to conclusions drawn by CLRAE almost three years ago, as progress since then has been insignificant. In mid-2001, many of the conclusions and recommendations made by CLRAE in 1998 remain valid, i.e. Ukraine has failed to honour most of its commitments reflected in the above suggestions. Almost the only exception is the Law on Kiev, which was passed by Parliament in early 1999. But even this was imperfect: the draft Law approved by the Parliament was amended before it was signed into law by the President without going through the proper parliamentary process. The final version set out a more centralised and controlled pattern of local government for the Ukrainian capital.

Despite these defects, there has been some progress in establishing local democracy. Local Councils are now chosen through elections involving multiple candidates, though even here the access to administrative resources granted to certain favoured candidates means that the playing-field is far from level.

Against this should be set the relative weakness of the elected bodies vis-à-vis the parallel organs of state executive power at the district and regional level. The heads of these (including regional Governors) are appointed by the President and can be removed by him at any time (theoretically on the advice of the Prime Minister). These bodies are the tool by which the President exercises power at the local level both directly and through pressure on the elected bodies.

Theory versus reality

In Ukraine today there is an increasing understanding of the concept of the municipality (*Hromada*) as the primary basis for genuine local self-government, and its place and role in local and regional development. Nevertheless, the country can boast little substantial progress in enabling municipalities to address effectively the issue of satisfying the basic needs of citizens. All this is happening against the background of deteriorating conditions and living standards in most parts of Ukraine. One major problem is the lack of a clear definition of the functions of elected local government bodies or any clear division between their responsibilities and those of the parallel state executive organs, for example in the provision of local services.

The Constitution of Ukraine guarantees each citizen the right to work, to a minimum social security, to 'satisfactory living standards', free health protection and medical care, and free education in state and local government institutions. These are generous provisions typically not found in Western Constitutions and could be extremely costly. However, the Constitution does not define at what level these services should be provided, or whether people can be expected to pay a proportion of the cost through some form of national or private insurance. Nor does it define the responsibilities of the tiers of governance for service provision, or make provision for the requisite funding.

Public expenditure constraints are forcing practitioners across the country to take difficult and unpopular decisions about which services they can afford, and which they cannot. Policy makers in national government, in particular in Parliament, have been slow, and even hesitant, to recognise this reality. Supporting legislation needs to be developed to clarify these issues. Without such guidelines, the service providers in region, district, city and village councils remain unclear as to how the Constitution should be interpreted, and the rationale behind executive decisions and priorities becomes increasingly more pragmatic, subjective and inconsistent.

Towards sustainable development: which way forward?

Are Ukrainian municipalities and regions mature enough to digest and implement the values of European local democracy embodied in specific patterns of citizen involvement, many of which are hundreds of years old? Overall, the answer to this complex and multi-disciplinary question is simple – no, they are not. Does it mean Ukraine should look for a third way, which would be its own 'Ukrainian' way, and give up the current, albeit controversial and inconsistent, and consequently not very successful, effort to Europeanise its local government? Again, the answer is no. There is no sound alternative.

What can realistically be done to help Ukraine's emerging local self-government? In what way could both domestic and outside institutions be instrumental in enhancing local and regional capacity for development in hundreds on Ukrainian communities that for many years have been surviving but not developing? What should be the priorities in rendering this assistance, and in which areas is impact achievable?

Currently, too much focus is given to the need to perfect local government legislation. Advocates of genuine European local self-government may be looking in the wrong direction when they identify this issue as central. Mostly the debate concentrates on the division of competencies between elected mayors and councillors, which competencies should be the exclusive prerogative of the Council, the Mayor's rights in appointing Executive Deputies, etc. No doubt a proper legal basis is a must for genuine local self-government. Municipalities and regions will not be able to operate efficiently without a sound enabling framework. However, if one compares the current Ukrainian local government legislation with that of some of its more successful neighbours in Central and Eastern Europe, one can hardly conclude that Ukrainian laws are worse, or less consistent with European values. The central problem lies in enforcing legislative provisions, creating an institutional infrastructure to support sustainable local and regional development, and enhancing the capacity of municipalities to ensure a decent level of service provision. In other words, this is a problem of governance, coupled with the low institutional and professional capacity of the local authorities.

There is also the problem of an integrated approach, or, to be more precise, the lack thereof. The available tools must be used in such a way as to bring together the various actors in partnership and co-operation. No single agency or institution, or sector of society, can alone successfully address the problems of a community suffering from industrial restructuring or economic decline. An integrated approach would recognise a leading role for the public sector (the municipality) in designing and implementing local development programmes and projects. At the same time it would make it absolutely clear that the private and voluntary sectors have their role as well, and should have their share in working in the public interest.

A sense of ownership, supported by 'bottom up' policies, should be cultivated among Ukrainian municipalities. All this should be done under the umbrella of local accountability. Efforts applied in this way will inevitably lead to increased examples of local best practice, which should then be rolled out nationally to help municipalities and regions take care of local service provision and development problems.

Ukraine's potential for transforming local government should not be overestimated, primarily due to its poor historical record of local democracy and accountability. However, the potential exists, but needs to be activated and supported. Since the Government has so far failed to do this, municipalities should, as far as is possible within existing legislation and the unfriendly national environment, take matters into their own hands. They should encourage the formation of a network of independent initiatives implemented locally, using mainly local resources. They should form regional associations both to carry out joint projects and to lobby at the national level. This is happening, but the process is slow, controversial and often over-politicised, i.e. those involved are more concerned with promoting their own political ambitions than supporting local authorities.

At the same time, central government should take action to encourage and support local initiatives and work towards the transformation of local government bodies from entities almost entirely dependent on resources from the centre into self-sustaining local communities with a proper local tax base, so that they have the resources to address both service provision and development issues, building consensus among key local stakeholders.

BETWEEN A (RUSSIAN) ROCK AND A (CRIMEAN TATAR) HARD PLACE?

ETHNIC, LINGUISTIC AND MINORITY ISSUES

Bill Bowring

Introduction

The European Union has not been concerned, as a first priority, with ethnic, linguistic and minority issues. But the year 2001 is the European Year of Languages, a joint initiative of the EU and the Council of Europe (CoE), against the backdrop of the EU's Charter of Fundamental Rights with its commitment to diversity. This is of particular significance both for the EU and Ukraine: the EU, as it seeks further to 'Europeanise' Ukraine, and Ukraine, as it struggles to consolidate its identity as an independent state. This short chapter seeks to identify and analyse some of the key issues, and in particular two of the most intractable problems for Ukraine. They are the problems, respectively, of the large Russian linguistic minority in Ukraine, and the small but well-organised Crimean Tatars in the 'Autonomous Republic of Crimea'. If these 'hot spots' are not resolved, they have potential for destabilisation and even conflict extending far beyond the borders of Ukraine.

Ukraine's divided population

At the time of the 1989 census (the most recent) the population of Ukraine was about 51.44m, including 37.4m (72.7 per cent) Ukrainians, 11.4m (22.1

per cent) ethnic Russians, 486,300 Jews (0.9 per cent), and significant numbers of Belorusians, Moldavians, Bulgarians, Poles, Hungarians, Romanians, Greeks, Germans, and Slovaks. The population began to decline from 1993, and on 1 January 1999 there were an estimated 50.1m people in Ukraine: but the relative proportions have remained largely the same, with the exception mentioned below. Another census is due to be carried out in late 2001, and the results may present a different picture. The Russian-speaking population is concentrated in Eastern Ukraine, where the city of Donetsk has a majority of Russians, and Kharkiv has 63 per cent Ukrainians, 35 per cent Russians and 4 per cent others. In Lviv, in Western Ukraine, there are only 7 per cent ethnic Russians. Given that the 'voluntary' union of Russia and Left Bank Ukraine – the Pereyaslav Treaty – took place in 1654, ethnic Russians and Russian-speakers have been living in the territory which comprises modern Ukraine for centuries.

However, there are more people who might identify themselves as 'Russians' than the figures above would suggest. Surveys carried out in February 1998 showed that 31 per cent of all inhabitants of Ukraine consider themselves to be to some extent Russian, including 11.5 per cent of inhabitants of Ukraine who claimed to be Russian, 5 per cent more Russian than Ukrainian, and 14.5 per cent equally Russian and Ukrainian. Read another way, the survey showed that only half of 'census' Russians claimed to be ethnic Russian. More significantly still, 55 per cent of all inhabitants of Ukraine prefer to use Russian as their everyday language – a fact which is immediately apparent in many Ukrainian cities. Nevertheless, Russians were for the most part in favour of Ukrainian independence. On 1 December 1991 an all-Ukrainian referendum took place, and as many as 90.3 per cent of Ukraine's inhabitants voted in favour of independence.

Crimea and the Crimean Tatars

The change in the population proportions mentioned above has been caused by the return, from the late 1980s onwards, of some 300,000 Crimean Tatars to Crimea. The peninsula, which was 'given' to the Ukrainian SSR in 1954 by Khrushchev to commemorate the Pereyaslav Treaty and was previously part of the Russian Federation, is otherwise more than 70 per cent ethnic

Russian. The Crimean Tatars themselves had suffered a great historical injustice: deportation en masse in 1944, primarily to Uzbekistan, for alleged collaboration with the Nazis. They suffered the deaths of between 22 per cent (official figures) and 46 per cent (their own) of their total population.

The 1996 Constitution proclaims that Ukraine is a unitary state, definitely not a federation (Article 2). Nevertheless, the administrative and territorial structure of Ukraine includes 'the Autonomous Republic of Crimea'. This ARC has its own Chapter (Chapter X) in the Constitution, and is described in Article 134 as 'an inseparable constituent part of Ukraine and [one that] decides on the issues ascribed to its competence within the limits of authority determined by the Constitution of Ukraine'. It has its own Supreme Soviet. This paradoxical formulation reflects the overwhelmingly Russian character of Crimea, and a long history since 1991 of constitutional and political clashes with Kiev, including substantial movements for reunion with Russia. Indeed, Crimean autonomy is, according to the Crimean Tatars, in reality the autonomy of the Russian majority (1.5m persons or 64 per cent of the population), who are settlers brought in after the deportation of the Crimean Tatars, or their descendants. Many are retired service personnel, given the presence of the Russian naval base at Sevastopol. There are only 600,000 Ukrainians in Crimea – 23 per cent of the population. And there are the 300,000 Crimean Tatars: the policy of the Russian authorities has been to prevent the returnees returning to their former homes, but rather to disperse them across the country.

The EU, Ukraine and minorities

Ukraine enacted in 1992 a *Law on National Minorities in Ukraine*. The 1996 Constitution makes provision both for the rights, including linguistic rights (Article 10), of national minorities and of indigenous peoples (Article 11). Ukraine has ratified most relevant international instruments, and has, to a greater extent than most post-Soviet states, made serious efforts to incorporate these into domestic law. Practice has proved more difficult.

The PCA entered into by Ukraine and the EU does not specifically mention minority issues. But the EU-Ukraine Summit on 15 September

2000 reiterated the importance of Ukraine to the EU. High on the list of priorities was the importance given to the development of stable institutions guaranteeing democracy and the rule of law, with recognition of the work of the Council of Europe and the OSCE. Indeed, even prior to the signing of the PCA, the European Parliament was showing special concern for minority rights. On 9 February 1994 it adopted a 'Resolution on linguistic and cultural minorities in the European Community'.

This pointed out again the need for Member States to recognise their linguistic minorities and to make the necessary legal and administrative provisions for them to create the basic conditions for the preservation and development of these languages. It stressed that all minority languages and cultures should also be protected by appropriate legal statute in the Member States.

Two other European inter-governmental organisations have played a much more important role with regard to minorities, and the European Parliament Resolution made express reference to them: the Council of Europe and the OSCE. Ukraine acceded to the Council of Europe (CoE) in November 1995, and immediately a European Commission/CoE 'Joint Programme for strengthening federal structures and local government, introducing human rights protection mechanisms, and supporting reforms of the law and legal system' was established as a response to accession to the CoE and the obligations Ukraine agreed to meet as a result. The programme was funded jointly, about 50/50, by the EC and CoE, with a budget of about three million euros for Ukraine.

Ukraine and the Council of Europe

Ukraine has had a stormy relationship with the CoE, and the issue of its exclusion is at the time of writing still under consideration. On acceding to the CoE in 1995, it committed itself to a long list of obligations, including ratification of the main CoE treaties. Ukraine has been threatened several times with exclusion from the CoE for non-compliance on a range of questions, most recently on 6 April 2001 by the Monitoring Committee of the Parliamentary Assembly.

But one of the Conventions it has ratified is the CoE's 1995 *Framework Convention for the Protection of National Minorities,* which it signed on 15 September 1995. The Framework Convention was ratified by Parliament on 9 December 1997 and entered into force on 1 May 1998. According to Article 9 of the 1996 Constitution, the Framework Convention is now part of Ukrainian law. It is a comprehensive instrument, covering a wide range of issues, including: non-discrimination; promotion of effective equality; promotion of the conditions regarding the preservation and development of the culture and preservation of religion, language and traditions; freedoms of assembly, association, expression, thought, conscience and religion; access to and use of media; linguistic freedoms: use of the minority language in private and in public as well as its use before administrative authorities; use of one's own name; display of information of a private nature; topographical names in the minority language; learning of and instruction in the minority language; freedom to set up educational institutions; transfrontier contacts; international and transfrontier co-operation; participation in economic, cultural and social life; participation in public life; and prohibition of forced assimilation.

Ukraine submitted its first Periodic Report on implementation of the provisions of the Framework Convention to the CoE in November 1999. This Report, on which the CoE's experts have not yet commented, provides a base-line for monitoring future developments. While there is a notable reluctance to mention the Russian-speakers, especially in matters of education, the Report does note that, according to the data of Ukraine' s State Committee on Statistics, in 1998/1999 there were in Ukraine 21,246 educational establishments of general education. These included 16,032 with Ukrainian language of teaching (4,421,265 pupils), Russian – 2,561 (2,313,901 pupils), Romanian – 108 (27,776 pupils), Moldavian – 18 (4,509 pupils), Hungarian – 65 (21,214 pupils), Crimean Tatar – 6 (4,071 pupils), Polish – 3 (1,109 pupils).

The Crimean Tatars' 'Foundation for Research and Support of the Indigenous Peoples of Crimea' prepared a lengthy Parallel Report, focusing on the situation in Crimea, and commenting in details on their many complaints, mostly against the Crimean authorities. They made the point that presentation of this Report and the use of the term 'national minorities' under the Framework Convention did not mean that the Crimean Tatar people agreed with their identification as a national minority. It is interesting that the Russian community provided no such 'parallel' report.

The Crimean Tatars and the OSCE's High Commissioner on National Minorities

The OSCE has played a very important role in reducing tension in Crimea. In 1996 the former OSCE High Commissioner on National Minorities (HCNM), Max van der Stoel, was asked by the then Ukrainian Minister of Justice to consider a Draft 'Concept of the National Policy of Ukraine in relation to Indigenous Peoples'. In his answer of 14 February 1997 he took the opportunity to make recommendations with regard to the Crimean Tatars, since they consider themselves to be the indigenous people of Crimea. In his view, an important difference between national minorities and indigenous peoples is that in contrast to a national minority, an indigenous people does not have a kinstate (the Russians in Ukraine obviously do have one – a large one).

But he was primarily concerned with the large number of returned Crimean Tatars who did not have Ukrainian citizenship, and were therefore excluded from voting, participating in privatisation, and many other important citizenship rights. The problem facing the Crimean Tatars who had returned after 13 November 1991 (when they would have become citizens automatically) was that they must renounce their Uzbek or other citizenship – Ukraine does not permit dual citizenship. And to renounce Uzbek citizenship was time-consuming and costly. This problem was in part resolved in August 1998, as a direct result of the HCNM's recommendation, by the Agreement on the Prevention of Dual Citizenship signed by the Ukraine and Uzbek Governments, which allowed for an accelerated and simplified procedure for renouncing Uzbek citizenship and acquiring Ukrainian citizenship. 25,000 Crimean Tatars have benefited from this change in procedure.

More seriously for the longer term, the Ukrainian elections held on 29 March 1998 left the Crimean Tatars with no representation in Crimea's Supreme Soviet – previously their elected body, the Mejlis, had 14 seats by way of a special quota granted to them after a prolonged campaign of civil disobedience. The quota was taken from them just before the 1998 elections. There are, however, two Crimean Tatar deputies in the national Parliament, Mustafa Djemilev (elected on the Rukh list) and Refat Chubarov (elected for a constituency seat). This means that at the next elections, in 2002, there is no guarantee that the Crimean Tatars will have any representation at all. The Ukrainian Government has shown sensitivity to the claims of the Crimean Tatars. A Council of Representatives of the Crimean Tatar People was established in July 2000, which has special access to and meets regularly with President Kuchma. Following a meeting on 17 September 2001, Kuchma stated that increasing their representation in public administration is an important and urgent issue – 5 per cent of all civil servants in Crimea was obviously too little. And the burning issue remains of Crimean Tatar participation in land privatisation, and indeed restitution of their land lost in 1944 – hotly contested by the Russian majority.

The Russians, the Charter, and the Constitutional Court

The Russian speakers of Ukraine as a whole – or more accurately their leaders, whose vociferous protests do not match the mood of most Russians – also have many complaints. Not the least of these is that Ukrainian is now required for entry to higher education as well as state employment. Furthermore, the three ethnic Russian groups in Ukraine, the Russian Movement of Ukraine, the Russian-Ukrainian Union, and For a Single Rus, fear that the number of Russian language schools is steadily diminishing. In September 2001 they stated that the Ukrainian Government had over the last decade changed the language of instruction in 1,300 schools from Russian to Ukrainian, and as a result only 10 per cent of schools in the country are now conducted in Russian. Of course, if this is accurate it may well be because Russian parents wish their children to have the best chances later in life. These leaders also fear – somewhat unreasonably, when Russian print and broadcast media are still dominant in Ukraine – that the Russian language and culture might be forced out. More trivially, perhaps, Russian names are now changed to their Ukrainian versions on official documents, for example passports and driving licences. Thus, S. A. (Alexandrovich) Pushkin becomes S. O. (Oleksandrovich) – a cause of some trauma. For all these reasons, these leaders have pinned their hopes of protection on a CoE instrument which has not received much attention in the rest of Europe.

On 24 December 1999 Parliament enacted a law to ratify the 1992 *European Charter for Regional or Minority Languages*. Ukraine signed it on 2 May 1996. It is a 'pick and mix' treaty covering education and other linguistic rights. The Charter's overriding purpose is cultural. It is designed to protect and promote regional or minority languages as a threatened aspect of Europe's cultural heritage. For this reason it not only contains a non-discrimination clause concerning the use of these languages but also provides for measures offering active support for them. The aim is to ensure, as far as reasonably possible, the use of regional or minority languages in education and the media and to permit their use in judicial and administrative settings, economic and social life and cultural activities.

But the Charter, unlike the Framework Convention, sets out to protect and promote regional or minority languages, not linguistic minorities. For this reason emphasis is placed on the cultural dimension and the use of a regional or minority language in all the aspects of the life of its speakers. The Charter does not establish any individual or collective rights for the speakers of regional or minority languages. Nevertheless, the obligations of the parties with regard to the status of these languages and the domestic legislation which will have to be introduced in compliance with the Charter will have an obvious effect on the situation of the communities concerned and their individual members.

The Law on Ratification set out precise percentages of minority population for each level of the Charter to come into effect. According to the Charter, in regions that are 20 per cent minority inhabited, minority languages shall gain official status. Enactment of this law was welcomed by the Russian community leaders, who had long been pressing for ratification of the Charter.

However, any euphoria was dampened by the advisory decision on 14 December 1999 of the Ukrainian Constitutional Court, with one strong dissension by Judge Mironenko, clarifying Article 10 of the Constitution, on the status of the Russian and Ukrainian languages in Ukraine. Ukrainian is stated in Article 10 to be the state language. Controversially, the view of the majority of judges went further. It was that the Ukrainian language was the only 'compulsory means of communication for officials of local government bodies and local self-government structures, and in all spheres of public life' including education. Consequently, according to a circular sent out by a government source, officials must use only Ukrainian, lack of knowledge of the language could lead to dismissal, and higher education must be in Ukrainian only, thus seeking to bring forward radically a hitherto gradual process. According to the dissenting judge, the Court paid too little attention to an important sentence of Article 10: 'In Ukraine, the free development, use and protection of Russian, other languages of national minorities of Ukraine, is guaranteed'. This decision played a part in further exacerbating tension between the linguistic communities, and preceded the death in Lviv of the Ukrainian popular composer Bilozir on 28 May 2000, as a result of injuries suffered allegedly at the hands of Russians in an open-air café - he was said to have complained about the Russian pop music. The Lviv authorities introduced, for a time, a decree banning the playing of 'low quality', that is Russian, music in public. And on 21 June 2000 the Cabinet of Ministers updated the 1997 'Measures concerning comprehensive development and functioning of the Ukrainian language', to provide not only for a 'wide interpretation' of the Constitutional Court's decision, but also for 'regular checks' of observance by state officials 'and in other spheres of social life'.

Even the apparent ratification of the Charter proved illusory. The instrument of ratification was never deposited in Strasbourg, and on 12 July 2000 the Ukrainian Constitutional Court ruled that the law on ratification was unconstitutional, on highly technical grounds – the law was not signed by the President as required by the Constitution. The Charter, which went out of force on 14 July, would have enabled minority languages to gain official status in 20 per cent minority-inhabited regions. The Ukrainian Government, however, remains committed to consolidating Ukrainian statehood and the position of Ukrainian as the state language, while protecting the legitimate interests of the Russian and other minorities. After all, Ukraine has rather a large neighbour.

Conclusion

Uncharitable commentators have wondered whether Ukraine is viable in the long term as an independent state. Some hotheads among the Crimean Tatars have found themselves gazing admiringly at Abkhazia across the Black Sea, where the 20 per cent Abkhazian population ethnically cleansed their territory of the 80 per cent Georgians. Lurid paranoid fantasies are rife among the Russians of Eastern Ukraine and the Ukrainians of Western Ukraine – words like 'apartheid' and 'cultural genocide' are heard too often. It is to the credit of the young Ukrainian state that none of these have led to other than very isolated bloodshed. The EU, CoE and OSCE all have the strongest possible interest in resolution of these tensions through the use of legal and political instruments and mechanisms. The short paragraphs above give a flavour of what has been done and can be done.

UNLEASHED, BUT STILL MUZZLED
THE MEDIA IN UKRAINE

Olexiy Solohubenko

'Ten years of independence in Ukraine have produced a multitude of different media, but does more mean free?'

Not long ago a respected British economist writing for a respected national broadsheet was taken for a weekend economics seminar in Kiev. The following week in his column the economist wrote that it was sheer pleasure to be able, in this day and age, to visit a capital city in Europe with no traffic. Simply, he had not been told that on Saturdays and Sundays cars were banned from the city centre. By Monday, traffic jams were back as usual, but by then the economist had flown back to London.

Something similar may happen if a visitor to Ukraine should decide to flick through TV channels, or try to listen to FM radio or look into a newspaper kiosk. There is so much of everything: there is more terrestrial television in Kiev than in London; there are more than two dozen FM stations and countless newspapers and magazines. In the provinces there will certainly be less choice compared with the capital. Nevertheless the sheer volume of the media is impressive.

When it comes to *choice* for an average Ukrainian, it is no worse than in many other countries, if that is a consolation. On television there will be lots of talking heads in live discussions about the meaning of life, national rebirth, fashion, spiritual values, family, traditions, sometimes politics. There will be lots of game shows, re-runs of old (sometimes Soviet-made) dramas and relatively recent Western TV shows, lots of rock and pop festivals and lots of programming in Russian and from Russia. News on TV will be sycophantic and stodgy on state channels, and loyal and bubbly on the commercial ones. Presentation techniques and studio design are as good as any.

On commercial radio the sound will be more homogenised: an abundance of pop, mostly in English and Russian, less often in Ukrainian, and linked by bubbly DJs whose winning formula is to speak fast. Jazz, classical music and, in particular, speech are a rarity on Ukrainian private radio. News on radio is patchy and parochial, with very few exceptions.

In print one would quickly notice that serious journalism is confined to a handful of low-circulation broadsheets (like *Den* or *Dzerkalo Tyzhnya* weekly) while tabloids like *Fakty* rule the roost. One would notice in them the abundance of stories about crime, celebrity gossip, and beauty contests. Here, too, there is not much difference to what a reader or listener can get in many other countries.

What is striking, however, is the inability of the average Ukrainian to get robust reporting on the workings of the President or his closest allies, to hear what opposition leaders have to say without editorialising by the presenters, to probe the powers-that-be on such issues as corruption, abuse of power, human rights, police abuse, prison reform, and, most recently, the Gongadze tape scandal known as 'Kuchmagate'. It is in independent political journalism that the state media and, to a lesser degree, commercial outlets fail their audiences. The pressure is too great for them to be able to meet the challenge.

Virtual dissent, actual control

Perhaps another striking thing is the complacency of Ukrainians with the degree of political control they allow the authorities to have over their media. In Prague, hundreds of thousands demonstrated because of the perceived threat to free reporting from the appointment of a pro-Government TV chief; in Ukraine the openly pro-presidential kow-towing of the 1st National Channel may spark occasional complaints from politicians and a string of censure motions from Parliament, but it fails to stir any popular protest. True, people do not believe what they get from it, but they lack the resolve and the democratic mechanisms to change the situation.

It is the subjugation of *independent* political journalism in both print and electronic media and persistent attempts at media control by the authorities that are the reasons why Ukraine's reputation and that of her leaders have been so seriously dented of late. Independent, probing political journalism is now confined mostly to the Internet and a handful of low-circulation newsletters with no mass impact – in a way a digital-age reincarnation of the Soviet-era dissident *samvydav* (literally self-publishing, better known by its Russian equivalent, *samizdat*).

The repercussions for the most daring critics of the regime (witness the conversations secretly taped in President Kuchma's office) can be harsh and even lethal. Over the last few years a number of high-profile journalists have been killed or have died in suspicious circumstances; dozens have been beaten, harassed or otherwise intimidated. Muted Western criticism of such strong-arm tactics is followed by standard rebuttals, by a rise in anti-Western feeling within Ukraine's ruling circles, and, often, by a step in the direction of Russia. In this balancing act Western criticism is muted even further to avoid antagonising Ukraine and provoking still more dramatic political shifts.

Lists of sins

Does Ukraine get a fair hearing, then? Is it true, as Ukrainian representatives often say, that 'all Ukraine gets is a list of sins'? After all, pressure on political journalists and spinning by governments is not unheard of elsewhere in the world, while game shows and tabloids are ratings leaders throughout Europe and America.

Many media gurus in Ukraine would argue that their country has merely joined the club. It has, but in a peculiar way, incorporating into the new scene many ideological carry-overs from Soviet times. One of them is a deeply held belief that letting the media operate freely will undermine the power of the state. This is why the imperative of political control underpins all legal regulation of the media, and probably serves as the biggest constraint on wider social and political reform in Ukraine.

Over the ten years of its independence Ukraine has adopted a number of legal documents that should, in theory, guarantee media freedom and independence. The Constitution, the Law on Television and Radio Broadcasting, the Election Law and many others proclaim freedom of the media as a pillar of the political system. But when it comes to the political will to observe these laws, then we see that the authorities often resort to arbitrary, extra-judicial moves in order to stifle the media they cannot control.

This may include closures of newspapers on the orders of the Information Minister (*Silski Visti,* closed for its support for the ex-Prime Minister Pavlo Lazarenko, is the most graphic example), crippling libel suits brought by powerful government and business figures, the refusal of largely state-owned printing houses to print offending papers or magazines, and intimidation of journalists through violence or threats of prosecution and imprisonment (usually for fiscal impropriety and underpayment of tax – never for political reasons). Ukrainian courts continue to give huge libel awards to local politicians and businessmen which often make a paper or TV station bankrupt. Lastly, the famous 'inspections' by tax authorities, fire brigades, environmental officers, etc., often arriving in clusters.

Recently, a new form of pressure has emerged in the form of the non-renewal of broadcast licences. This has happened to Kiev's *Radio Continent* where the murdered journalist Heorhiy Gongadze used to work and which re-broadcast Western stations including the BBC. But the most effective way of controlling the media is through covert political pressure and the surviving Soviet habit of self-censorship.

There are many forms of media control through self-censorship, the most common being an 'understanding' between the proprietor, publisher or controller and the editorial staff that the names of certain politicians should not be mentioned at all or mentioned in a negative context. At one respected TV channel a specially appointed editor-at-large acting on behalf of the proprietor was employed to vet all the pieces in news bulletins, removing or re-wording references to opposition leaders. When journalists challenged the practice, the head of the station – incidentally, one of the best in Ukraine – responded by saying that by yielding to the control he was 'saving the channel'.

The vetting may apply not only to opposition leaders, but even to the Prime Minister himself. This happened to Viktor Yushchenko, who complained to President Kuchma about the deliberate tarnishing of his Government's record by state television and its boss Vadym Dolhanov. The President did not dismiss Dolhanov. Instead it was Yushchenko himself who was removed from office shortly after a libellous piece about him produced by Russia's ORT television was re-broadcast nationally by its partner channel in Ukraine, INTER.

Money talks, in a subtle way

Politics has played a much greater role in the Ukrainian media to date than economics. Few if any of the national commercial TV channels are profitable. Most radio stations are struggling on meagre budgets and are lucky to break even, and many papers rely on regular financial injections by their proprietors. Nothing surprising if one compares the annual advertising turnover in Ukraine (circa $35 million in 2000) with that in neighbouring Romania ($100 million, with less than half the population) and much more prosperous and again less populous Poland ($400 million and rising).

In Poland and even in Russia the media, particularly television, is a money spinner, whereas in Ukraine financial gain is often secondary. Most of the media moguls *earn* their money elsewhere, and *spend* it on the media. The low disposable incomes of vast numbers of Ukrainians make advertising revenue a precarious gamble; for instance, had market conditions been applied, most of the 20-odd FM stations in Kiev would not have survived, as their outgoings on electricity, production and staff (though not on copyright fees) are usually greater than any income they can raise from advertising. With the printed media the situation is made easier as they can recover some costs through sales, yet even the relatively small list price of many newspapers is prohibitive to many Ukrainian citizens.

The key media tycoons who are commonly referred to in Ukraine as *oligarchs* – like Hryhoriy Surkis, Olexander Volkov, Viktor Pinchuk, Viktor Medvedchuk – have most of their financial interests in property, football, pipe manufacturing, banking and breweries, and use their media interests for political ends, often as *add-ons* to their main business. They may have rivalries of their own and there may be competitive pressures between them, but they secure their financial and business standing by being part of the President's circle, by supporting him through the media they control. In neighbouring Russia there have been recent precedents of media tycoons surviving for years in opposition to the authorities. In the early stages of wild privatisation they managed to become rich by *not being part* of the ruling circle. In Ukraine this was not possible, and business success could be achieved only through political loyalty.

When President Kuchma was challenged by a journalist in Lithuania who asked about the lack of free media in Ukraine, the President replied that many of the media in Ukraine were privately owned, and so, by definition, they were free. Projected onto the Ukrainian situation, however, media ownership matched with political loyalty results in exactly the opposite.

Small steps, quiet voices

To a large extent this explains why Ukraine's media are so timid and also why attempts to reform the media through the legislative process have proved futile. On the surface, Ukraine has the laws – often compatible with European legislation – and the necessary regulatory authorities, like the State Committee on Information Policy (successor to the Information Ministry) and the National Council for Radio and Television. However neither can disengage itself from the control of the authorities, and while the former (headed until recently by the poet Ivan Drach) acts mostly as a funnel for venting anger at the dominance of Russian-language media in Ukraine, the latter (headed by Borys Kholod) acts as licensing authority on behalf of pro-presidential groups.

A major player with substantial financial and political backing, the INTER TV channel has so far managed to keep its licence, even though its term has expired and even though most of the channel's programming is in Russian – in contravention of Ukrainian language law and the provisions of the licence itself. However when it comes to more vulnerable outlets – like the FM station *Nikopolskiye Izvestia* or the *Ishtar* Company from Vinnytsya, the wrath of the regulator is formidable. Similarly, the financial debts of some become the main reason for depriving them of licences, whereas the biggest debtors – among them state radio and TV – are judged by different criteria and get away with being in the red for years on end.

The issue of the language of broadcast is perhaps as contentious as political content, and it merits a special study. However, any controversy connected with it and the power of the Ukrainian regulators to deal with it in accordance with the media law are swept under the carpet when big-time politics and real heavyweights are in play. An example of this is the agreement signed in Moscow in October 2000 by the Foreign Ministers of Ukraine and Russia, which in effect legalised the Russian media presence in Ukraine. The fact that it offered similar possibilities for the Ukrainian media in Russia is quite meaningless as the Ukrainian media are unlikely ever to realise those possibilities.

The vulnerability of the Ukrainian media to external competitive pressures (mostly from Russia, but also, to a smaller degree, in the news market from Western broadcasters) together with internal weaknesses arising from low investment, lack of talent and a repressive climate have resulted in attempts at 'ring-fencing', known in Ukraine as 'protection of the national media space'.

Many institutions and individuals have been involved in elaborating the 'concept of national media space' over the past few years, and perhaps the fact that it has not so far materialised can be explained not by the poor performance of the elaborators, but rather by the fact that the concept flies in the face of media globalisation and of growing trans-frontier access by Ukrainians to the media they want.

Instead of unleashing creative freedom and encouraging competition, the Ukrainian authorities seem to have opted to fence off what they understand as their 'national media space' by transplanting the idea of 'national air space' into broadcasting. While national air space can be managed by banning unwanted aircraft, it is difficult to see how national media space can be protected. This is not just because airwaves, satellite signals and, more recently, the Internet reach users directly wherever they are, but also because Ukraine has proclaimed its European credentials and is a signatory to the European Convention on Trans-frontier Television, whose very essence contradicts the spirit and mentality of media restrictions.

Similarly unsuccessful have been the numerous attempts to devise a concept of public service broadcasting. On every occasion the stumbling block has been the devolution of broadcasting from the state. Typically, there has been talk of a 'state-public' television, with the *state* as the dominant partner and with no real mechanisms or legislative tools left for the *public* to play a role in shaping broadcasting policy. Indeed, the reality in Ukraine is that the President now rules the media by decree – appointing key managers in national television, radio and regulatory bodies, and leaving Parliament very few options and mechanisms for removing them.

Another attempt to develop a concept of public broadcasting is now being developed by a group headed by the Ukrainian specialist in media technologies and PR techniques, Professor Heorhiy Pocheptsov. Even if his team comes up with a coherent concept of open public service media (which is not certain as many of the professor's views centre round conspiracy theories and hidden media agendas) it is unlikely that anything major will happen before the parliamentary elections in March 2002 and the presidential elections two years later. The political culture of control and domination now prevalent in Ukraine will determine the role of the media for the entire election period. It seems unlikely that any opposition group or party will be able to finance and sustain a meaningful media presence in the parliamentary elections in 2002; as for the presidential race of 2004, there is a possibility that some media moguls may decide to reassign their loyalties and swap allegiances, particularly if President Kuchma fails to change the Constitution and does not run for a third term.

Supply and demand

Over the past ten years Ukraine has had some spectacular achievements in its media development. For instance, some of the investigative reporting on social issues and the environment on the *1+1* channel by Olha Herasimiuk was truly outstanding – as was the camera work. Some political programmes, like *The Fifth Corner* on the same channel, were innovative and fresh. The slick design of news and current affairs programmes as well as talk shows on *Novy Kanal* (The New Channel) were as good as any. One can also cite political programmes on *Radio Continent* in Kiev or some excellent reporting in the press, radio and television in Lviv, Odessa, Ivano-Frankivsk and the Crimea.

Special credit should go to Ukrainian web-designers, who may have started late but are now on a par with the best in the world: they have style, vision and subtlety that set them apart. There is perhaps less sparkle in the print media, but there are some excellent papers published both in Kiev and in regional centres.

Alas, the supply of such quality material is rather limited, and the Ukrainian media market is still one of imports rather than exports. For some, sadly, this may be a reflection of what is known in Ukraine as *'menshovartist'*, i.e. something home-grown but qualitatively inferior to the model which inspired it. For others it proves that there is a good deal of talent in Ukraine, but that conditions are not right for it to blossom.

Whatever the reason, one thing is seldom disputed: as in other areas, Ukraine has dithered too long and, as a result, has failed to realise its full potential. The void has been filled with imports from abroad, mostly from Russia, and it is not at all clear that this trend will ever be reversed.

The recipe for media success anywhere is to set talent free, and this has particular significance for Ukraine which has traditionally found itself under a double cultural pressure from Russia and from the West. It seems that more deregulation, more competition, more opportunity and more freedom should be the answer. The authorities in Ukraine tend to think differently: in their quest for a 'national media space', the recipes they offer are often simplistic and hark back to the Soviet past.

Speaking in 2001 on the occasion of Ukraine's national press day, President Kuchma said that the prime task of Ukrainian journalists was to 'create a positive image for Ukraine'. While this kind of view of the role of the media in society prevails at the top, journalists will continue to face an uphill struggle to maintain freedom of speech on the ground.

NGO DEVELOPMENT IN UKRAINE
THE BEGINNINGS OF CIVIL SOCIETY

Vira Nanivska

This article examines the development of the civil society and NGO sector in Ukraine as its government moves from a totalitarian to a democratic system. It deals with the structures of civil society and their role in strengthening the Government of Ukraine's transition towards democratic functioning, discusses trends in the number, membership and types of activity of Ukrainian NGOs, and analyses the challenges and problems of civil society development in Ukraine. Further, evidence shows the necessity of establishing public policy procedures to strengthen governance and democracy building. This chapter therefore assesses the role of the public policy process in facilitating democratic transformation in Ukraine, through a comparison with developments in this sector in Central and Eastern Europe under EU guidance.

Historical overview

Repression in the former USSR

For most of the twentieth century totalitarian rule in Ukraine excluded civil society development. In the former Soviet Union, civil society was repressed and indeed criminalised; therefore, there was a low level of public participation and awareness of citizen rights. During the Soviet era, public engagement methods such as demonstrations and meetings did exist, but were used to control and required mandatory participation. Prior to Ukraine's independence there was no modern history of voluntary or spontaneous public participation. These factors had a negative impact on human development in Ukraine and were destructive for both civil society and social capital. Finally, non-government organisations were unthinkable in a system in which the government was ubiquitous.

Civil organisations in Soviet Ukraine

Communist ideology only accepted civil society organisations (CSOs) created and controlled by the party-state. Mass organisations did exist, like the *Komsomol*, a youth institution preparing young adults for future Communist Party involvement. Such structures reinforced the values and objectives of the system, playing an important role in disseminating ideology; membership was valued for personal advancement. Typically, participation in such organisations was merely formal, indicating most clearly Party control.

'Amateur clubs' were also popular, targeting athletes, hunters, musicians, etc; they operated on a non-profit basis. These groups were created and maintained by the state to facilitate the talents and interests of the population and to control their gatherings. These groups were non-political; they were simply interest clubs with no advocacy or social justice mandate.

New challenges since 1991

Change came in the late 1980s due in part to the economic, environmental and social problems exacerbated by the Chernobyl catastrophe. The Government was not able to control the spontaneous increase in civil movements challenging the communist structure and demanding government accountability. With the fall of the USSR, basic democratic rights including freedom of speech, freedom of information and the right to associate were quickly recognised in the newly independent Ukraine. The law 'On Unions of Citizens' (1992) became a catalyst for the rapid growth of CSOs. New opportunities to establish open organisations were capitalised on by Ukrainian citizens.

The third sector

NGOs

Newly emerging NGOs represent society's response to the challenges of transformation and the responsibility for co-creating good governance. Many

NGOs work to fill those niches where the state no longer supplies services it was responsible for in the past. Further, Ukrainian NGOs are beginning to serve as an instrument for increasing public awareness and fulfil the democratic task of holding the Government accountable for its decisions. However, the poor level of skills and training for this work demands immediate intervention.

Local NGOs are proving to be more successful than national ones, due to shared community interests and accessibility. Trust is slowly increasing between the Government and citizens as NGOs collaborate with municipal governments. Further, the development and support of community initiatives that take into account citizen interests and the input of local NGOs creates an important dialogue between the citizen and the public service. This is accomplished by monitoring service delivery at the municipal level and building NGO capacity to provide citizen engagement in the policy process. This includes:

- training in public hearings
- facilitation of questionnaires on service delivery
- sectoral 'report cards'
- civic journalism training
- establishing advisory committees including public officials and local NGO representatives

Projects focusing on such practical outputs, such as the 'People's Voice Project' (WBI/CIDA funded), achieve tangible results and create a positive response towards NGO development in Ukraine. Although such public/private engagement in the stuff of 'everyday' democracy in the West, it is an area of capacity building that Ukraine dramatically needs.

NGO development

When compared to EU candidate countries, the NGO sector in Ukraine is small. According to official statistics, in 2000 there were approximately 25,500 civic organisations operating in Ukraine *(Figure 1).*

Figure 1. Number of NGOs in Ukraine

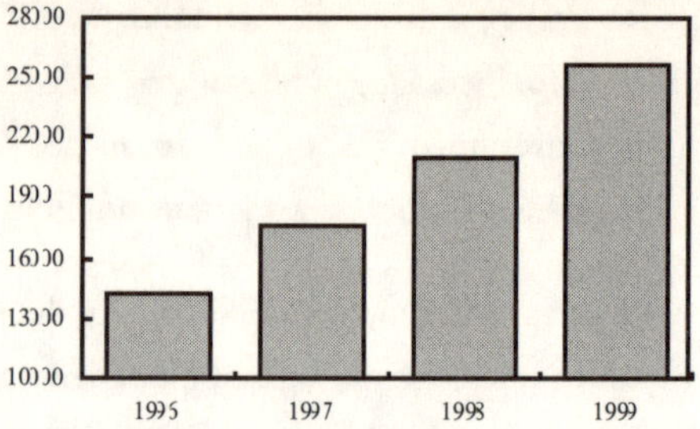

Source: GolovDerzhSluzhba

In comparison, in 1994 the Czech Republic had more than 30,000 CSOs; in Poland, about 20,000 were registered. Hungary had 43,000 CSOs in 1995. CEE countries are mandated and supported by the EU in the development of their third sectors. To facilitate this, the EU established Phare, targeting social solidarity, civil society and networks between NGOs, particularly between European Union organisations and their CEE counterparts. Mirroring Phare's methods in Ukraine could establish similar results and facilitate Ukraine's alignment with EU standards.

Participation in NGOs

The Democratic Initiatives Foundation (DIF) opinion polls show that third-sector membership in Ukraine remained constant from 1994 – 2000, with no major changes: in 1994, 82 per cent stated they are not members of any civic or political organisation and in 2000, 83 per cent. Because Ukrainian citizens are not fully aware of the third sector's role they are reluctant to participate. Other causes are:

- Lack of experience, desire, time;
- Economics: the need to earn a living;
- FSU 'volunteering' undercuts involvement;
- Distrust reduces participation.

NGO activities.

Most NGOs in Ukraine are public health, social welfare, social/political, advocacy or cultural/arts organisations (Figure 2).

Figure 2. Types of NGO activity

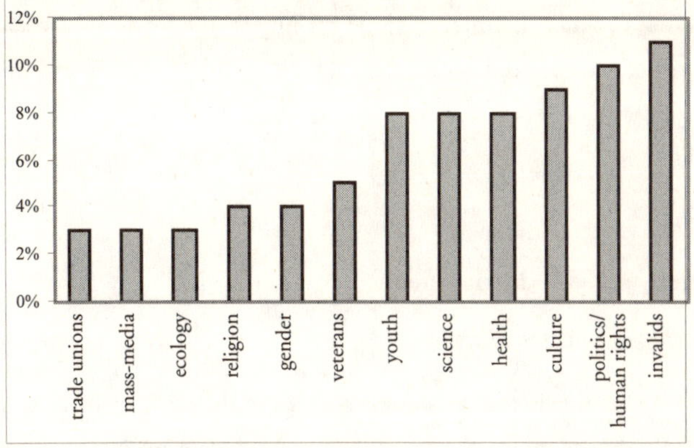

Source: UNDP

Such groups focus on the disabled and war veterans; supporting culture, children, youth and students; and assisting victims of ecological catastrophes. Public/private interest is in increasing the services previously monopolised by the state. Advocacy structures continue to grow; there has been a steady development in religious organisations, including NGOs (Figure 3).

Figure 3. The dynamics of religious organisatons

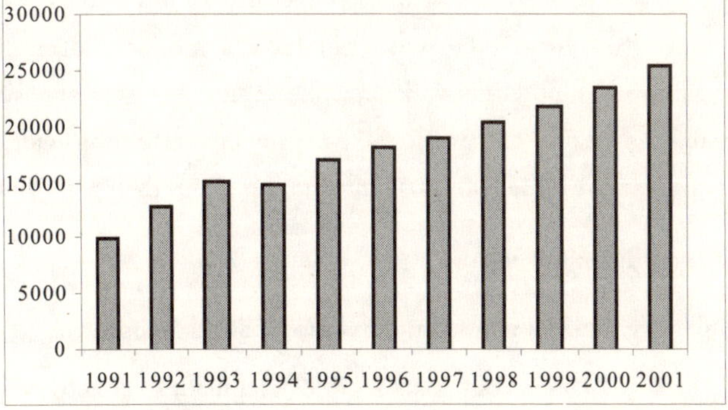

Source: State Committee on Religious Issues

There is a concomitant increase in the growth rate of associations for youth and women. New political/social structures enable the women's movement, which is proving to be an important force of advocacy. More than 4 per cent of NGOs deal directly with women's issues and promote the development of legislation and mechanisms for the improvement of their status.

Barriers to NGO development

Information accessibility

There is a generally low awareness about the third sector in Ukraine, due to the limited availability of official and reliable data on NGO developments; such information appears on a sporadic and irregular basis. New sources of information are:

- Directories: *NGO Guide in Ukraine; Ukrainian Third Sector Framework; Civic and Charitable Organisations in Ukraine; Ukrainian NGO Directory.*

- NGO Websites: www.ngoukraine.kiev.ua; zurc.org; www.freedomhouse.kiev.ua; www.gurt.org.ua.

- Periodicals: *Civic Initiatives; NGO News; Crossroad; Counterpart Alliance for Partnership News.*

- Resource Centres: *Gurt Resource Centre; Western Ukrainian Resource Centre; Counterpart Creative Centre.*

This does not provide a complete picture of third sector operations in Ukraine. Most local NGOs do not have a modern communication infrastructure; computer networks, telephone and fax systems are simply too expensive. As a result, they are not able to provide their nation-wide partners, or anyone else, with the necessary information about their activities.

NGO Legal Background

Ukrainian legislation provided the basis for CSO development:

- Law 'On Unions of Citizens' (1992), regulating the activities of social-political groups, parties and civic organisations;

- The Constitution of Ukraine (1996);

- Laws 'On Charity and Charitable Organisations' and 'On Creative Workers and Creative Unions' (1997); and
- Law 'On Youth and Children Civic Organisations' (1998).

This legislation made possible the diversity of non-governmental structures in Ukraine. However, problems regarding definitions of third sector players and their status still create unnecessary confusion, due to gaps in legislation. For instance, multiple terms, such as 'non-government,' 'civic' and 'public' are used, but are not legally defined.

Third sector taxation must be regulated and aligned with EU standards. At present, Ukraine has not developed the concept of 'the public good;' tax regulations for charitable donations have not been fully introduced. NGOs are exempt from profit or value-added taxes, but they must not engage in commercial activities. Some provisions in tax law are inconsistent and contradict provisions of other, non-tax, laws; as a result, the legislation is confusing. Ukrainian legislation is without clear concepts and criteria to define non-profit activities.

There is a global trend, initiated by the International Red Cross, towards establishing NGO 'Codes of Conduct'; several voluntary and self-policing codes have been adopted. Although non-legal, they establish precedents that protect donors, governments, and the public. Such codes improve NGO credibility, authority and transparency in their activities. It would be very helpful if the Ukrainian NGO community adopted their own code, and when relevant, participated in international ones.

Third sector capacity

The role of public policy in democratic capacity building

To increase Ukrainian social capacity to perform its democratic function, training in the institutions, practices and procedures of public policy are required. Through projects providing training in public policy mechanisms and procedures, civil society is empowered and transparency, accountability and increased government effectiveness is achieved. In Ternopil and Ivano-

Frankivsk, local authorities and NGOs are engaging in new decision-making processes, through training from ICPS's 'People's Voice Project.' Local NGOs work in a variety of sectors, including gender advocacy, implementing public monitoring initiatives. The Project held a number of workshops to help these NGOs, covering issues of strategic and operational planning and management; media relations; teamwork skills; proposal writing and fundraising.

Essential skills for the policy process

The main obstacle to NGO participation in public policy is a lack of training in the mechanisms and procedures required. Many NGOs in Ukraine are still characterised by:

- Weak institutional capacity for the decision-making process;
- Poor management and professional expertise;
- Undeveloped planning, development and budgeting skills;
- Lack of training in public consultations and debate;
- Inexperience with evaluation and monitoring;
- Poor analytical skills.

These are all teachable and learnable skills; Ukraine needs Technical Assistance providing skills-based training to the NGO sector. Then it will fulfill the mandate for citizen engagement.

Technical assistance and third sector capacity building

The role of Technical Assistance in civil society capacity has two aspects:

- To stimulate the growth of NGOs in Ukraine and facilitate their organisational structure and management, through providing them with training, information and experts sharing the best concepts and practices.
- To build the Government's capacity to encourage civil society through developing appropriate financial and legal environments and strengthening dialogue with civil society organisations.

Conclusions

Achieving democratic governance through civil society empowerment is critical to Ukraine's future. This process can be accelerated through strengthening the third sector and developing its close co-operation with government at the national and local levels. NGOs activities increase the potential for better government performance, facilitating a transparent and sustainable democratic transformation. Therefore, Ukraine's capacity in the following sectors must be encouraged:

- Stimulating citizen participation;
- Public monitoring of government policies;
- Developing democratic norms and values through existing democratic institutions.

These recommendations are targets for the EU's involvement in candidate countries and are supported by generous funding. Their NGO sector has a trajectory of growth and development unseen in Ukraine. If similar targets and methods were adopted, Ukraine's NGO capacity would improve substantially. When citizens are empowered to take up their democratic responsibilities in a skilful and competent way and participate in public policy development, then democracy in Ukraine will flourish.

3

Ukraine: Economic Progress and Prospects

UKRAINE
THE EVOLUTION OF ITS ECONOMY SINCE INDEPENDENCE

Edilberto Segura

Introduction

When Ukraine declared its independence in August 1991, it became the second largest European country in landmass and the fourth largest in population, with 50 million people. Ukraine's agricultural soil is extensive and rich: it used to be the breadbasket of the former Soviet Union, providing a large portion of its agricultural needs. Ukraine also has good mineral resources (iron ore, coal) and an adequate infrastructure. It has a well-educated and skilled labour force, with significant engineering and scientific foundation. All this permitted Ukraine to supply much of the heavy industry of the former Soviet Union.

Despite these favourable conditions, Ukraine has had one of the most difficult economic challenges in Eastern Europe, with a long economic recession that lasted eight years. From independence in 1991 up to 1999, gross domestic product (GDP) declined every year, with a cumulative decline of about 60 per cent.

The recession in Ukraine from 1991 to 1999 lasted so long because the country's initial conditions after independence were quite unfavourable, with major structural weaknesses and an economy highly dependent on the other former Soviet Republics. The collapse of the former Soviet Union cut these production and trade relations. In addition, the country had a large percentage of military industries (25 per cent of all companies produced military goods), which found themselves without markets after the end of the Cold War.

Furthermore, due to negligible energy costs during Soviet times, many industrial processes were very energy intensive (in the early 1990s, Ukraine consumed 6 times more oil per unit of GDP than Western Europe). Energy imports are still important; in 2000, import of oil and gas represented 43 per cent of merchandise imports and 19 per cent of GDP. These energy-intensive firms became unprofitable when energy costs increased 5-10 times after independence. Although the cumulative decline in GDP after 1991 was 60 per cent, about one-half of this decline was offset by expansion of the informal or shadow economy. This has helped to contain the decline in living standards. But it has also reduced the tax base and fiscal revenues.

Although the initial fall in GDP was amplified by unfavourable initial conditions, the slow economic recovery from 1991 to 1999 was due principally to the very slow, piecemeal, and uneven implementation of economic reforms. This was due to lack of political consensus and to opposition from some groups in Parliament and vested interests. This situation has led to a perception of Ukraine in the West as a country plagued by economic chaos, corruption, flight of capital, political infighting and an unstable legal environment.

But few people in the West are aware of the enormous developments that have taken place over the last two years. In fact, in 2000, after nine years of poor economic performance, the economy began a strong recovery. GDP grew by 6 per cent in 2000, with the pace of growth accelerating to 10.8 per cent in the first eight months of 2001 compared to the same period the previous year. This GDP growth was widespread, supported by expansion in industrial and agricultural output. In January-August 2001, industrial output increased by 16.9 per cent compared to the same period in 2000, while agricultural output increased by 27.7 per cent during the same period.

This impressive economic performance did not happen by accident. As will be discussed below, sound monetary and fiscal policies as well as a significant number of economic reforms implemented over the last two years finally produced the critical mass of economic changes needed to break a transition economy out of the doldrums of post-communist decline.

The early economic reform programme

The structural weaknesses of Ukraine during Soviet times meant that major corporate restructuring was needed after independence. Unfortunately, from 1991 to 1995, very little was done: the Government followed a 'preservation' strategy. That is, it tried to maintain the status quo through the payment of large, direct subsidies.

Relying on Government subsidies for their existence, state-owned enterprises had little incentive to restructure themselves and remained largely inefficient. These Government subsidies led to large fiscal budget deficits, monetary financing of these deficits, and hyper-inflation. During 1992 and 1993, with total fiscal expenditures at about 65 per cent of GDP, the fiscal budget deficit reached 25 per cent and 16 per cent of GDP respectively. The monetary financing of these deficits led to very high annual rates of inflation which peaked in 1993 at 10,160 per cent and which remained above 100 per cent per annum in 1994 and 1995.

In 1994, Leonid Kuchma was elected President on the basis of a reform agenda. During 1996-1998, under President Kuchma, significant progress was made in many areas of economic reform:

- Prices and international trade were liberalised.
- Small and mass privatisation programmes were completed successfully.
- The National Bank of Ukraine (NBU) was strengthened and monetary policy was implemented wisely.
- A new currency (Hryvnia or UAH) was introduced successfully in September 1996, without confiscation.
- Inflation was reduced to 10 per cent by mid-1998.
- The exchange rate was maintained within a narrow corridor around 1.9 UAH per dollar from 1995 to mid-1998.
- The NBU's international reserves increased to $2.3 billion by the end of 1997.
- Ukraine accepted IMF obligations under Article VIII (which requires foreign exchange convertibility for current account payments).
- A new Constitution was approved in 1996, which guaranteed private property and market-based principles for the country's economy.

Tight monetary policies imposed by the NBU were responsible for the significant progress made by Ukraine towards financial stabilisation from 1996 to mid-1998. In fact, the annual rate of growth of money supply declined from 540 per cent in 1994 to 25 per cent in 1998. These monetary policies brought annual inflation rates down from 10,160 per cent in 1993 to 40 per cent by 1996, to 10 per cent by 1997 and to 7.5 per cent by mid-1998.

Financial stabilisation from 1996 to mid-1998 took place despite the fact that up to mid-1998 the Government continued to run large fiscal budget deficits, exceeding 6 per cent of GDP in all years. From 1991 to 1998, fiscal budgets were prepared unrealistically, with overestimated revenues and excessive expenditures. In addition, the tax base was reduced by innumerable privileges and exemptions.

Up to the end of 1997, a large portion of the fiscal budget deficits was financed by foreign borrowings. Although foreign financing was key to stabilising the economy in those years, the level of foreign debt increased rapidly. External debt increased from $4.4 billion in 1994 to $11.5 billion in 1998. Domestic Government short-term obligations (Treasury bills) increased to UAH 10 billion ($5.2 billion equivalent) during the same period. Although the absolute size of foreign debt was not excessive, this debt was of short maturity. Therefore, the level of annual debt service payments was quite high, reaching $3.2 billion in 1998, and put heavy pressure on Government finances. In addition to debt issuance, the fiscal deficit was also financed through the accumulation of wage, pension and budgetary arrears (such as non-payment of utilities by public entities).

In early 1998, the Asia Crisis, large repayments on foreign debt, and delays in implementing fiscal and structural adjustments in Ukraine began to change investor perceptions of Ukraine. Furthermore, structural reforms had not reached the critical mass needed to revive confidence, investment and growth on a sustainable basis. Given Ukraine's large fiscal deficits, slow implementation of structural reforms, and large short-term debt repayments, the country was vulnerable to negative external events. This led to the Financial Crisis of 1998, as discussed below.

The financial crisis of 1998 and subsequent recovery

During the first half of 1998, with investor sentiment becoming more negative, capital outflows accelerated and the NBU had to sell a considerable amount of its foreign reserves to protect stability in the exchange rate. Foreign reserves declined from $2.3 billion at the beginning of the year to about $1 billion by mid-year. To protect the exchange rate, the use of foreign reserves was supplemented by the placement of two large Eurobond issues for a total of $1.1 billion. But it was the Russian crisis of August 1998 that triggered a financial crisis in Ukraine, which was already vulnerable. In August 1998, Russia simultaneously defaulted on much of its domestic government debt, declared a moratorium on debt principal payments to foreigners by Russian firms, and devalued its currency. These moves prompted a run on Russian banks, a sharper fall in the exchange rate (from 6 Rubles/US$ in mid-1998 to 22 Rubles/US$ in March 1999) and an acceleration of inflation.

Following the Russian crisis of mid-1998, investors' sentiment about Eastern Europe became negative and foreign financing became unavailable to Ukraine. With international reserves declining rapidly, in September 1998 the NBU had to stop selling foreign exchange. The results of the financial crisis were far reaching, with the following outcomes:

- The exchange rate came under pressure with the Hryvnia depreciating sharply from about 1.9 UAH/US$ in December 1997 to 3.4 UAH/US$ by the end of 1998.
- International reserves fell sharply from $2.3 billion in December 1997 to $0.76 billion in December 1998.
- Large foreign debt service obligations, amounting to $3.2 billion, that were due in 1998 could not be rolled over or repaid.
- Capital inflows dried up completely.
- The refinancing annual interest rate of the NBU increased sharply from 35 per cent to 60 per cent per annum.
- The annual rate of inflation, which was running at an annualised rate of 7.5 per cent during the first half of 1998, reached an annualised rate of 34 per cent during the second half of 1998, giving a yearly rate of 20 per cent for 1998.

Despite the severity of the 1998 financial crisis, Ukraine was able to deal with it successfully and without resorting to the printing of money. The success in handling the crises was due to the following measures:

- The country was able to negotiate voluntarily the restructuring of its public debt.
- Monetary policy was handled effectively with the aid of some exchange controls (particularly the obligation of exporters to sell 50 per cent of their foreign currency proceeds at official exchange rates), which were introduced as 'temporary' measures.
- From September 1998, the fiscal accounts were kept in balance. The deficit for 1998 was contained at 2.1 per cent of GDP (compared to 6.8 per cent in 1997).

As a result of these measures, by early 1999 Ukraine had overcome the risk of a financial collapse. Furthermore, during 1999 the country went through a period of recovery and consolidation of its fiscal accounts. In fact the major achievement of the Government in 1999 was control of its large fiscal deficit, the major source of Ukraine's economic imbalance in the past.

As noted earlier, weaknesses in public finance were at the core of the economic difficulties that Ukraine experienced from 1992 to 1998, despite the progress made in other economic areas. Since 1999, the execution of the Government's fiscal budget has been improved significantly. Fiscal expenditures are better controlled and the transparency of Government fiscal operations has improved with the strengthening of the Treasury, which took over the recording of most central cash and non-cash expenditures and gradually took over budgetary payments at the central and regional levels. Other important fiscal measures have included the adoption of a new budget classification system, creation of an external fiscal auditing function, and improved availability of fiscal budget information.

As a result of these measures, the fiscal budget deficit since 1999 has been kept under control, reaching only 1.5 per cent of GDP in 1999. In fact, the major benefit of the 1998 financial crisis was the adoption of fiscal discipline. This crisis brought wide recognition among most branches of Government that the fiscal deficit had to be maintained within limits that could be financed on a sustainable and non-inflationary basis (around 1.5 per cent to 2 per cent of GDP).

Economic developments since 1999 and prospects

The year 2000 started with a number of positive political and economic developments. President Kuchma was re-elected for a five-year term in November 1999 on a platform calling for an acceleration of economic reforms. Since then, fiscal and monetary policies have been satisfactory. The fiscal budget balance showed a small deficit of only 0.5 per cent of GDP in 2000, should show a sustainable fiscal deficit of about 1.5 per cent of GDP in 2001, and should have a deficit not exceeding 1.7 per cent of GDP in 2002. Monetary policies have been somewhat expansionary, with money supply increasing by 45 per cent on 2000 and 25 per cent from January to September 2001. These increases in money supply were caused principally by the heavy purchases of foreign exchange in the inter-bank market made by the NBU to serve large amounts of foreign debt due during this period. However, these increases in money supply have not led to high inflation, as inflation from January to September 2001 was only 3.7 per cent (or about 5 per cent on an annual basis). This is because the increases in money supply were absorbed by increases in money demand derived from high rates of growth of the economy.

In addition to sound fiscal and monetary policies, since the beginning of 2000 the Ukrainian Government has implemented an impressive number of important economic reform measures: a land reform that transferred land ownership to individual farmers; the elimination of Government intervention in the agricultural market and its commercialisation; a significant reduction of barter in public utilities and international trade; elimination of Government pension arrears; simplification in business inspections and registration requirements; introduction of European import certification standards; approval of the Banking Law, the Criminal Code and the Budget Code; successful external debt restructuring including the Paris Club and the gas debts to Russia and Turkmenistan; and the renewal of lending programmes by the IMF, World Bank, EBRD, and European Commission.

The control of the fiscal deficit and the above implementation of economic reforms have had a major impact on the economy, including the following:

- GDP grew by 6 per cent in 2000, with the pace of GDP growth accelerating to 10.8 per cent during January to August 2001, compared to the same period the previous year.
- Industrial output expanded by 13 per cent in 2000, and continued at an even higher rate of 16.9 per cent from January to August 2001, year-on-year.
- Agriculture, a long depressed sector, grew by a healthy rate of 9 per cent in 2000 and continued to grow by 27.7 per cent during January-August 2001 (with grain output increasing from 24 million tonnes in 2000 to an estimated output of 38 million tonnes in 2001).
- Since the beginning of 2000, the country has had a positive foreign trade and current account balance.
- The foreign exchange rate has been quite stable at about 5.4 UAH/US$ since early 2000.
- Foreign reserves increased from $1 billion in early 2000 to $2.7 billion in September 2001.
- The size of external public debt declined significantly, representing now only 25 per cent of GDP.
- Growth of 45 per cent in the population's deposits in commercial banks.
- Control of inflation with the rate of inflation at only 3.7 per cent during the period from January to September 2001.

The above progress achieved over the last two years has been outstanding. Eighteen months ago, this outcome would have been considered just a dream. A lesson for other countries is that this economic performance was not due to chance. It was largely due to the implementation of sound economic policies. It is a good example of the view that good economic policies do work.

But not everything is perfect in Ukraine. Additional significant improvements are still needed to sustain long-term growth. In particular, there is a need to revive the level of investment in the economy. Given the high level of unutilised capacity, over the short term economic growth can be based on better utilisation of existing investments. Current levels of capacity utilisation suggest that economic growth should be able to continue well into 2002. However, beyond 2002 or even sooner, growth based on improved utilisation of existing capacity will slow down. Therefore, in order to continue the high rate of growth new and significant additional investment will be necessary, particularly foreign investment since domestic savings are low.

The level of foreign investment has, however, remained low. A recent study carried out by the International Private Capital Task Force (IPCTF), under the chairmanship of SigmaBleyzer, identified the main causes of the lack of investment in the country. It found that, despite the reforms undertaken over the last few years, Ukraine's business climate is still fundamentally unsatisfactory. Based on statistical work in 50 emerging economies, the study found that differences in the flow of foreign capital into these countries could be explained by differences across countries in nine policy areas or investment 'drivers'. These nine investment drivers, ranked according to their statistical impact on capital flows, were as follows: (i) liberalisation and deregulation of business activities; (ii) stability and predictability of the legal environment; (iii) soundness of public and corporate governance, including public administration reform; (iv) extent of restrictions on international capital and foreign trade; (v) availability of financing of businesses by the financial sector; (vi) degree of corruption; (vii) level of political risk; (viii) extent of government business promotion; and (ix) rationalisation of investment incentives. The first three items explained almost 60 per cent of the differences in capital flows across the 50 countries.

The study then compared the performance of Ukraine in these nine investment drivers with the performance of other benchmarked countries, including Poland, Hungary, Russia, Chile and Argentina. It found that in almost all of the nine policy areas that are key drivers for foreign investment, Ukraine ranked at or near the bottom of these countries.

Based on extensive analysis and discussions with the Ukrainian international community, the study outlined the specific actions in the nine policy areas that were needed to improve the business climate and attract more foreign investment into the country. It also quantified the impact that the implementation of these actions could have on the scale of the flow of foreign direct investment. It concluded that, without a deepening of reform, Ukraine would continue to receive very limited amounts of foreign investment, putting in jeopardy the ongoing recovery. On the other hand, Ukraine could increase the flow of foreign direct investment from its current annual level of less than $1 billion to $3.4 billion per year in five years, if it were to narrow the policy differential with the best of the benchmarked countries by 50 per cent. Under more optimistic policy scenarios — narrowing of the policy differential by 80 per cent — capital inflows to Ukraine could increase to $6 billion per year in five years. These levels of capital inflow would make the current economic recovery sustainable over time, adding several percentage points to GDP growth. Therefore, the implementation of the IPCTF measures is essential to put the economy on a sustainable path of growth.

The IPCTF report was recently presented to the President, the Prime Minister and other Ukrainian officials. They are now fully committed to accelerate the implementation of reforms that would bring foreign investment to the country. A July 2001 Presidential Decree outlined a plan to improve the investment climate in Ukraine based on the IPCTF recommendations. It appears now that there is a window of opportunity for the country to move forward on a sustainable basis.

Nevertheless, in addition to the implementation of the measures identified by the IPCTF, in order to ensure future sustainable economic growth, Ukraine will require the support of Western Governments and institutions. Ukraine has taken many of the steps required to put its economy in order. There is a window of opportunity now to implement further reforms. It is now time for the West to provide the moral and financial support necessary to ensure economic stability and growth over the medium term. In fact, the extraordinary economic performance of Ukraine over the past 18 months has given the country a unique opportunity to break through its past economic difficulties and sustain growth. The West should embrace this possibility since a strong and economically independent Ukraine is critical to stability in Europe.

ENERGY
CURRENT PROBLEMS AND LONG-TERM STRATEGY

Volodymyr L. Saprykin

On independence Ukraine found itself with substantial energy resources and a well-developed energy sector, but with a system inextricably entwined with that of the rest of the defunct Soviet Union and suffering from years of under-investment. Ten years later, the situation is close to critical. Ensuring stable development of the energy sector is indispensable to Ukraine's economic revival as it joins the global economy, and to the country's economic and political independence. A long-term strategy is badly needed.

Key facts and figures

Ukraine's energy sector supplies only 47 per cent of the national demand for fuel and energy. Ukraine will remain a net importer of fuel and energy for the foreseeable future, and will require annual imports amounting to 70-100 million tonnes of oil equivalent.

The last decade has seen a decline in output in nearly all branches of the energy sector. This trend persisted in 2000 with production of oil (including gas condensate) falling 2.9 per cent compared with 1999, natural gas 0.4 per cent, electric power 0.5 per cent, and coal almost 2 per cent.

- The national integrated energy system provides energy for domestic consumers and is responsible for power export and imports. Over 1990-2000 period, electricity production fell by

42.8 per cent. In 2000, 48 per cent of electricity came from thermal, 45.3 per cent from nuclear and 6.7 per cent from hydroelectric power plants. Over 95 per cent of power units have completed their planned operational life. The four nuclear power plants have been in operation for some 15 of their designed life of 30 years. The age of current plant, lack of financing, and absence of a national development programme make prospects for this branch dim.

• At Ukraine's eight large and ageing hydroelectric power plants, plant and hydraulic engineering equipment are largely worn out and require upgrading.

• Coal output fell rapidly after 1990 and reached an all-time low (70.5 million tonnes) in 1996. After subsequent modest increases, production in 2000 was 80.3 million tonnes – 1.4 million tonnes less than in 1999 due to a shortage of funds for capital construction. Given the low rate of commissioning of new extraction capacities, a further decline in coal output can be predicted. Ukraine already has a substantial trade deficit in coal, with imports four times as high as exports in 1995-1999.

• In recent years, the load of domestic refineries has been falling: in 1999-2000 it fell from 18.6 per cent to 14 per cent. The depth of oil processing remains low – 63 per cent on average, against 90 per cent at the best US factories.

• The relatively good figures for oil and gas mask an impending decline due to the decommissioning of obsolete assets, a decline in raw materials, both in quality (higher share of less accessible resources) and quantity (less reserves), a fall in investment and lower return from geological prospecting. Domestic production already covers only 24 per cent of Ukraine's need for natural gas and 12 per cent for oil.

• Ukraine is one of the world's most important gas transit countries, carrying more than 90 per cent of all Russian gas exports. But many pipelines, compressors and other equipment require modernisation. Close to one third of all gas pipelines have been in operation for decades, and many facilities are obsolete and/or worn out.

• The core of Ukraine's oil transportation system is two autonomous pipeline systems, 'Druzhba' running westwards and 'Prydniprovsky' running South and East; and petroleum product supply pipelines and oil terminals. The construction of Pivdennyi oil terminal near Odessa and the Odessa-Brody oil supply pipeline (from Odessa to 'Druzhba') is nearing completion. (See map on page opposite)

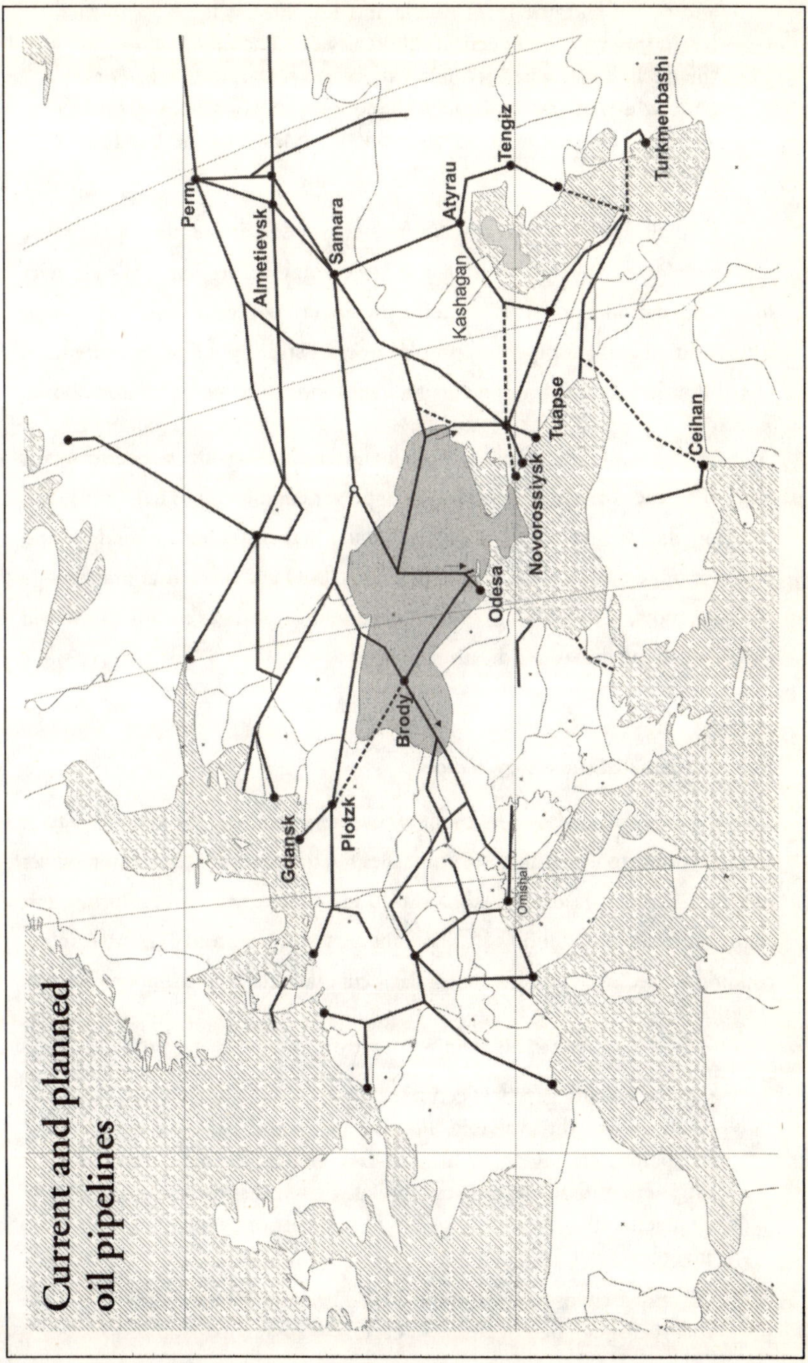

Current and planned oil pipelines

- Over the period 1991-2000 the amount of oil transported to and across Ukraine from Russia and Kazakhstan fell by a third (including by 2.2 per cent in 2000 alone). The main reason for the decline was a reduction in supplies to Ukraine's refineries. Meanwhile, oil transit through the country rose by almost a third, and has been stable at 53-56 million tonnes over the last four years.

Overall, the potential of Ukraine's energy sector is rather high; some sub-sectors (especially oil refining and power engineering) have idle capacity surpassing national needs. Even in the present critical conditions, the nuclear sector and oil and gas pipeline complex operate steadily, while there are signs of stabilisation in coal mining and geological prospecting for hydrocarbons.

At the same time, most equipment and technology in the energy sector is obsolete and worn out. Investment in power engineering is negligible, and this (together with a crisis of non-payments) makes its stable operation and progress impossible. As a result, in 1990-2000 Ukraine's fuel and energy complex (power engineering, coal industry and oil and gas complex) showed a steady decline in basic indicators.

Key problems in the enegy sector

The situation that emerged in Ukraine's energy sector over the last 5-6 years is a serious threat to its national security. Despite the potent energy sector, power supply is limited, leading to disconnection of hundreds of enterprises and transport facilities. Million of Ukrainians are not guaranteed even basic living conditions: electricity and gas are regularly cut off, and homes are poorly heated.

These negative trends stem mainly from the following problem areas.

- An increasing gap between the sector's financial needs and the funds and credit available, because of unpaid debts to energy companies arising from interest-free credits to cash-strapped suppliers and some households, and to the spread of barter arrangements (amounting to 20-25 per cent of payments in the energy sector).
- Excessive energy consumption arising from industry's inefficiency and technical backwardness, excessive losses in production,

mismanagement and direct and indirect theft. Ukraine uses 2-3 times as much energy per unit of GDP as Western Europe.

• Lack of an independent, accountable and effective energy regulator – the National Electricity Regulatory Commission (NERC), put under the President's supervision in October 2000, does not provide a relevant system of checks and balances.

• Poor legislative base. Legislation governing the energy sector is fragmentary and inadequate for the effective regulation of market relations. No fundamental law on the oil and gas complex has yet been adopted, and the law on production sharing agreements does not work. Energy consumers, even those who pay regularly, are defenceless against suppliers who do not perform their contractual commitments.

• A real threat of collapse in electricity supply due to lack of fuel, inability to regulate peak and semi-peak loads, obsolete equipment, lack of proper maintenance and safety precautions.

• Lags in the development of new sources of raw materials, especially oil and gas. In 1990-1999 the intensity of deep drilling fell 46 times, seismic prospecting 15 times; the growth in explored reserves did not even make up for their current extraction.

• Large debts for imported energy resources. As of November 2000, Ukraine's debt for Russian gas consumed in 1998-2000 alone amounted to $1.362 billion.

• Critical dependence on supplies of energy resources from one country, Russia (close to 60 per cent of imports in 2000) – see below.

• A chronic lack of investment in all parts of the sector. Investment in 1999 was only a half to a third of that in 1990. This is not enough to compensate for decommissioned production capacities.

• Ukraine's non-compliance with its international undertakings. For instance, some projects in power engineering with foreign partners have been suspended because Ukraine has not fulfilled its own funding commitments. Delayed payments for imported energy resources and unauthorised siphoning off of transit Russian gas have become common. This raises doubts as to Ukraine's reliability as a trading partner.

• A deepening scientific and technical lag in all branches of the energy sector, with low-quality domestic equipment preventing steady economic growth.

• A low level of environmental safety in energy sector enterprises.

• A significant lag in the pace of privatisation. 27.6 per cent of companies in the fuel industry and 16.2 per cent in the energy sector have been privatised, against 55.5 per cent in industry as a whole. Privatisation in the energy sector is accompanied by a covert division of former state property. For example, the privatisation of electricity distribution companies was undertaken by offshore companies at understated prices under pressure from lobby groups. This led, among other things, to a sharp decline in the collection of fees for electricity consumed.

• Poor social protection and labour safety, with substantial wage arrears and one of the world's worst records for industrial injuries. Deaths at Ukrainian mines are 100 times higher than in the USA per unit of output.

• Unrealistic medium-term planning and forecasting. Most targets have never been met, and no sectoral or national energy programme has been realised in its entirety. In fact, there is no systematic national energy policy in Ukraine.

• Lack of readiness to adopt EU norms and standards. Even specialists do not understand the essence of reforms to be made by countries aspiring to join the EU. This is not yet hampering Ukraine's energy sector, but it may hinder the fulfilment of EU requirements in the future.

In addition to these general problems there are specific issues that require immediate resolution: the inadequacy of national price, tax and tariff policies in the energy sector; the immaturity of the competitive energy market and market infrastructure; the non-transparency of business activity, which hinders the development of competition.

All this shows that Ukraine's energy security is close to critical. The sector's inability to meet the demands of the economy and population for fuel and energy, the accumulation of enormous debts for energy resources consumed, and the piling up of unresolved problems could undermine the fundamentals of economic security and bring about social destabilisation in Ukraine. Resolute action by the Yushchenko Government in 2000 produced improvements, for instance an increase in the level of cash payment and reduction in barter in certain branches, but the general situation remains very unstable and complicated.

Resolution of the problems is hampered by the excessive politicisation of the energy sector, and the struggle of influential political forces, financial and industrial structures and criminal groups to gain control over its multibillion cash flows.

Despite this complex situation, Ukraine can escape its energy crisis and ensure its energy security. Stabilisation requires systematic, co-ordinated action by all branches of government within the framework of a well-thought-out national energy policy.

A national energy policy for Ukraine

Ukraine's long-term energy policy should aim for effective co-operation between all government bodies and enterprises of different forms of ownership. This section sets out the fundamentals of such a policy for the next twenty years, and defines the directions and main tasks in its implementation.

Creation of liberalised and competitive markets for energy (by 2005) to encourage efficiency at energy sector enterprises. This requires the creation of a competitive environment in the production and consumption of energy; the establishment of real business entities; the liberalisation of pricing on energy markets; the development of a market infrastructure; the limitation of state interference in the work of energy producers; the predominant use of market levers for regulation.

Deep structural changes in the production and consumption of energy (by 2010), creating the economic and legal conditions to encourage efficiency and reduce energy losses in industry, so bringing Ukraine's fuel and energy balance into line with available resources. Profitable coal enterprises should be expanded and hopelessly loss-making mines closed. The excessive share of natural gas in the national fuel and energy balance should be reduced by increasing coal production, improving the quality of mined coal, commissioning new reactors at nuclear power plants, and using non-conventional and renewable sources of energy.

An increase in domestic extraction or production of energy (by 2005) to help reduce dependence on imports. This requires an increase in domestic production of coal, natural gas and oil (through increased geological prospecting); fuller exploration of hydrocarbon deposits; recruitment of foreign companies to search for and extract mineral resources on the basis of product-sharing agreements; improved oil processing (through modernisation of refineries); and the use of non-conventional and renewable sources of energy.

Maximum energy conservation (by 2005) to bring Ukraine's energy consumption into line with developed countries, including through improved technology and equipment and the mass installation of meters and thermostats in homes.

Enhancement of the safety, durability and viability of power industry sites to secure stable supplies, reduce accidents and minimise environmental damage. Attraction of foreign investment to bring the domestic energy sector to a qualitatively new level. Strategic foreign investors would not only provide critical funds but also management and marketing skills. Working under transparent schemes within the framework of applicable laws would help to bring Ukraine's power industry out of the 'shadow' economy. (According to official statements, the size of Ukraine's shadow (illegal) economy is roughly equivalent to the official economy, accounting for 45-60 per cent of GDP.) This requires broad privatisation of energy enterprises with the participation of foreign investors and the creation of a favourable investment climate – including transparent procedures for privatisation, a drive against corruption among officials, and a limit to administrative interference in the activity of joint ventures.

Enhancement of export potential (by 2005), increasing energy transit across Ukraine; the export of coal, electricity and power engineering equipment; the export of services, such as exploration, development and exploitation of deposits; and the construction of energy projects in foreign countries. Ukraine needs to apply a flexible tariff policy for energy transportation; attract Russian and Western companies into joint gas transportation operations; privatise refineries with the participation of foreign oil suppliers; make active use of information, organisational, diplomatic, political and other types of state support; and ensure participation by Ukrainian enterprises and scientific research institutions in international projects.

Dependence and diversification

Ukraine imports 53 per cent of its energy resources. By international standards this is not excessive. However, Ukraine obtains the bulk of its energy resources (close to 60 per cent of imports) from one country – Russia (either directly or via its territory). Such critical dependence carries the following risks:

- complications in the development of equal bilateral relations;
- monopolistic raising of prices or restrictions in supply if relations deteriorate. (According to Petroleum Argus, France and Germany obtain Russian natural gas for around $77 per 1000 cubic metres, while Ukraine pays $80);
- reductions in supply because of reduced Russian output (this is already happening);
- irregular supply as a result of large-scale pipeline accidents resulting from natural or man-made emergencies, subversive activities, ageing etc.

Thus, as would apply to any other state in this situation, reducing Ukraine's dependence on energy supplies from Russia is a task of strategic importance. Diversification would give Ukraine increased reliability of energy supply and lower prices due to competition between suppliers, permit truly equal co-operation with Russia, and provide a higher level of domestic energy security.

But there are major obstacles to diversification. First, the cost – the construction of oil and gas pipelines and creation of a national nuclear fuel manufacturing cycle or elements thereof would run into hundreds of millions or even billions of dollars. Second, in view of the critical state of Ukraine's economy and the unfavourable investment climate (and correspondingly high risks for investors), it would be impossible to establish fully-fledged alternative sources of all types of energy resources by 2020. Third, new sources may initially be more expensive than current supplies from Russia. Fourth, diversification could complicate relations between Ukraine and Russia; to cease imports of energy from Russia would be not only economically inexpedient but also politically unacceptable.

Natural gas

Russia possesses the world's largest gas resources, borders Ukraine (so transportation costs are minimal) and is already connected to Ukraine by a powerful gas transit pipeline system. In these circumstances, Russia will remain the main supplier of natural gas to Ukraine at least up to 2020. At the same time, Ukraine has a favourable geographical location and can diversify its gas supply to include Turkmenistan (as happened in 2000), Kazakhstan, Uzbekistan, and also Norway, Azerbaijan and Iran.

At the first stage of diversification, Ukraine should import gas from Russia, Turkmenistan, Uzbekistan and Kazakhstan. Although gas from the last three can be supplied only via Russian pipelines, these alternative sources would mean that gas supply from one source would not exceed 51 per cent of all imports.

Over the longer term (up to 20 years), Ukraine needs to develop gas supply routes that do not cross Russia, thus achieving true diversification of supply. Later on, use of new sources of gas would be determined exclusively by economic expediency.

All this will require substantial Western credits and international consortia. In addition, liquid natural gas supplies require the creation of a Black Sea market for liquid gas and participation of the leading multinational oil and gas corporations in the construction of a receiving terminal and installation of a liquid gas re-gasification plant in Ukraine. With the creation of such an infrastructure for receiving liquid gas, the number of potential gas suppliers would include not only Caspian countries but also Oman, Libya and others.

Oil

The completion of the Odessa-Brody pipeline will open up the possibility of new supply routes across Ukraine. Use of these could increase the utilisation of national oil refineries, cut the price of crude oil on the domestic market and provide transit fees for Ukraine's budget. Ukraine's geographical location theoretically enables it to draw on oil from a variety of regions: Russia, Kazakhstan, Azerbaijan, Middle East countries and others.

Today, Russia dominates the CIS energy market. It exports the lion's share of energy resources from the region to world markers and retains control of their supply from other CIS countries. Almost all CIS countries depend on Russia – either on supplies of Russian energy resources or on Russia's permission for their transit. Creation of a capacious oil transportation corridor independent of Russia will help the project participants (Ukraine, Azerbaijan, Kazakhstan, Georgia) reduce their energy dependence on Russia and improve their competitiveness.

Ukraine's location on the route of Caspian oil exports to Europe means that new oil routes can avoid both Russia and the overcrowded Bosphorus. (See map on page 105). The oil supply route suggested by the Ukrainian Government to the countries of Central Europe would carry oil across the Black Sea, through the Odessa-Brody system (scheduled for completion at the end of 2001) and on to the port of Gdansk (Poland). This route has economic and political advantages over the Baku-Ceyhan route from Azerbaijan to Turkey being advocated by the USA, including low transit tariffs. Poland, Slovakia, the Czech Republic and Hungary have already shown interest in the Ukrainian proposal, while Croatia and Germany would be potential customers in the future.

Some Ukrainian non-government oil experts believe the route from Brody via the Druzhba pipeline directly to European countries, with subsequent access through an expanded pipeline to the port of Omishal (Croatia) on the Adriatic, would be more advantageous to the consumer than the above route terminating in Gdansk. Omishal can take large tankers (up to 500,000 tonnes), which would permit them to carry oil to the USA. (Once the embargoes against Iran and Iraq are lifted, the Mediterranean market will be oversaturated.) Access to the Baltic ports (Gdansk and others) is restricted by the depth of the Danish Straits (maximum tanker dead-weight 120,000 tonnes).

Commissioning of the Odessa-Brody system will resolve the issue of diversification of both transit routes and oil supply to Ukrainian refineries. However, this project is likely to be delayed due to the absence of signed agreements on use of the Odessa-Brody system; insufficient oil (primarily from Azerbaijan, not from Kazakhstan) to load the route; and the availability of other competitive routes (through Turkey, Iran and other countries). Implementation of the Odessa-Brody project requires urgent negotiations leading to the signing of agreements with transnational corporations and countries which supply oil to the Black Sea (including Russia), with countries on whose territory the connecting oil pipelines will be constructed and connected to the Ukrainian oil pipeline, and with potential consumers for this oil (the volumes and transit tariffs for which need to be determined).

Most Ukrainian oil experts consider that Ukraine should shift the emphasis in negotiations away from interstate talks with Kazakhstan and Azerbaijan towards agreements with the transnational corporations which own 75-80 per cent of their oilfields. These countries have an interest in supplying oil to Ukrainian oil refineries, some of which have been taken over by Russian and Kazakh companies on privatisation.

Once the relevant contracts and agreements are signed, Ukraine needs to complete the construction of the Odessa-Brody system, including the Pivdennyi oil terminal, and, for maximum benefit, to build its own tanker fleet to ship oil to Odessa from the oil ports on the East coast of the Black Sea.

There is no point in continuing construction of the Odessa-Brody oil pipeline before these contracts and agreements are signed. However, construction of the Pivdennyi oil terminal can be regarded as an independent project to supply oil to nearby Ukrainian refineries. If it proves impossible to load the Odessa-Brody oil pipeline, the construction of the terminal should still go ahead once oil supply agreements have been negotiated.

The Ukrainian Government has floated and should pursue more energetically the idea that Ukraine's pipeline network should be managed by an international consortium.

Nuclear fuel

Russia at present supplies all the nuclear fuel to Ukraine's nuclear power plants, and undertakes the storage and processing of spent fuel. In 1998 Russia ceased supplies of nuclear fuel in compensation for nuclear weapons transferred from Ukraine, and once Ukraine's stocks are exhausted it could be vulnerable to economic pressure from Russia as a monopoly supplier of nuclear fuel.

The importance of nuclear power in electricity generation, as well as the need for energy security, militates for the creation of a domestic nuclear fuel cycle in Ukraine. However, with no national nuclear power programme to look at prospects for the next 30-40 years, and the high cost of creating a nuclear fuel cycle, construction of such a complete cycle would be economically risky. In the period up to 2020 it would be more expedient to create only separate components of such a cycle.

Once a joint project with Westinghouse is completed in a few years' time, Ukraine will be able to use nuclear fuel purchased from other countries, thus achieving diversification of supply in the nuclear field.

EU energy legislation, norms and standards

EU membership has been proclaimed as a priority goal of Ukraine's foreign policy. This would require, among other things, compliance with EU legal, organisational and technical requirements in the energy sector and related branches. Progress in reforming the energy sector is an important element in Ukraine's adoption of EU legal and regulatory standards – the a*cquis communautaire*.

In adapting to EU norms and standards, Ukraine needs to limit administrative interference by the state in the energy sector; liberalise energy markets; create a favourable investment climate for foreign capital; promote energy efficiency and conservation; enhance nuclear safety; reduce negative environmental impact; create strategic reserves of oil; and so on. Over the next 10-15 years, energy efficiency, nuclear safety and environmental protection should become priority spheres for Ukraine's co-operation with the EU in the energy sector.

Adapting domestic legislation to EU norms and standards, and especially implementing the relevant changes, will require significant resources and government-wide action. As a first step, the drafts of all regulatory and legal acts dealing with the energy sector should be subject to obligatory preliminary review to ensure their compliance with EU norms and standards, while taking into account Ukraine's interests and peculiarities.

Conclusions

Unfortunately, overseas investors are deterred from investing in Ukraine because of the unstable economic situation; non-payments in the energy sector and more generally; a heavy tax burden; endless changes in legislation; large state debts; energy prices and tariffs unrelated to the cost of extraction and production; non-transparent rules of the game on energy markets; and the slow pace of privatisation in the energy sector. Further uncertainty on these and other issues, the majority of them general rather than specific to the energy sector, makes prospects for the energy sector dim for the foreseeable future.

Inadequate modernisation and restructuring in the energy sector could become a serious impediment to joining the EU. Ukraine, with one of the largest fuel and power industries in Europe, still lags behind even Central and East European countries on a number of indicators. This is largely because of the absence of a clear policy and plan for reform, together with the politicisation of operations in the energy sector.

The resolution of virtually all the problems of the energy sector lies in Ukraine's hands alone. The survival of the state depends on whether the country's leadership and Ukraine's political elite can meet those challenges.

We need to consider our energy sector from three critical angles: energy conservation, open markets for energy resources, and diversification of energy supply. These are the cornerstones of our times and will remain so in the future, both in the EU and Ukraine.

Parts of this article were published in the *National Security and Defence Journal*, Kiev, No 2, 2001.

GAS TRANSIT
A CRITICAL STRATEGIC ISSUE FOR UKRAINE

Frank Duffield

Ukraine sits astride the main pipeline network carrying gas from Russia, produced by the Russian company Gazprom, which holds the world's largest reserves of gas, to its biggest customers, in Western Europe (see map on the next page). Can it make use of this to strengthen its own economy and consolidate its position in the wider European community?

Gas currently accounts for 21 per cent of Western Europe's primary energy supply, and this is likely to increase because of its advantages in environmental and efficiency terms. Current estimates are that the proportion will grow, perhaps to as much as 30 per cent by 2020, though this will depend on economic growth rates, relative energy prices, and developments in other energy technologies.

At the same time domestic production is expected to decline with the depletion of North Sea gas, so increasing demand will have to be met through imports. Gazprom already supplies 25 per cent of Western Europe's gas and, given its massive reserves, a significant if not dominant proportion of new gas supplies could be expected to come from there. However this will require resolution of a number of problems.

The existing pipeline system bringing Russian gas to Europe was developed and financed in the days of the Soviet Union, when it was managed

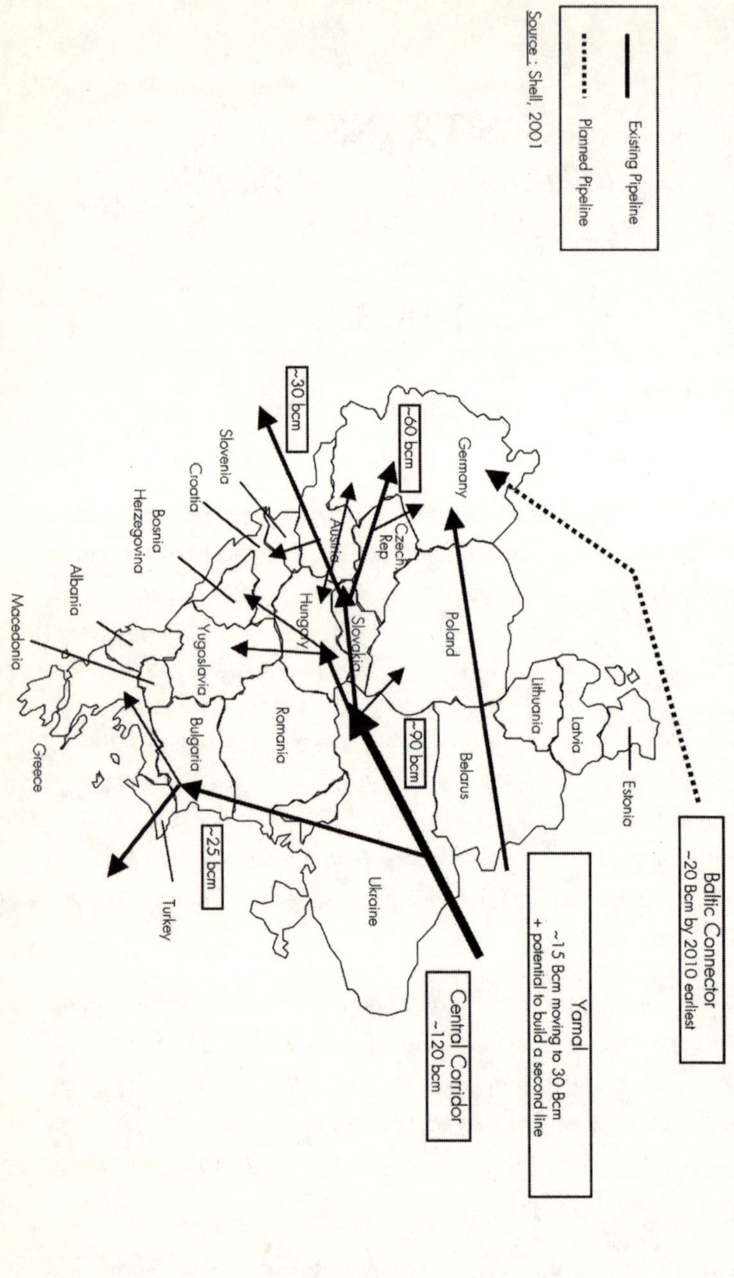

Transnational pipelines
Supplying Russian gas to Western & Central Europe and Turkey

and operated on a totally integrated basis. Since independence Ukraine has had control of and responsibility for that part of the system passing through its territory. The pipelines through Ukraine carry 90 per cent of Russia's gas supply to Europe. There have been problems in the management and operation of the system over the last 10 years, although it should be stressed that while these have created great difficulties for Gazprom, and sometimes between Russia and Ukraine at the political level, Western Europe has never failed to get its contracted gas. These problems have arisen mainly because arrangements between Gazprom and Ukraine have operated on a barter basis: Ukraine receives part of its domestic gas requirements from Gazprom in return for providing transit rights for Gazprom gas, and contracts for additional supplies. This has resulted in persistent problems in accounting for the gas supplied to Ukraine, leading to the growth of substantial Ukrainian debts to Gazprom. Furthermore, the barter arrangement contributed greatly to the system not being able to generate funds to keep it fully maintained. Although Ukraine has recently made determined and successful efforts to address operational problems, there remain sufficient grounds for concern for Gazprom to wish to reduce its dependence on the Ukrainian pipelines by looking for alternative routes.

Any new Russian gas supplies for Europe will have to come from distant fields, which will require substantial investment in development of the fields and in additional delivery infrastructure. This will all have to be financed. But finance will only be forthcoming if it is covered by long-term gas contracts from reputable creditworthy buyers who will guarantee to take or pay for a minimum amount of gas at an agreed price. As well, new supply projects will take considerable time to develop, so financial commitments will need to be made well in advance of the need for new supply.

At the same time the market in Europe is changing. A policy of liberalisation in the energy sector is being pursued with the object of removing market inefficiencies and enhancing competition in order to achieve the lowest possible price of energy for European consumers. This makes it more difficult to predict the rate of growth in demand for gas. It also means buyers will be looking for shorter-term contracts to maintain their flexibility to switch suppliers to take advantage of changes in relative price between different energies. There is a clear tension here between the flexibility achieved by liberalisation and the need for long-term commitments to underpin essential investment. This tension will need to be resolved, but in any case it will be essential to ensure that investment in new supply and infrastructure is made in good time to meet demand and that costs are kept to a minimum in order to minimise financing needs and the cost of supply that the market will have to pay.

Additional gas from Russia will mostly reach clients in Europe by pipeline. This can be done by upgrading existing pipelines and building new pipelines. Both will be necessary. In view of the difficulties it has encountered in Ukraine over the last decade, Gazprom is understandably keen to diversify its supply routes – this is already happening with the construction of the new Yamal pipeline across Belarus and Poland. This line has a current capacity to convey 15-20 billion cubic metres (bcm) a year, and is ultimately capable of carrying 30 bcm. The cost of such investment is massive, and even this will not be sufficient to meet expected extra demand. Current purchase commitments show Russian gas supplies to Western and Central Europe increasing from 100 to 140 bcm. This may well rise to 180 bcm by 2010. Additional capacity will be essential. A second Yamal pipeline can be considered, and Gazprom is actively promoting an additional pipeline through the Baltic.

Given the huge costs of these new schemes and energy market developments in Europe, and despite the diversification of routes that the schemes bring, it makes sense to maximise use of what already exists, for both cost and environmental reasons. A recent survey shows that the Ukrainian system is in a better state than previously thought, but that it needs significant investment in maintenance. If Russia, Ukraine and European partners work together, they could arrange for viable and economic investment which would produce the optimum benefits. Such a project would also be a major driver for economic transformation in Ukraine, bringing a double benefit.

However, one essential condition for such investment must be that Ukraine eliminates once and for all the type of problems that have occurred in the past. Without certainty of this Gazprom would be wise to seek options to limit its exposure to Ukraine. A sustainable long-term solution can only be based on the monetisation of the system within a proper legal, regulatory and operational framework founded on principles similar to those in the European Energy Charter. It would also require the development in Ukraine of a properly functioning energy market in which energy is priced at a level reflecting its true cost of supply and the cost of alternatives and in which that price is in fact recovered from end-users. Ukraine has made considerable progress towards these objectives over the past year.

Another essential condition is that Gazprom, the sole user of the transit, fully supports and participates in any investment proposal.

These requirements raise big challenges, but with co-operation and careful thought they can be overcome. Once they are in place then there is every reason to believe financing to maintain the system can be attracted. When all is said and done, such financing would have the security of the transit revenues deriving from the flow of Gazprom gas to its customers in Europe, a flow that has never failed in the past.

A satisfactory resolution of this problem would be in the interests of Europe at both a political and a security of energy supply level, and the EU can play an important role in meeting these challenges.

First, it could seek to facilitate an agreement between Naftogaz of Ukraine (NAK), Gazprom and potential foreign investors. A preliminary framework agreement between NAK and Gazprom, building on the recent settlement of gas debt issues, could form the basis for inviting proposals from foreign investors for investment in the management and maintenance of the system. Such a framework agreement need not itself propose solutions. It need only outline a credible basis on which investors could be invited to make proposals. The proposals from investors should contain the specific measures for resolving the issues and providing the investment.

Secondly, the EU could through an appropriate support programme provide funds to enable Ukraine to access world-class advice to support it in any negotiations. For Ukraine to be well advised is essential if a long-lasting solution is to be found.

Thirdly, the EU could identify and provide support to Ukraine, directly or possibly through the EIB, for programmes that run parallel with the implementation of an investment proposal relating to the transit system. An example is a programme further developing the efficient operation of the gas market in Ukraine. If such a programme were developed parallel with investment in the transit system, the two programmes would mutually reinforce each other's objectives and increase the probability of success of both.

A domestic market programme need not be capital intensive. For example it could be directed at further improving NAK capability in the areas of metering, billing, and payment collection.

In the recent report on the EU/Russia Partnership on Energy reference was made to the possibility of the development of a non-commercial risk mechanism to enhance capacity for financing energy projects. An investment proposal relating to the transit pipeline in Ukraine could be an early beneficiary of such a mechanism.

The EU could also seek to promote parallel support through the programmes of other international financial institutions such as the IMF, World Bank and EBRD.

Another way in which the EU could help would be in providing an effective and speedy dispute resolution procedure to support any agreement that is made.

With this kind of effort a solution can be found which would increase energy security for suppliers and consumers, postpone the need for hugely expensive new pipelines, and boost Ukraine's economy: a win-win-win situation for Ukraine, Russia, and their business partners and customers in the rest of Europe.

BEYOND CHERNOBYL
A WAY FORWARD?

Michael McCulloch

Introduction

Ukraine's evolving relationship with the European Union in nuclear safety mirrors its wider links with European partners since achieving independence in 1991. The key themes, embracing politics, law, finance, technology, culture, and institutions, represent Ukraine's transition in microcosm. Its processes have engaged the interests of a range of participants that would have been unthinkable a decade earlier. They include the Ukrainian authorities and Energoatom, the nuclear utility; the Member States of the European Union; the European Commission through its Tacis programme; Euratom; international institutions, notably the European Bank for Reconstruction and Development and the International Atomic Energy Authority; non-European G7 countries, particularly the United States; and, never far from the action, Russia. Despite some successes, it is not clear that Ukraine has yet defined a coherent and consistent pathway to improved nuclear safety.

Background

The explosion at Unit 4 at Chernobyl in April 1986 symbolised much that was wrong about the Soviet system. The disaster spurred public criticism, which contributed to dethroning the Communist Party and dismembering the Soviet Union. As Ukraine disengaged in 1991, it inherited a substantial portion of Soviet nuclear capacity, and became overnight one of the world's main nuclear power producers (today producing over 40 per cent of its power from nuclear generation).

Although later Soviet plants were safer than Chernobyl, much still fell short of international standards. Ukraine's problems were compounded because, in the nuclear as in other sectors, it inherited less than a complete system, without roles and institutions previously concentrated in Moscow. Besides the damage of Chernobyl, therefore, Ukraine faced the challenge of creating the legal, policy, and institutional framework for an entire nuclear sector, and its relations with the energy sector and economy at large. Assisting this process became a priority for Ukraine's new external partners, including the EU.

Components of partnership

There have been three main elements:

- Making Chernobyl safe: urgent safety upgrades, a permanent shelter for the damaged Unit 4, closure of the remaining Units 1-3, and initial decommissioning
- A proposal to complete two partly-built nuclear power plants, of Soviet-era but safer design, Khmelnitsky Unit 2 and Rovno Unit 4 (K2R4)
- Improving safety standards and performance throughout the Ukrainian nuclear sector.

Another, arguably more urgent, programme aimed to remove safely from Ukraine the nuclear weapons which it had also inherited. Here the United States took the lead and main financial responsibility. The programme had practical and political significance for civil nuclear collaboration. It explored and demonstrated how specialists and decision-makers, whose relations had been distant and by intent hostile, could work together. It invented means of inter-state partnership, and sealed bargains that set expectations about subsequent co-operation. Its successful completion contributed to later Ukrainian perceptions that they had delivered more than they gained, a recurring theme in their approach to civil nuclear safety.

An important earlier prelude was the opening of contact with the Soviet Union after the Chernobyl disaster. The Soviet authorities' first reaction was to keep news of it from their own people. Still less were they inclined to share information with scientists from the West, turning down several offers of help. Slowly, however, attitudes changed. Exploratory contacts launched by Hans Blix of the IAEA burgeoned into deepening scientific relations, and the benefits of sharing expertise partly eroded the Soviet obsession with security. Though limited in scope, this initial post-Chernobyl collaboration proved a helpful introduction to the larger task that arose after Ukraine became independent.

Chronology

We can distinguish three main phases in Ukraine's co-operation with the EU:

- From Ukrainian independence to the G7 Summit at Munich in July 1992, which established the framework for co-operation in nuclear safety matters with Central and Eastern Europe
- The subsequent period culminating in the G7/Ukraine Memorandum of Understanding (MoU) of December 1995, which incorporated commitments to energy sector reform, the completion of K2R4, and assistance for a shelter and decommissioning at Chernobyl
- A third stage, implementing the MoU, marked by the G7 Summit at Denver in June 1997, which committed financing for the Chernobyl Shelter Fund

It is no coincidence that each milestone was an event in the G7 calendar. Although the European Commission and EU Member States bilaterally took initiatives to improve nuclear safety in Ukraine, the most significant steps occurred within the G7 framework.

Independence to the Munich Summit: Finding a Framework

After the Soviet Union disintegrated, both assessment and activity in nuclear safety expanded rapidly, prompting attempts to establish a framework to co-ordinate the multiplying projects. It was clear that, whatever the wider strategy, Ukraine had high priority.

The outcome of months of negotiations was the G7/European Commission agreement, endorsed at the 1992 G7 Summit in Munich, on an overall framework within which to promote improved nuclear safety in Central and Eastern Europe. This agreement launched the Nuclear Safety Account, through which much of the money offered would be channelled, in pursuit of a structured programme of projects across the main nuclear power-generating countries of the region. In Ukraine, a series of short term safety upgrades for Unit 3 at Chernobyl, which continued to operate, and decommissioning facilities for units closed down, were identified as priorities.

Munich to MoU: deepening commitment

Over the next three years, two issues dominated collaboration: closure of Chernobyl, and fundamental reform of Ukraine's energy sector. Two previously separate strands, nuclear safety and energy sector reform, became closely linked. Ukraine's partners had broached this already. Concern to secure and diversify energy sources had prompted President Kravchuk to sponsor, to widespread surprise, the one comprehensive reform initiative of his administration, the restructuring of Ukraine's power sector. But it was external efforts to gain commitment to shut Chernobyl that brought energy sector reform to the heart of nuclear safety negotiations.

Interdependence took two forms. The first revolved around overall demand for electricity. The Ukrainian authorities argued that, if Chernobyl were closed, alternative capacity must be available, to underpin the anticipated economic recovery and to counter political opposition to closure. But Ukraine's partners doubted the 'Chernobyl replacement' case, pointing to probable constraints on demand if thoroughgoing reforms, including progress towards market-based pricing, were pursued.

The second linkage was financial. Ukraine and its EU partners were digesting the first serious measure of what a full nuclear safety agenda might cost. Concern in foreign capitals at the potential price echoed growing Ukrainian anxiety about the costs it would face. The discovery that the emergency sarcophagus at Chernobyl Unit 4 was deteriorating dangerously underlined the urgency of arranging finance. Given the parlous state of

Ukraine's public expenditure, however, domestic funding could come only from reform of pricing and revenue collection in the power sector.

For Ukraine's partners, economic arguments for advancing energy sector reform coincided with their reluctance to carry the full burden of financing improved nuclear safety. For Ukraine, foreign eagerness to see Chernobyl shut permanently offered a fertile opportunity to negotiate aid for a new shelter and initial decommissioning at Chernobyl, and for investments in new generating capacity.

In 1994 the European Commission proposed a plan to reform Ukraine's energy sector, linked to early definitive closure of Chernobyl. The deal struck, again after long negotiations, was incorporated in an MoU between the G7, the European Commission and Ukraine, signed in December 1995. Ukraine agreed to close Chernobyl by 2000, and to pursue energy sector reform. The G7 and the European Commission undertook to finance energy sector investments meeting cost effectiveness criteria, and to help secure finance for a new Chernobyl Shelter and for initial decommissioning. European countries, bilaterally and through the Nuclear Safety Account, would support improved safety at Chernobyl pending its closure. The EU would contribute to some decommissioning costs, and provide the technical assistance to launch and solicit financing for the Chernobyl Shelter Fund, as well as for regulatory development. The 1995 MoU has become the reference point for subsequent EU/Ukrainian co-operation.

MoU to Denver, and beyond: delivering commitment

Since 1995, Ukraine and its partners have made substantial progress in implementing the MoU:

- Safety upgrades at Chernobyl Unit 3 pending its closure
- Chernobyl closed, definitively, in December 2000
- Provisional approval, by the EBRD and the European Commission, of financing to complete Khmelnitsky 2 and Rovno 4 to international safety standards, subject to conditions that include confirmed complementary funding from export credit agencies

- Ukrainian agreement to far reaching improvements in safety throughout the nuclear power sector, including an independent and adequately-resourced regulator
- Ukrainian commitment to progressive reform of the power sector, including tariffs, revenue collection, and some privatisation
- An emergency programme to prevent further deterioration of the existing sarcophagus over Chernobyl Unit 4 successfully completed
- The Shelter Fund launched and largely financed
- Progress in preparing the permanent replacement shelter, notably approval of the design choice in early 2001.

The tally, though impressive, is also misleading. For it does not convey any sense of the immense effort, challenges, misunderstandings, controversies, or reverses along the way, which characterised its realisation.

For example, the Ukrainian authorities, notwithstanding their MoU commitment, held out until late 2000 before naming a firm date to shut Chernobyl. Some observers believe Ukraine sought to exploit its partners' attachment to closure to extract beforehand the maximum financial assistance. External commitments to the Chernobyl Shelter Fund might easily be presented in this light. Fear that at the last moment President Kuchma might concede to pressure in the Rada, Ukraine's Parliament, to keep Chernobyl open, undoubtedly prompted renewed efforts to reach a decision on financing for K2R4.

Developing the Chernobyl Shelter project was far from straightforward, even though all agreed on its urgency. Ukraine's partners initially came up with about half the estimated cost, expecting that some of the balance could come from the private sector. This hope proved illusory, and a second round of pledging concluded only just in time to avoid prejudicing implementation. Ukraine, wanting perhaps to promote domestic procurement, held up for several months approval of a shelter design that was clearly preferable against all main criteria.

The proposal to complete Khmelnitsky Unit 2 and Rovno Unit 4 deserves a longer account of its own. The conditions for confirming provisional approval of the EBRD Board and for declaring the financing effective have yet to be met. Not all the outstanding action rests with Ukraine. Ukraine has continued work at the sites, with its own resources, raising fears that one or both plants could be completed without meeting international safety standards.

The outcome of the K2R4 proposal will be a key indicator of Ukraine's longer term direction. For the proposal incorporates and reinforces adherence to the primary goals evolved during several years of collaboration with Ukraine. The deal represents the closest Ukraine has come to a comprehensive statement of its commitment to see international safety standards met throughout its nuclear sector, and to enforce market-based operations within a restructured energy sector. Proceeding with K2R4 as negotiated would thus be a major step towards attaining these two goals.

Assessment and Prospects

When Ukraine began to integrate itself with the international community and European countries responded, few understood the magnitude or complexity of the challenge of modernising its nuclear sector. Many technical and scientific issues had yet to be properly assayed. How far Ukraine fell short of international standards and practice became apparent only as work proceeded. Most of the legal, political, institutional, financial and cultural differences that have encumbered co-operation were still to be encountered.

Against that baseline, much has been achieved in ten years. Against international benchmarks, much remains to be done. However, Ukraine and its European partners now have the institutions, and a culture, of co-operation in nuclear safety. They can address the outstanding agenda better and more realistically equipped. What remains elusive is confidence that Ukraine is irrevocably committed to reaching the standards with which its partners would be comfortable: whether indeed it has chosen its route map, or might still prefer to go backwards to the future.

4

Foreign Policy, Defence and Regional Relations

TEN YEARS ON
UKRAINE'S FOREIGN POLICY PRIORITIES

Anatoliy Orel

Ukraine has entered the new millennium as an important new reality in the world's politics. This is a country of almost 50 million inhabitants with the second largest territory in Europe. It possesses considerable industrial and technological potential and has attained the necessary dynamic for its development. The nation has chosen a democratic path and is striving to achieve the highest standards of human rights and fundamental freedoms. Last but not least, Ukraine is uniquely located at a strategic crossroads in the geographical centre of the European continent.

Because of all these features it is always imperative to see and understand Ukraine's foreign policy in its entirety, and especially when reflecting on its strategic goal – European integration. Of course this policy is based on national interests, but it is also greatly inspired by a sense of responsibility going far beyond the country's national borders. The recent tenth anniversary of Ukraine's independence offers a good opportunity to take a look at the country's foreign policy priorities.

From the very first day of its independence Ukraine was confronted with three major challenges. First, the country had to consolidate its statehood and sovereignty with practically no previous experience in that area and under unfavourable international conditions. The second critical task was to keep step with political, economic and technological developments in the world, not to be left in the back yard of civilisation by the powerful forces of globalisation and by the country's own difficulties in the transitional period.

Finally, Ukraine's independence coincided with a world-shattering shift from the Cold War to the global age. Together with new opportunities it has brought unforeseen problems: a resurgence of ethnic, racial, and religious conflict; the danger of proliferation of weapons of mass destruction; international networks engaged in terrorism, crime, and drug trafficking; environmental degradation; the spread of infectious disease. The devastating terrorist attacks in New York and Washington on 11 September 2001 highlighted the urgent need for all states to look at each other less through the prism of traditional state-centred concerns and more in the light of their *existential interdependence*.

For Ukraine, developing a foreign policy with the European Union, the Russian Federation and the United States as its three cornerstones was, first and foremost, an endeavour to meet all those challenges effectively. Time has never brought into question the wisdom of the choice made in the early years of Ukraine's independence. Yet even now occasional experts attempt to compare a foreign policy based on these three foundations with Buridan's ass, caught between the bales of hay. This is both narrow-minded and shortsighted as a view of Ukraine's international stance.

Ukraine is a European nation, and always has been. Ukrainians substantiate their *European-ness* with their lifestyles and principles; their enthusiasm and creativity in building a free, peaceful and prosperous society; their resolve to triumph over the remnants of the totalitarian legacy; their approach to tackling interethnic and interconfessional relationships; their responsible and visionary diplomacy.

This predetermines Ukraine's only strategic goal, which is fully-fledged integration into European political and economic institutions. Ukraine does not ask for permission to enter Europe – it is already there; but the nation aspires to be fully integrated into the European mainstream, not isolated from it.

Significant progress has been registered in the Ukraine-EU dialogue over the past decade, but the hardest part still remains to be achieved by both sides. For its part, Ukraine is determined to continue its social and economic transformation, which will bring it closer to the EU accession criteria. However, the Ukrainian people still await a clear and distinct EU statement on the future of Ukraine-EU relations.

Of course giving Ukraine an unambiguous prospect of EU membership would commit the Union to a major policy shift from the current co-operation to a comprehensive pre-accession strategy. But the future will confirm that this would be one of the most far-reaching decisions taken by the Europeans since the end of the Cold War.

Indeed, membership of the EU for Ukraine presents a historic opportunity for the whole of Europe. The issue is not so much that the European Union would be poorer for Ukraine's absence (though it is easy to anticipate that the EU will derive considerable economic and political benefits from Ukraine's membership).

The real issue has been repeatedly explained by EU politicians and scholars themselves. 'The EU had to open up to the East, otherwise the very idea of European integration would have been undermined and eventually self-destructed. An EU restricted to Western Europe would forever have had to deal with a divided system in Europe... A divided system of states in Europe would in the long term make Europe a continent of uncertainty...' These are the words of the German Foreign Minister, Joschka Fischer, at Humboldt University in Berlin on 12 May 2000. They sound especially relevant if applied to the question of Ukraine's place in the process of European integration.

It is an absolutely false notion that Ukraine cannot effectively pursue its European choice and develop a strategic relationship with the Russian Federation at the same time. Quite the opposite – the quality of these relations increases the country's relevance to the EU. It also opens unprecedented opportunities to the European continent.

The significance of Russia, not only to Ukraine but also to nearly every country in Europe, has frequently been emphasised, and it is indeed a vital interest to both Ukraine and the EU to have Russia as a democratic and friendly partner and ally.

By contrast, Ukraine's capacity to shape Russia's evolution is almost completely ignored. Yet no historian would deny the profound influence exercised by Ukraine over Russia in the 18th and 19th centuries when this country was one of the most influential participants in the Concert of Europe. Without Ukraine the Soviet superpower could not have maintained its strength in the 20th century. It is legitimate to assert that Ukraine's future will have a deep impact on the future of its Northern neighbour in the new century as well. This impact will largely depend on Ukraine's place in European integration.

It is true that over the past decade Ukraine and the Russian Federation have had to deal with a number of difficult issues in their relationship. Yet the way they have resolved their disagreements in most cases could stand as an exemplary model of responsible international behaviour. As Henry Kissinger once observed, 'Mankind will never know what it was spared because of risks avoided or because of actions taken that averted awful consequences – if only because once thwarted the consequences can never be proved'.

As most of the thorniest problems in Ukrainian-Russian relations have been settled, the way is open to strengthen bilateral ties on the basis of sovereign equality and internationally recognised norms. The stronger Ukraine becomes, the greater its interest in deepening mutually beneficial co-operation with the Russian Federation. And this understanding is reciprocated – there is a growing realisation among the Russian leadership that a strong and confident Ukraine with a proper place in Europe would be a better partner for their country.

This is equally true with regard to Ukraine's relations with its other strategic partner – the United States. Ukraine's rating as a valuable partner to the USA is in direct proportion to the country's internal strength and stability, its consolidation as a regional leader, its engagement in the process of European integration and, of course, the dynamism of its bilateral relations with the Russian Federation. Ukraine and the USA will continue to be united by common values, shared interests and their resolute stance on building a powerful Europe without creating new dividing lines on the continent.

Through the years of independence the strategic structure of Ukraine's foreign policy has been complemented and reinforced by the country's commitment to effective co-operation with Nato; its active stance in the United Nations and OSCE; its participation in a complex network of multilateral arrangements at sub-regional level, such as GUUAM (Georgia, Ukraine, Uzbekistan, Azerbaijan, the Republic of Moldova), the Central European Initiative, and the Black Sea Economic Co-operation Organisation.

Having left behind the first and most difficult period of its nation-building, the country has formulated an ambitious foreign policy agenda for the future. The major objectives include creating favourable international conditions for sustaining its economic growth; ensuring the success of its course towards European integration: restoring peace and stability in its immediate vicinity from the Balkans to the Caucasus; developing its enormous transit potential; and strengthening its capacity to resist the threats and side-effects of globalisation.

Ukraine has always aspired to take due account of the fundamental interests of her strategic partners. This has secured the country a reputation as a partner to be relied upon. At the same time, a strategic relationship is a two-way street and imposes certain obligations on both sides. Ukraine has a legitimate right to expect from all her strategic partners not only an understanding of her vital national interests, but their active participation in their realisation.

UKRAINE AND NATO
A REVIVING PARTNERSHIP?

James Sherr

Ukraine's partnership with Nato is rightly called 'distinctive'. The Charter on a Distinctive Partnership signed in Madrid on 9 July 1997 not only formalised an intensity of co-operation unique between Nato and a non-candidate state, it established several new mechanisms of co-operation which do not exist between Nato and any other country. At the same time, this partnership is problematic. Despite Ukraine's consistently declared 'strategic course of entering Europe', Ukraine's President, Leonid Kuchma, has with equal consistency since his election in July 1994 pursued a multi-vector policy. The principle aim of this policy is to reconcile Russia to Ukraine's European course and make Ukraine's 'strategic partnership' with this neighbour a mutually beneficial one. It is also problematic because the impending enlargement of the European Union is ample indication that Nato is not the only Western institution whose interests and policies matter. A strong Nato-Ukraine relationship does not guarantee strong or even good relations between Ukraine and the EU.

Three paradoxes

It is therefore not surprising to find that there are several paradoxes in the Nato-Ukraine relationship. For one thing, unlike the Russian Federation, Ukraine has officially set its sights on becoming an EU Member State. But with respect to Nato, it has expressed no aspiration beyond 'special partnership'. Yet until mid-1999, it had been Nato, not the EU, which served as Ukraine's primary vehicle for integration into Europe. This is the first paradox.

Between 8 February 1994 (the date Ukraine joined Partnership for Peace) and 28-31 May 1997 (dates concluding, respectively, the Black Sea Fleet accords and the 'Big Treaty' between Russia and Ukraine), the paradox had two sound justifications. On the one hand, from the time of the USSR's collapse, the key question for Ukraine was, 'will Ukraine remain an independent state?' Nato played an instrumental role in ensuring that the answer would be 'yes'. Well before the Charter on a Distinctive Partnership was signed, the Nato-Ukraine relationship had already become unique. The only states of the former Soviet Union which could claim to enjoy relations with Nato of equivalent intensity and closeness, the three Baltic states, had made Nato membership the cornerstone of their foreign policies. Such was the momentum of the Nato-Ukraine relationship, and such was the skill of Ukraine's Ministry of Foreign Affairs in exploiting it, that by spring 1997, Russia had concluded that lack of agreement on the Black Sea Fleet, state borders and Ukraine's territorial integrity was 'pushing Ukraine towards Nato'. In fact, by affirming with the Polish and three Baltic Presidents their 'common position that Nato should remain open for all countries aspiring for membership', President Kuchma led Russia to believe that it might be pushing Ukraine to actual membership of the Alliance.

The second justification was the European Union's relative coolness. Whereas Nato had committed itself to a form of enlargement, Partnership for Peace, as early as January 1994, the European Union had made no such commitment. The March 1994 EU-Ukraine Partnership and Co-operation Agreement (PCA) – which only came into effect in June 1998 – neither echoed Nato's repeated affirmations of Ukraine's 'key' importance, nor did it welcome Ukraine's officially proclaimed European vocation. Even in the wake of the December 1997 decisions of the Luxembourg European Council inviting six states to begin accession negotiations, the EU took no measures to develop an analogue to PfP, which Nato hoped would soften the distinction between 'membership' and 'partnership'.

After 1997, the wisdom of placing so much emphasis upon Nato became questionable. By then it was true, as President Kuchma affirmed, that 'the transitional period in the self-determination of the state is over'. But what type of state would Ukraine be? The key questions were now distinctly different from what they had been in the post-independence period. Would Ukraine be part of Europe or part of Europe's grey zone? Which Western institution, Nato or the EU, would play the decisive role in answering that question? And if the European Union mattered most to Ukraine, then what mattered to the EU? By the time of Kuchma's re-election, it had become clear that what mattered to the EU was not Ukraine's foreign policy, but its internal policy.

In sum, the temporary diminution of the Russian factor had brought the Ukrainian factor to the foreground. This in turn demanded a readjustment of priorities. In response to the collapse of the Soviet Union, Ukraine had rightly given priority to developing its *nezalezhnist*, its formal independence. But very little attention had been given to developing the country's *samostiynist*, its 'ability to stand'. The relative absence of *samostiynist* – the weakness of state and society, the alienation of ordinary people from the political order, the contradiction between 'European' aims and Soviet-era (and increasingly criminalised) practices – had by 1997 been identified not only as barriers to Europe, but as threats to Ukraine's national security. Ukraine's official National Security Concept, drawn up by specialists from the National Security and Defence Council (NSDC) and ratified by Parliament in January 1997, went so far as to define 'strengthening civil society' as the first of nine national security challenges. One year after President Kuchma's re-election, it had become obvious, in the words of a confidential Ukrainian assessment, that 'the principal security threat to Ukraine is Ukraine itself.'

When these factors are brought into the equation, it becomes clear that between 1994 and 1997, Ukraine's hopes in Nato exceeded Nato's potential. At the same time, Nato's actual potential was never realised. This is the second paradox characterising Ukraine's relations with the West.

Until recently, the paradox was not an obvious one. Between 1994 and 1997, much of Ukraine's political establishment rightly perceived that the

Nato-Ukraine relationship was establishing networks which institutionalised as well as personalised Nato's commitment to enhance what the former Secretary of the NSDC, Volodymyr Horbulin, called Ukraine's 'role in ensuring European political and economic stability'. These networks in turn reinforced the standing of those inside Ukraine who believed that national security structures, without losing their distinctiveness or their pertinence to local conditions, should evolve in ways compatible with Nato patterns of co-operation, professionalism, transparency and democratic civilian control. Not least, such networks appeared to reduce the risk that Ukraine would find itself isolated in disputes with neighbours and correspondingly increase the risk that threats to Ukraine would set off alarms throughout the 'common European house'. Indeed, it was hoped that Nato's enlargement, along with the scale and depth of Nato's defence co-operation with Ukraine (and the Baltic states) could gradually blur the practical distinction between full PfP participation and Nato membership, particularly if Nato continued to acquire more of a military-political and less of a military orientation.

Yet as Ukraine's focus shifted from interstate threat to integration and economic well-being, the limitations of this relationship became more apparent. The limitation is not only straightforward, it is unalterable. Nato is a security organisation, and it is doomed to remain one. Nato-Ukraine co-operation cannot make Ukrainian goods competitive in European markets, stimulate domestic entrepreneurship or decrease unemployment. Moreover not even a comprehensive and intimate Nato-Ukraine relationship will attract Western finance to Ukraine, let alone enable Ukraine to integrate with Europe in the terms that matter most – through business, trade and investment. The success of Ukraine's most committed partner, Poland – a Nato member state since March 1999 – only reinforces the point, for the formula which produced the 'Polish miracle' was economic transformation and security, with security being the dependent variable.

Nevertheless, as a security organisation encompassing not only a vast multilateral structure, but 19 separate defence establishments, Nato also constitutes an unrivalled repository of expertise which, thanks to PfP, is open to exploitation by those seeking to create defence and security establishments appropriate to democratic norms and the post-Cold War security environment.

By focusing so heavily on the political significance of co-operation with Nato, Ukraine's exploitation of this opportunity, whilst impressive in breadth, lacked depth and focus. Today, this is no longer the case.

This change in focus – from politically driven participation in 'programmes' to intensive military-technical collaboration – has created a third paradox. For the new direction and vigour of co-operation with Nato has arisen at a time when, thanks to the Kosovo conflict, Nato's stock has fallen in the country at large; when, thanks to President Putin's 'tougher', 'more pragmatic' and 'more aggressive' policy, Kiev has made several geopolitical accommodations towards Russia; and it continues despite the fact that the tape scandal has further damaged Ukraine's standing in the West – not to say President Kuchma's relations with reformists and Westernisers in his own country.

To this day, most Nato members fail to appreciate the damage which the Kosovo bombing campaign inflicted not only upon Nato's standing in Ukraine, but upon the security of Ukraine itself. From the vantage point of Kiev, the launch of Operation Allied Force had three deleterious effects. First, and for the first time, it presented Nato in a provocative and even threatening light to a population which for the most part had viewed it in benign, favourable and even protective terms and which had been encouraged to do so by a Government firmly convinced that Nato 'projected security and stability in Europe'. Misconceived this shift of perceptions might have been, but it was based, as in Russia, on sentiments of Slavic (and Orthodox) kinship, on deep fears of any state or coalition prepared to violate the sovereignty of small powers and (contrary to hysterical accusations of 'Ukrainianisation' by Russian nationalists) by the disproportionate influence in the country of the Russian media and its slanted portrayal of events. Second, it raised the fear that continued co-operation with Nato could put Ukraine and Russia diametrically at cross purposes. Third, it exposed Ukraine's impotence: its failure to influence Western 'partners' (and be included in the decisions that matter), the failure to 'integrate' in anything more than cosmetic terms and the failure of these partners to treat Ukraine's 'pivotal' role in European security as anything more than a slogan.

By the close of the operation, these effects were supplemented by three more:

- The operation sharply heightened concerns that Ukraine could be drawn involuntarily into disputes and conflicts outside its borders. Russia's dispatch of a 'humanitarian' convoy to Yugoslavia (halted on the Hungary-Ukraine border) in April 1999, its redeployment of the intelligence ship Liman (and initial preparation to redeploy other vessels) from Sevastopol to the Adriatic and its plans to transit Ukraine with Airborne Troop reinforcements after the 'brilliant dash to Pristina' in June 1999 provoked anxiety and, in some quarters, alarm.
- It created precedents which Ukraine feared could be used by other states to weaken its own sovereignty in the name of human and minority rights. Shortly after the bombing campaign commenced, the staff of the NSDC undertook an examination of scenarios for possible employment of coercive diplomacy by the Russian Federation in event of a separatist challenge in Crimea.
- It created concern that the scale and complexity of commitments in the Balkans could diminish Nato's attentiveness to Ukraine and its responsiveness to pressures which other states might put upon it.

When these factors are added to Ukraine's increased sensitivity to Russian interests, how is it that Nato-Ukraine co-operation has intensified rather than disintegrated? Counter-intuitive as this change might appear, there are three compelling reasons for it. First, whilst conceding to Russia what he must, President Kuchma wishes to preserve as much of the multi-vector policy as he can and therefore has a clear incentive to reinforce the few channels of the Western vector – the Polish-Ukraine relationship being another such channel – which produce benefits for Ukraine. Second and no less important, the worsened geopolitical climate finally persuaded Kuchma that serious defence reform could no longer be postponed. This conclusion is powerfully reinforced by the economic condition of the country, which persuaded a critical mass of key players that a bloated and underfinanced defence establishment could become a social and, ultimately, a national security problem for the country.

Defence reform and refocused co-operation

Today, as opposed to 1997, the prime goal of Nato-Ukraine co-operation is not advancing Ukraine's 'European course' but, in the words of the Minister of Defence, Army General Kuzmuk, 'supporting defence reform in the country'. Now as well as then, no equation is made between co-operation with Nato and future membership. Indeed, the military leadership, like the political leadership, is as opposed to Ukraine joining Nato (on grounds of external security and internal concord) as it is supportive of closer ties with it. The conclusion innocently and widely drawn that those opposed to Nato membership are necessarily anti-Nato is therefore misconceived.

It is often forgotten that Ukraine did not inherit an army in 1991. What it inherited was a force grouping – without a Defence Ministry, a General Staff and central organs of command-and-control. Moreover, this grouping, its formidable inventory of equipment and its highly trained officer corps were designed for one purpose: to wage combined arms, coalition, offensive (and nuclear) warfare against Nato on an external front and under somebody else's direction. In 1991 these formations were not equipped, deployed or trained to provide national defence or, for that matter, integrated military operations of any kind. As they stood, they were bone and muscle without heart or brain. In the post-independence period, therefore, Ukraine did not merely face the task of 'reforming' an army, but creating one. Having accomplished this far from straightforward task, Ukraine's Armed Forces entered a period of stagnation whose ills only began to be addressed after President Kuchma established an interdepartmental commission on defence reform in December 1999, chaired by Army General Oleksandr Kuzmuk (Minister of Defence) and Yevhen Marchuk (Secretary of the National Security and Defence Council). To understand what has and has not been achieved (as of October 2001), it is essential to analyse defence policy as well as its implementation.

Unlike the operation of a market economy, national defence must be a planned activity. Failure to produce a tight correspondence between national security policy, military doctrine (the purpose and the priorities of armed forces) and military programmes (detailed schemes for their development) will lead to waste, confusion and, in the worst case, breakdown. Producing such a correspondence is not easy, particularly in the radically transformed circumstances confronting newly independent states, and in nearly all of these states it has not been achieved because old mentalities and strong interests continually intrude. Programmes therefore matter, because nothing sensible can be accomplished without them.

In contrast to the post-Soviet norm (which, according to President Putin, applied to Russia until last year), Ukraine adopted a National Security Concept (approved by Parliament in January 1997) which was a model statement of first principles. It assaulted the general war ethos (which had been inculcated in the Soviet-trained officer corps of Ukraine) by stipulating that in conditions where both state and society were weak, the prime security challenge would be to forestall and resolve local crises, emergencies and conflicts and prevent them being exploited by actors (internal and foreign) with ulterior political ends. Proceeding from this analysis, the Concept identified 'the strengthening of civil society' as the first of nine security challenges for Ukraine. Ukraine's first State Programme of Armed Forces Development (1997) had its merits, but was not consistent with these principles. A far more impressive consistency has been achieved in the current State Programme of Armed Forces Development and Reform 2001-2005, which was submitted to President Kuchma in May 2000.

The capabilities mandated by the Programme furnish obvious incentives to exploit Nato's post-Cold War expertise in joint operations, complex emergencies and 'operations other than war'. Therefore, at the same time as it was submitted to the President, the State Programme (minus a classified geopolitical assessment) was submitted to Nato for analysis and comment. In April 2001, Nato presented its recommendations at a meeting of the Joint Working Group on Defence Reform (a body established under the Nato-Ukraine Distinctive Partnership, which has no analogue between Nato and any other country). On the basis of Nato's assessment that stipulated force levels would still be grossly out of balance with resources, Ukraine is now considering a more intense schedule of reductions.

Co-operation with Nato has now moved beyond the formal exchange of ideas to a scheduled process of audit and consultation. In 2001, Ukraine became an active participant in Nato's Planning and Review Process: a PfP programme requiring each participating country at regular intervals to supply Nato with a detailed inventory of its military assets and, jointly with Nato, identify real costs, as well as capabilities in short supply or surplus to needs. Ukraine will also draw up a detailed package of National Defence Reform Objectives for initial review by Nato in December 2001. A mechanism has also been devised for keeping Nato advised on a regular basis of the Programme's implementation. These are significant steps for a military establishment schooled to regard transparency as a threat to departmental interests and national security.

These steps have also given more focus to the considerable volume of activities which take place between Nato and Ukraine each year. More than 500 bilateral activities are scheduled between Nato Allies and Ukraine in 2001, as well as 250 multilateral activities with Nato. These numbers in themselves, of course, say very little about the value of co-operation: e.g., the establishment of the Polish-Ukrainian battalion (POLUKRBAT) has been worth several dozen such 'activities'. Although the volume of Ukraine-Russia military activities is comparatively modest (in stark contrast to co-operation in the military-industrial sector), this is not to say that Ukraine sees no value in such co-operation. As a case in point, Russia's merger of Air Forces and Air Defence Forces is being closely studied. But few believe that the Russian Armed Forces are an attractive model for the conduct of joint operations and the regulation of civil conflicts. Additionally, as the issue of the joint naval force demonstrates, many question whether Russia's military co-operation goals are compatible with Ukraine's. As Leonid Polyakov, Director of Military Programmes at UCEPS, maintains:

> So far, Russian officials, unlike Nato's, have never voiced their concern about the weakness of Ukraine's defence or the slow pace of its military reform. One might infer that Ukraine's problems in building its Armed Forces are simply more acceptable to Moscow than Ukraine's success in that area.

The agenda of challenges

Only nine months into the Programme, the catalogue of measures implemented is necessarily sparse. Troop reductions have begun, front-line organisation is being overhauled, reorganisations of the Air Force and Air Defence Forces are in train (possibly as a prelude to merger), and preparations for the closure or merger of surplus facilities are proceeding. A major training command for peace support operations has been established, and a Nato bloc of courses is being established at the National Armed Forces Academy. Moreover, every new officer is now obliged to learn English, French or German as part of his academic curriculum. Yet there must be several areas of major concern.

The first, still, is the awesome imbalance between plans and resources. This is a long-standing concern inside Nato HQ, where it is often pointed out that with a budget 75 per cent larger than Ukraine's $450 million, Hungary is reducing the size of its armed forces to 45,000 and Ukraine, at the very most, to 200,000 servicemen. Yet where force levels are concerned, the Nato approach ignores two compelling factors. The first is that Ukraine, unlike Hungary, is a non-aligned country bordering seven states (and the Black Sea) and lying in the vicinity of several conflict zones. Even as harsh a critic of Ukraine's defence policy as Anatoliy Grytsenko (former Director of Analysis at the NSDC) believes that the strength of MOD armed forces should not fall below 150,000 (although he also believes that the defence budget should not fall below 2.5 percent of GDP). Second, conscripts are an extremely cheap component of Ukraine's armed forces (the wage per conscript being $50 per annum). Ukraine's entire conscript cohort of 130,000 (nearly half the army) costs the defence budget $6.5 million, roughly 1.5 per cent of the total. It is reductions, not high force levels, which are expensive, because any serious reduction scheme must involve reorganisation, base closures and, by law, the retraining and resettling of officers, which is already an acute and sensitive issue.

Yet the professionalisation mandated by the Programme (at wages of $50 per month) is even more expensive. Whilst force levels as low as 200,000 are under discussion, the MoD rightly refuses to commit itself to reduce below 295,000 until the Government provides a defence budget projection to 2005. This explains the decision to defer large-scale professionalisation to 2010 (50 per cent of the force) and 2015 (100 per cent). Unless the budget is steadily and substantially increased, these 'plans' will remain wishes. But even if they are implemented, the mere replacement of conscripts with *kontraktnikiy* (contract soldiers, who now make up 10 per cent of the force) will not itself provide the improvements sought, for without a substantial improvement in conditions of service, the overhaul of the training regime and a vast expansion of the NCO corps, these professionals are unlikely to have the commitment or skills expected of them. Moreover, without budgets approaching Grytsenko's figure, the provision of Forward Defence Forces will be minimal at best and certainly far below the extravagant capabilities officially envisaged for it. On the whole, the imbalance between plans and resources is at least as much a reflection of a lack of understanding (and responsibility) inside Ukraine's political establishment as of a lack of realism on the part of its military establishment.

The second area of concern is civilian democratic control, now officially deemed a priority in Ukraine. Priority it might be, but the starting point is a military establishment still inclined to equate 'civilian democratic control' with control by an elected President. The presidential tapes published in small doses since November 2000 – which allegedly link the President to serious abuses of power, including the murder of the journalist Gongadze – are forcing people to re-examine this simple equation. For if it is the case, as several opposition figures allege, that the President ordered the Ministry of Interior (MVS) to murder Gongadze and put pressure on other critics and rivals, then the difference between presidential control and democratic control of force structures is very clear. But if the President did not actually order or intend Gongadze to be killed, then it is clear that presidential control is insufficient.

But how is civilian democratic control of Ukraine's force structures to be established? Despite a growing pool of civilian specialists – some of extremely high calibre – there is a serious deficit of civilian expertise in the fields of security and defence. Even the Parliament – which has a Standing Commission on Questions of Security and Defence and budgetary powers denied to the British Parliament – suffers from this deficit, for the Commission does not employ specialist advisers, its relationships with NGOs are limited, few of its own members can be considered experts, and not all of them are committed to exercising the prerogatives which they have. The Parliament might have powers, but it has very little capacity. What is more, Ukraine lacks a professional civil service. It has civilian functionaries. There is still limited awareness of the need for a corps of experienced administrators, 'above politics' and immune from political pressure, who are expert enough to implement government policy and help the Government frame it. The administrative culture of Ukraine – oppressively bureaucratic and hierarchical, distrustful of initiative and outsiders (even from the next office) – weakens transparency by definition; and by weakening transparency – the ability to see – it weakens the ability to monitor and control. The quality of decisions is also weakened when there is little integration within institutions, not to say between them. The contrast with the working culture of Nato HQ – where most decisions are made at mid-level, by interdepartmental (and civil-military) committees with full access to relevant information – could not be more profound. It will be a long time before a critical mass of Ukrainians understand that their declared objectives are undermined by their own administrative culture.

The final area of concern is the failure of reform to touch the non-MOD force structures, particularly the Ministry of the Interior (MVS) and the Security Service of Ukraine (SBU). The former service (as well as emergency services and border guards) have been identified by the Nato-Ukraine Joint Working Group as areas into which reform and Nato-Ukraine co-operation must extend, whilst the European Union has undertaken a programme to help bring Ukraine's border regime into line with its own standards. But with the exception of the emergency services and border guards, the Joint Working Group has handed itself an agenda of struggle and frustration.

The overwhelming obstacle to serious transformation is the continuity between these services and those that existed before. Whereas the USSR Ministry of Defence and General Staff were centralised, all-Union institutions, the MVD and KGB had analogues at the level of Union Republic. These bodies survived the Soviet collapse relatively intact. The custodians of independent Ukraine therefore faced a stark choice: either to dismiss the greater proportion of those who worked in these services and construct security establishments from scratch – a course pursued only in the Baltic states and post-Communist Czechoslovakia – or to do what all other successor states have done: eliminate the overtly disloyal and proceed to 'reform' the structures inherited. Ukraine made the conservative, understandable but fateful choice. It took what was available. Unlike Estonia, Ukraine could not rely upon a vigilant civil society to mount guard over 'their' state whilst a committed corps of citizens was first identified and then laboriously turned into professionals. Unlike Czechoslovakia, Ukraine faced security threats. It still faces them. The reasons which make it difficult to reform Armed Forces during a war – though unless they are reformed by war, they are often defeated – make it difficult to reform security services under threat. Now that the dish is cooked, the country has to eat it: security services dominated by members of the former KGB and MVD which have preserved much of the mental inheritance of these services and some of the methods, too.

The second factor is the 'objective logic' of the methods themselves in contemporary Ukrainian conditions. Unlike the FBI, MI5, Special Branch and other Western analogues, the internal services of the KGB (and much of the MVD) were instruments of administrative control over society. Today their successors remain networks of influence, not only in state structures but in partnership with regional authorities and with much of the 'private' sector. Thanks to this influence – their ability to advance careers or obstruct them, grant licenses or deny them, provide tax privileges or dispatch tax inspectors – these services not only moderate heterodoxy, they provide themselves with informers, collaborators and surrogates. How is one to overcome this state of affairs? To be sure, the position of Western security services presents a radically different picture. These services have no 'presence', let alone influence in society. Unlike SBU employees (who are paid 40 percent more than their military equivalents), they have very moderate salaries and only a moderate social status. The overwhelming majority of citizens – those who are neither subversives nor candidates for jobs requiring a security clearance – will live out their entire lives without coming into contact with them. But can Western security services be a model for Ukraine? If these services could not rely upon voluntary co-operation, let alone other features of a strong civil society – a coherent, effective legal order, the vigilance of NGOs and journalists and a large degree of transparency in politics and business – they would swiftly find themselves overwhelmed. The methods of the SBU and MVS reflect the weakness of civil society in Ukraine. But they also prolong its weakness. It remains to be seen whether the Gongadze affair produces a more assertive civil society or a more submissive one.

In creative but at the same time unanticipated ways, the Nato-Ukraine partnership has evolved to reflect the changing priorities of each party and their respective views of the 'art of the possible'. The suppleness and flexibility of this relationship, maintained despite several blows inflicted upon it, might suggest that Nato-Ukraine co-operation has an intrinsic viability, even a permanence in what is plainly a rapidly changing Europe. Nevertheless, the partnership also reflects the expectations of the partners, along with a balance of political forces inside Ukraine and the Western world which is far from unalterable. It would be unwise to draw too much comfort from the resilience of this comparatively short relationship and conclude that it will survive every shock to the international system, let alone mutual disillusionment.

TWO EAGLES
STORY OF THE POLISH-UKRAINIAN BATTALION

Robert Pszczel

It was a strange, almost surreal juxtaposition. One rainy evening in October 2000, Polish television showed two clips in one edition of the evening news. The first recounted the box office success of film epic 'By the Fire and the Sword'. Three hours in length, shot with great panache, it portrayed (in Hollywood style) the adventures of a gallant Polish officer involved in heroic battles with the Ukrainian Cossacks challenging the Polish crown in the 16th century. The second clip, shown in the world news part of the programme, was a short reportage on the joint work of the Polish and Ukrainian peacekeepers in Kosovo.

Surreal or not, those two items, shown almost together, captured the very essence of the dramatic evolution that Polish-Ukrainian relations have undergone in the last 10 years. The turbulence of these nations' history can hardly be matched by any other example in Europe. Poles and Ukrainians have fought against each other for centuries, but they have also shared much misfortune, most strikingly during the second world war or during communist times. The outbreak of Polish democracy at the end of the 1980s and declaration of Ukrainian independence in 1991 provided the two neighbours with an excellent opportunity to begin a completely new chapter in the old saga. Starting with the fact that Poland was the first country in the world to recognise Ukraine's independence, one can find many examples demonstrating a very optimistic thesis: that both Poles and Ukrainians have seized this opportunity. The joint battalion is an excellent illustration of this.

It actually began with an idea floated among politicians and independent commentators in the mid-1990s. Why not create a living and concrete proof of flourishing bilateral co-operation, a kind of good-neighbourhood project *in corpore*? The idea was picked up by the respective Ministries of Defence in 1995 and after the inevitable bureaucratic phase bore fruit in an agreement signed by the two Ministers on 26 November 1997. The agreement (subsequently ratified by the Polish Sejm in 1999 and the Ukrainian Rada in 2000) established a joint unit to be deployed for peacekeeping missions under the authority of the UN. POLUKRBAT achieved operational readiness by 1999 and in July 2000 began its mission as part of KFOR's Multinational Brigade East in the US-led sector.

How does it work? Well, given that neither side suffers from a surplus of funds for defence, pragmatic solutions had to be applied. First, the composition. To save on transport costs (which can be a very expensive item) the two components of the battalion were picked from units stationed near the Polish-Ukrainian border. The Polish contribution comes from the 21st Brigade of Podhale Riflemen (based in Przemysl, location also of the headquarters), the Ukrainian from the 208th Independent Special Battalion (based in Yavoriv, where the joint battalion does a lot of training together). In total there are about 900 soldiers currently serving in POLUKRBAT in Kosovo, at least a third of them professionals.

Second, the structure and procedures. A simple rule is observed: if a given cell is commanded by a Pole, a Ukrainian acts as his deputy and vice versa. Currently POLUKRBAT is commanded by a Pole, Lt. Col. Bogdan Tworkowski. Logistic channels are kept separate as each side is responsible for the establishment, maintenance, equipping and functioning of its contingent. A visit to the battalion's base (named 'Two Eagles') in Kosovo would quickly show that the rule is not strictly applied. The Ukrainian contingent is the only one in KFOR to have its own bakery – freshly baked Ukrainian bread is thus very popular among the Polish soldiers (in fact its fame extends even to the main US base, Camp Bondsteel).

And what about the language? Written orders and communications at higher level are all in English. And Nato procedures are applied – after all both countries are participants in the Partnership for Peace programme, which places a high premium on inter-operability. However, below command level the soldiers use their own languages. Bearing in mind the common Slavic roots of both Polish and Ukrainian, it is not an uncommon sight to see a Pole and a Ukrainian engaged in lively conversation, with an extensive use of hands and body language to help reach understanding.

Third, actual performance in Kosovo. Those who had expected major problems – Poland is a member state of Nato, Ukraine is not – were severely disappointed. The battalion has quickly won the trust of the local population (both Albanian and Serb). Patrolling is easy – no signs of resentment are encountered, on the contrary soldiers have a difficult time extracting themselves from the company of locals, who are usually able to address each member of the patrol by name. As far as the mission is concerned, once KFOR increased its workload through tasks related to patrolling the former Yugoslav Republic of Macedonia side of the Kosovo border, POLUKRBAT efforts became the centre of international attention (their zone of responsibility lies directly in that area). The facts speak for themselves – as of autumn 2001 the battalion has one of the best records in terms of interdiction of illegal weapons or armed extremists across the border.

There is no doubt that POLUKRBAT has lived up to expectations. At Nato it is regarded as an excellent proof that multinational units, irrespective of composition, can improve dramatically integration into Nato-led operations (by the way POLUKRBAT in KFOR also includes a Lithuanian platoon). The Polish and Ukrainian authorities, encouraged by results so far, have decided to propose a full-sized brigade for the EU's Headline Goal catalogue of forces. In the future, POLUKRBAT may even serve as a nucleus for an even larger multinational formation comprising units from other countries in the region. But perhaps the most important evaluation was offered by the Ukrainian Defence Minister, Oleksander Kuzmuk, who at the ceremony at the end of July 2001 marking the rotation of the battalion said: 'We do not divide the battalion soldiers into Ukrainians or Poles. It is not even one team, it is in fact one family. We are proud that the sons of Poland and Ukraine are working shoulder to shoulder together to bring peace to the Balkans.' Much had to change in the bilateral history of the two nations, and indeed the history of Europe, for such a statement to be made. And European security is in a much better shape for that.

RUSSIA AND UKRAINE
A GEOPOLITICAL TURN?

James Sherr

In Ukraine, it has long been accepted that whilst many Russians love Ukraine, very few love its independence. Nevertheless, the Russian Federation recognised Ukraine's independence as long ago as 1992, and as recently as his first summit with President Kuchma on 17-18 April 2000, President Putin affirmed that its independence was 'irreversible'. But what does independence mean in practice? Not until the signing of the Tripartite Accord on 14 January 1994 did Russia pledge to respect Ukraine's territorial integrity – and not until the 'Big Treaty' was signed on 31 May 1997 were Crimea (and its largest city, Sevastopol) conclusively recognised as part of this territory. To this day, the Russian Federation refuses to demarcate the border between the two states; many of its official representatives speak of Ukraine as an 'ally' (thus refusing to recognise the country's non-aligned status); and several of its actions (e.g. the use of Crimean bases to train troops for combat duty in Chechnya) suggest that there might be more respect for Ukraine's sovereignty *de jure* than there is *de facto*. More fundamentally, the Russian authorities see no contradiction between independence and '*integratsia*'. In his last interview as Director General of the SVR (Foreign Intelligence Service) on 26 December 1995, Yevgeniy Primakov stated that his service had used 'all possible means to strengthen centripetal processes in the former Soviet Union.'

Even prior to becoming President of the Russian Federation, Vladimir Vladimirovich Putin let it be known that Russia's policy towards its former Soviet neighbours would become 'more active', 'more pragmatic', 'more aggressive' and 'far tougher'. Does that mean that he is pursuing a new policy or giving fresh impetus to an old one? How is Ukraine responding to what many privately view as a new regime in Russia and a more intense mode of engagement? How might the EU's interests be affected by changes in the relationship between Ukraine and Russia, and how might such changes affect Ukraine's chances of realising its long proclaimed 'European choice'?

Continuities in thinking and practice

The continuities in the Ukraine-Russia relationship are defined by identity, sentiment and interdependence. Both identity and sentiment are expressed in the old maxim that 'St. Petersburg is the brain, Moscow the heart and Kiev the mother of Russia': a maxim which reveals that, from the point of view of the vast majority of Russians, Ukraine is not the lodestar of the Russian Empire, but the birthplace of the Russian state. Yet from a Ukrainian perspective, this 'truth' not only ignores those Ukrainians from the six Western regions of the country who never lived in a Russian state until 1939-40; as the Russian historian Georgiy Fedotov noted, it also ignores 'three to four centuries of history that had made the Ukrainian people and their culture different from the Great Russians'. That Ukraine and Russia – like England and Ireland, Sweden and Norway, Germany and Austria – have a related history is indisputable. But Russian insistence on a *common* history is a key reason why many Ukrainians share the verdict of another Russian historian, Vernadskiy, that 'Russian democracy ends where the question of Ukraine begins.'

A second reason for Vernadskiy's verdict is that the growth of the Russian state and empire were coterminous processes. Russia has limited historical experience of living with neighbours who are at one and the same time friendly and independent. This fact in itself would explain the integrationist bias in policy and the tendency, not only amongst Ukraine's enemies in Russia, but its friends, to equate good relations with 'drawing closer' and 'firm good neighbourliness'.

The issues of sentiment and identity are aggravated by at least one additional factor: the large number of ethnic Russians on Ukrainian territory

(19 per cent of the population, according to the last Soviet census): 'compatriots' who, according to two Concepts of Foreign Policy, the Russian Federation is obliged to 'protect'. Yet with the revealing exception of Crimea – 90 per cent of whose ethnic Russians arrived only after 1944 – those who identified themselves as Russians in the Soviet census are well assimilated into their regions, are in large part ethnically mixed and in even larger part resentful of ethnic labels. To be sure, the 'Russian dominated' regions of the East overwhelmingly favour close linkages, if not 'union' with Russia, yet this is as true for the ethnic Ukrainians living there as it is for ethnic Russians. In regions wary of Russian influence, the picture is the same: ethnic Russians generally share the orientation of ethnic Ukrainians from the same generation, profession and social background. For the vast majority of Ukrainian citizens, *nalezhnist* (belonging) matters more than *poskhodzhennya* (origin), and there is no contradiction between being pro-Russian and distrustful of the Russian state.

Ukraine's economic dependency on Russia – demonstrated obviously and oppressively by the question of energy – plainly compounds the difficulties of a state with aspirations of 'living apart' from its more powerful and vastly larger neighbour. Yet the difficulties are both more subtle and more serious than this dependency suggests. For one thing, it is more accurate to speak of an uneven interdependency than a dependency – as revealed not only by Ukraine's extensive energy transport and refining infrastructure (still vital for Russia's gas shipments to Europe), but its substantial and highly specialised capabilities in what had once been a tightly integrated 'all Union' defence-industrial complex. No less significant are all the linkages – in loyalties, values and working culture – of many of the elites who dominate the economic, political (and military and intelligence) structures of a state determined to become a 'full member of the European family of civilised nations' and, eventually, the European Union. These Soviet and post-Soviet realities give point to the vital distinction between a country's *nezalezhnist* (its 'independence') and its *samostiynist* (its 'ability to stand'); they have prolonged the life of the old Russian conviction that '*samostoyatelnoy Ukrainiy nikogda ne budet* ('Ukraine will never be able to stand alone'); and they have even persuaded many Russian democrats (to quote Yeltsin's State Secretary Gennadiy

Burbulis) 'that there is a logic that will bring the former republics back again our way.'

The Putin factor

To be sure, Putin's policy is not exclusively Putin's. Like President Putin himself, this policy is a reflection of moods, interests and the balance of forces within Russia's policy-making elite and, to a considerable extent, the country as a whole. Thanks to a variety of internal and external factors, these moods and forces were shifting over the course of the Yeltsin era. By the time Vladimir Putin became Acting President in December 1999, they had combined to produce a paradigm shift. Four of these factors have proved particularly influential in Russia:

- The 1998 Financial Crisis was rightly or wrongly seen as a damning, definitive demonstration that Western economic models and 'remedies' had not advanced the development of Russia. To Putin and his entourage, the diminution of the state is the most flawed feature of these Western models. Nevertheless, Putin is determined that Russia benefit from 'globalisation processes' rather than find itself isolated by them. Reconstructing the 'vertical of power' is seen as indispensable to making Russia a capable actor in the international system.

- Nato enlargement, even where not seen as a military threat to Russia, is widely seen as a means of excluding it from Europe and de-legitimising its interests.

- EU enlargement, whilst appraised far more positively than Nato enlargement, is none the less regarded with some ambivalence. There is growing recognition that the EU is not exclusively, or even primarily, a 'counterbalance to US dominance', but a mechanism of integration. Whilst on the one hand believing in the merits and possibility of 'strategic partnership' with the EU – a matter of high politics – there is reasoned scepticism that integration – a course requiring profound micro-level change – can be anything more than a very distant prospect.

- Kosovo: in military terms, Nato's intervention was widely seen as a rehearsal for more ambitious exercises in 'coercive diplomacy' and in political terms as a testing ground for using human rights as a flag of convenience for breaking up 'problematic states'. This perception has greatly sharpened the geopolitical stakes for Russia in Central Asia and in the Caucasus (where the 'rights' of Chechens and small states might provide a useful pretext for Nato to advance its geoeconomic interests). To those conscious of these interests in the 'Black Sea and Caspian region', Ukraine's location and its oil refining and transport infrastructure are hardly of peripheral importance.

As a result of these international developments and internal reverses, President Putin came to power convinced that Russia was under geopolitical pressure from the West and especially from Nato and the United States. Given these developments, the transformation of the CIS into a bloc and an internationally recognised 'zone of interest' is seen not only as a defensive and urgent measure, but as a precondition for giving Russia 'equality' in the international system. In the words of Andrey Fedorov, former First Deputy Foreign Minister,

> Today we are speaking more or less openly now about our zones of interests. In one way or another we are confirming that the post-Soviet territory is such a zone. In Yeltsin's time we were trying to wrap this in a nice paper. Now we are saying it more directly: this is our territory, our sphere of interest.

These perceptions have affected Russian policy towards Ukraine at three levels. First, President Putin has disciplined – though certainly not eliminated – the *mnogogolosiye* (multi-voicedness) of the Yeltsin era and has succeeded in producing a tighter correspondence between Russia's commercial, geoeconomic and geopolitical objectives. Second, he has been more pragmatic (and sceptical) than his predecessor about the merits of the traditional Soviet concept of integration – a concept which implies burdens for Russia as well as benefits – whilst focusing more intently on the *subordination* of Ukraine in concrete areas relevant to Russian interests. Finally, consistent with his KGB background, he has intensified covert means of influence, placed greater emphasis on internal Ukrainian allies and has endeavoured to turn weakness, division and even scandal inside Ukraine to Russia's geopolitical advantage. These shifts in focus and method can be seen in three key areas: Ukraine's energy debt, the fate of the Yushchenko government and the tape scandal known as 'Kuchmagate'.

Where debt is concerned, the switch to a 'cold', 'specific' and 'pragmatic' policy became apparent when Russia cut the oil supply to Ukraine in December 1999 (which, not incidentally, is the start of winter). Although this was the fifth major oil cut-off since Ukraine became an independent state, those given responsibility for resolving the matter (notably the leadership of the National Security and Defence Council) soon sensed that the rules had changed: that Russia would inflict pain and continue to inflict it until the necessary conclusions were drawn. At the outset of the dispute, Russia's Acting Prime Minister Kasyanov declared that there would be no further deliveries until Ukraine entirely halted diversions of Russian gas supplies transiting Ukraine: in essence, officially sanctioned (but officially disavowed) theft from the *Druzhba* pipeline, then running at 185 million cubic meters of gas per day. When Ukraine's authorities took measures to control what they could control, reducing diversion to 35 million cubic meters, Russia continued to withhold deliveries, and Kasyanov restated his terms. At the same time, he sounded a new note: Ukraine would find it easier to avoid such difficulties in future if it joined the CIS Customs Union, an invitation which on political as well as economic grounds, Ukraine has steadfastly declined since this 'Union of Five' was established in March 1996. During his summit with President Kuchma in April 2000, President Putin made a broader and more direct linkage between energy and Ukraine's geopolitical course. It was only after this summit that deliveries resumed and only after a second summit in August that a mechanism was put in place to resolve the issue of debt. Russia's management of this dispute illustrates three features of the Ukraine-Russia relationship:

> 1. 'Promoting Russia's economic interests' in neighbouring states, including 'joint rational use of natural resources' – priorities established by Russia's June 2000 Foreign Policy Concept – are tasks which Putin has pursued with rigour and determination. In the process he has demonstrated that state interests and private enterprise can be linked when circumstances require it. The Russian state faced no insurmountable difficulty halting deliveries by *LUKoil* (a joint stock company) in a dispute involving *Gazprom* (a separate joint stock company) and *Itera* (an ostensibly private concern) – and maintaining suspension of deliveries until a wider set of economic and political conditions were met. In February 2001 in Dnepropetrovsk, President Putin tied the establishment of a debt clearance mechanism to the 'privatisation' of Ukraine's energy and refining infrastructure by Russian commercial concerns.
>
> 2. Economic pressure is being used to advance political aims, not merely economic ones. In June 2000, Ukraine made a further

exception to its opposition to participation in CIS security structures (the 1995 CIS Air Defence Agreement being the first), joined the newly established Anti-Terrorism Centre and took further steps to enhance intelligence collaboration with Russia. In September 2000, within days of the Yalta summit, President Kuchma dismissed Foreign Minister Borys Tarasyuk and several other key officials whom Moscow had long identified as impediments to 'good neighbourliness'. Since the presidential summits, where several key security issues are concerned – e.g. the activities of the Black Sea Fleet and its Naval Infantry – Ukraine has overlooked gross infractions and ceded ground.

3. The opacity of the Russian and Ukrainian energy sectors – so opaque that the 16 agreements concluded between the two presidents in Dnepropetrovsk were kept secret from the Ukrainian government – pose a threat to Ukraine's *samostiynist* as well as its security. There is no conclusive way of establishing who owns what – or who owes what to whom – in a 'market' characterised by arbitrary price levels, hidden payment mechanisms, invisible partners, tax fraud and an extensive barter trade. In such a milieu, the counter-intuitive is far from abnormal: hence the suspicion, privately expressed by Ukrainian officials and partially substantiated, that Gazprom siphoned off some of its own gas in order to prolong the dispute and enhance Russia's bargaining power. If the Ukrainian state controls 'its' energy sector, it does so on the sector's terms.

That there has been a growing 'commercialisation' of Russia's priorities in the 'near abroad' is beyond doubt. But if the reduction of Ukraine's debt were Russia's principal priority, one would expect to find the latter supporting efforts to diversify Ukraine's energy suppliers, develop its indigenous resources and strengthen its solvency. In all three spheres, Russian entities and their Ukrainian allies have sought to obstruct rather than facilitate. The conclusion one is led to is that dependency, rather than solvency, is Russia's principal priority, and that the principal advantage of Ukraine's debt is that it is unpayable.

The fate of Prime Minister Viktor Yushchenko, appointed on 21 December 1999 and dismissed by Ukraine's Parliament on 26 April 2001, reinforces this conclusion. Yushchenko's government was the first in Ukraine determined to introduce the structural changes required to realise the 'European choice' in practice. Had Yushchenko failed simply because he failed – because his reforms had negligible or deleterious results – then his fall would serve as a commentary on the intractability of Ukraine's economic problems. But because his reforms had measurable and positive results – because they eliminated pension and wage arrears *and* secured, for the first time since 1991, economic growth, and because Yushchenko secured unprecedented levels of popularity and trust compared to other office holders in Ukraine, then a different commentary is needed.

At one level, Yushchenko's dismissal is a commentary on the degree to which the interests of Ukraine's oligarchs differs from the interests of the country as a whole. But it is also a commentary on the importance of the Russian factor. On 19 January 2001, Prime Minister Yushchenko's close ally, Deputy Prime Minister Yuliya Tymoshenko, was dismissed and on 26 January replaced by a figure perceived as friendly to Russian energy interests, Oleh Dubyna. Despite her previous incarnation as a leading energy oligarch, Tymoshenko had amply demonstrated that she had since become unfriendly to these interests, as well as to those inside Ukraine who believe that the energy market should remain a closed shop, immune to taxation. Allegations of gas smuggling on her part whilst head of United Energy Systems of Ukraine (UES) in 1996-7 were far from new and therefore do not explain the timing of Kuchma's decision. More interesting is the timing of allegations by Russian military prosecutors that she had sold an 85 per cent stake of UES to the Russian Ministry of Defence during the same period and then subsequently misappropriated the funds. Did it really take the Russian prosecutors four years to realise what had occurred during a time when she and her ally, former Prime Minister Pavlo Lazarenko, enjoyed close ties with Russian power structures? On 13 February, Tymoshenko was arrested. On 14 February, Gennadiy Seleznev, Speaker of the Russian State Duma, praised President Kuchma for this latest 'example of how to deal with corrupted persons'.

Seleznev's assessment is particularly noteworthy given Russia's response to the scandal which erupted in November 2000, when a former officer of the SBU published tapes allegedly implicating President Kuchma in the murder of a journalist as well as other serious abuses of power. Far from joining the chorus of protest and recriminations (including moves to expel Ukraine from the Council of Europe), Russia in a striking reversal of roles portrayed Western entreaties and pressures as blatant attempts to interfere in Ukraine's internal affairs and alter its economic and foreign policy course. The scandal – which has not only weakened Kuchma, but the legitimacy of Ukraine's political order – presented Russia with yet a further opportunity to increase its influence. This is because the scandal has driven what appears to be an immovable wedge between the President and those most capable of advancing Ukraine's 'strategic course of entering Europe.' By the same token, it has made him dependent on those whose commitment to this goal is merely declaratory as well as on those who oppose it altogether.

Russia's exploitation of these difficulties was so artful and methodical that even the influential Russian newspaper *Izvestiya* (13 February 2001) dropped hints that Putin, his special services and their allies in Ukraine might have played a role in recording the tapes and distributing them. Whatever the truth of the matter, the scandal demonstrably accelerated the shift begun in August 2000 in the main method of Russian policy: from pressure to support. Within three months of the 'new principles' that Yushchenko noted in September, the dynamic of relations substantially changed. The 24 December Minsk accords deferred Ukraine's gas debt to Russia for ten years and under remarkably lenient terms, but at a price: conclusion of agreements (November 2000 and February 2001) transferring to Russian entities *de facto* ownership of most of Ukraine's energy transport infrastructure. The conclusion on 14 May of a five-year gas supply agreement with Turkmenistan – presented by Ukraine's state television as a means of diversifying gas supply and by Kuchma as a 'historic event' – is a further sign of such support, as Turkmen gas must transit the same Russian owned distribution network which blocked the conclusion of similar deals in the past.

The appointment of Russia's former Prime Minister, Viktor Chernomyrdin, on 10 May 2001 as Ambassador and Special Envoy for the Development of Russian-Ukrainian Trade and Economic Ties, is clearly designed to consolidate these gains. Chernomyrdin is widely expected to be as much an 'arbitrating judge' as an ambassador, bridging what in post-Soviet conditions is often unbridgeable: the gap between agreements and their implementation. He is likely to be a powerful ally in residence for those who want to see Ukraine anchored in Russia's business networks — and who, by the same token, feel threatened by European standards of openness, competitiveness and transparency. As noted by Anatoliy Grytsenko, President of the Ukrainian Centre for Economic and Political Studies:

> 'He is a man who knows exactly the economic value of everything that exists in Ukrainian-Russian relations. He knows not only the official reports of the State Committee for Statistics and the CIS Interstate Economic Committee, but also the shady schemes out of which both the Ukrainian and the Russian businessmen who now influence politics made their first capital. He knows exactly who owes how much to whom, which means that in this regard it will be both easy and difficult for the Ukrainian side to work with him.'

A compatible but less problematic assessment of Chernomyrdin's role and potential was provided by Dmitriy Rogozin, Chairman of the Committee on International Affairs of the Russian State Duma, on 15 May 2001:

> 'Of course, Chernomyrdin should not just conduct himself as an ambassador in Ukraine. He should be taking a more active part in the solution of, well, I am not afraid to say this, some Ukrainian problems, too…I think that Viktor Stepanovich will have to act as a kind of arbitrating judge in the solution of numerous conflicts, even those of an internal political nature. Here he will have to display such high statesmanship and wisdom as will make it possible for him not to involve Russia directly in the internal affairs of Ukraine.'

Intervening but in ways which do not 'involve Russia directly' is a well established art, but it has not been always delicately performed by Russian emissaries or graciously received by their hosts.

Ukraine: retreat and manoeuvre

The principal foreign policy challenge for Ukraine is to give substance to its declarations. The realisation of Ukraine's 'European choice' not only demands support from the West, it demands that Ukrainians who believe in this choice have a fair degree of control over the country's affairs. Post-Soviet realities have not afforded them this luxury. In Ukraine as in other newly independent states, the problem is not simply that civil society is weak, but that other people and interests are strong. Many of these interests - the fuel and energy complex, the financial and banking sector, the security and intelligence network – are transnational structures *de facto*, moreover not transnational *European* structures, but structures of the former Soviet Union, whose attitudes to transparency, competition, entrepreneurship and contract enforcement are very different from the EU norm. In view of these realities, it is an illusion to believe that a pro-Western foreign policy can provide a substitute for the arduous task of Westernising Ukraine.

In the eyes of its Westernising proponents, President Kuchma's 'multi-vector' policy has been a means of buying time for pursuing this arduous task. Yet Ukraine is neither skilful nor powerful enough to create its own geopolitical environment. The Kosovo conflict appeared to confront Ukraine with the worst of both worlds: a breakdown of Nato-Russia co-operation (hence, heightened Russian opposition to the Nato-Ukraine relationship), coupled with a simultaneous diminution of Nato's attentiveness to the country's interests and concerns. At the same time, it was becoming apparent that the European Union was determined to pursue a model of enlargement, exemplified by the Schengen accords, which threatened to shut Ukraine out of the 'greater Europe'. Therefore, Western policy as much as Russian policy persuaded President Kuchma that he had no alternative but to make a number of strategic concessions to Russia. Justifying his opposition to 'Ukrainian patriots' like Tarasyuk on 28 August 2000, Kuchma asserted that 'Ukraine would gain nothing from a confrontation with Russia', but then added 'besides, the West is closed to us now'.

Nevertheless, two years after the conclusion of the Kosovo conflict and nearly one year after the 'Gongadze affair', it is clear that the multi-vector policy is very much alive. For this there are three clear reasons. First, according to the most cynical reading of his character, President Kuchma will sacrifice Ukraine's interests to the preservation of his own political power. But he is not pro-Russian, and there is abundant indication that he is not only wary of Putin, but afraid of him. He is therefore determined to make only those concessions which he *must* make. Beyond this, he will seek counterpoises and compensations, lines of retreat and room for manoeuvre – and in this respect, he is a classically Ukrainian president. Second, as an astute Ukrainian and an astute politician, he knows that a Belorusian course would tear the country apart, enable Ukraine's 'patriots' – Yushchenko, Tymoshenko and Tarasyuk – to detach his centrist supporters and leave him totally at the mercy of President Putin. Third, he knows that in practical ways – military-technical assistance and defence reform – the Nato-Ukraine relationship has benefited the country; moreover, it remains Ukraine's one solid anchor in the West. Despite Russian pressure, in this sphere he has held firm.

Challenges for the EU

The certainty that, sooner or later, the Western frontier of Ukraine will become the Eastern frontier of the EU has focused minds in Brussels as well as in Kiev. If the apprehension in Kiev is that the Schengen frontier could become a new 'iron curtain', the apprehension in Brussels must be that if Ukraine were to fail – if it became a zone of turbulence, lawlessness and unrest – Schengen could become the economic equivalent of a Maginot line, providing limited security or only an artificial sense of it. How does the relationship between Ukraine and Russia relate to this concern?

The European Union – and for that matter Nato – have wisely refused to support Ukraine on an anti-Russian basis. Yet until the Gothenburg Council many EU members erred in the opposite direction, insisting on maintaining a link between Ukraine and Russia, despite the fact that Ukraine has consistently declared a vocation for EU membership and Russia has not. This linkage has had two damaging consequences. First, it has persuaded those Ukrainians most capable of realising the 'European choice' that whatever steps are taken, Ukraine's prospects will be linked to that of another country. Second, it suggests that the European Union regards the former Soviet Union as Russia's rightful 'zone of influence' and that it regards newly independent states as states of a lesser order. There could be no better way of strengthening those who would define Russia's interests in neo-imperial terms or, on the other hand, weakening Russians who rightly perceive that their country has no imperial future.

The dangers inherent in such perceptions are not only profound for Russia, but for Europe. A large proportion of Ukraine's elite (and its alienated society) is European in orientation and pro-Western by conviction. The mainstream perception in Russia – that as an 'East Slavic people' Ukraine and Russia 'belong together' – is adamantly rejected by a large proportion of the country. Amongst the population as a whole, 30 per cent believe that Ukraine should never join the Tashkent Collective Security Treaty. In Western regions, this perception is vastly higher. If there is a Belorusian course for Ukraine, it is unlikely to be a peaceful one. Western policies which strengthen Russian misunderstanding of these realities can only lead to trouble.

The second concern for the 'greater Europe' must be the synergy which exists between Russian influence, collusive and opaque norms of business, the 'domination of authoritarian tendencies' in Ukraine and the criminalisation of the state. In Ukraine as in Russia, the reality of economic and, by extension, social life is laws which are so stultifying and contradictory as to make corruption unavoidable, the absence of mechanisms (local and judicial) to enforce contracts, a taxation regime designed to penalise business rather than encourage it, and a business class predatory rather than entrepreneurial and more skilful at extracting wealth than creating it. Efforts along the lines of Yushchenko's government to address these deficiencies run into greatest resistance from the structures which dominate trade within – and sustain the interdependence of – 'former Soviet space'. Transparency – the ability to know *what* decisions are taken, *where* decisions are taken and *by whom* they are taken – is anathema to these structures. It would be heroic to assume that the further maturation of these pathological conditions will simply affect Ukraine and other newly independent states, rather than prove (to quote Anatoliy Grytsenko) 'a source of additional threats to European countries in terms of drugs, weapons, illegal immigrants, prostitutes and ecological disasters [and, he might have added, money laundering].'

Third, the foregoing concerns are made especially acute by the character of Ukraine's Eastern border, which is the point of entry for two thirds of contraband and 90 per cent of the country's illegal migrants. By definition, this border must be properly controlled if Ukraine is to harmonise its border and customs regimes with Schengen criteria. Yet Ukraine's fixed and consistent official position – that all of its borders must have the same legal status – is flatly unacceptable to Russia, which has consistently maintained that the 'internal' borders of the CIS should have a different status from its 'external' borders. Although over 90 per cent of the Ukrainian-Russian border is delimited (drawn on maps), Russia has steadfastly refused to demarcate the border on grounds which its Ministry of Foreign Affairs reiterated on 16 August 2001 – *viz.*, that 'the Russian-Ukrainian border should be a border of peace, accord and interaction; it should unite not separate the people of our countries.' Although Ukraine's MFA holds the view that 'demarcation does not require the construction of walls or any obstacles', the dialogue on demarcation has become a *dialogue des sourdes*.

The location and condition of Ukraine is one of several reasons why the European Union now perceives a security gap which Nato earnestly believes that it cannot fill alone. Overdue as the development is, the Gothenburg Council boldly parted ways with habit and prejudice and gave a clear signal that, henceforth, the European Union would approach Ukraine's problems and its potential on its own merits. The establishment of an EU pilot scheme to modernise Ukraine's border regime is consistent with this change in rhetoric. Whether that change acquires sufficient momentum to alter Kiev's conclusion that 'the West is closed' to Ukraine remains to be seen.

UKRAINE
POLAND'S FAILING PROJECT

Roman Wolczuk

In 1991 an independent Ukraine joined the international system of states. Perhaps nowhere was this event observed and analysed more closely, and with a greater degree of apprehension and excitement, than in Warsaw. For a Poland embarking on its 'return to Europe' via membership of key regional institutions such as Nato or the EU, an independent Ukraine could be one of two things. A pro-Western and pro-Polish Ukraine could act as a 1000-mile wide 'firebreak' between Poland and Russia. Conversely, if Poland attained Nato membership, a pro-Russian Ukraine would once again make Poland a front-line state should there be a renewal of Cold War hostilities. It is therefore perhaps all the more surprising that in the early years following Ukrainian independence, Poland chose to allocate Ukraine a distinctly secondary status to its relations with Russia. It was only once Poland's place in Western institutions, namely membership of Nato (and eventually the EU) was effectively assured, as it was from 1994, that Poland prioritised relations with Ukraine over those with Russia. The aim of this chapter is to chart the contours of Poland's relations with Ukraine in the context of its developing relationship with Western institutions. Kiev was of course not a passive actor in this process and had firm expectations as to the role Poland could play in Ukraine's own 'return to Europe.'

Ukraine's unfulfilled high hopes

Through its emergence as a new non-aligned state in the centre of Europe, independent Ukraine redefined the geopolitics of the region and negated long established regional norms. Such change is destabilising at the best of times, but was especially dangerous in Central and Eastern Europe where Ukraine was bordered by states with historical grudges against it and which had previously used their power against it. In order to counter threats that could conceivably lead to the country's fragmentation, Kiev developed a multi-pronged foreign and security policy. Firstly, it pursued harmonious bilateral ties with all its regional neighbours, the most important of which was Poland. Secondly, it saw relations with Warsaw as a means of facilitating membership of subregional and regional institutions in the West. The desire to integrate with subregional institutions reflected Ukraine's recognition that key regional goals were effectively unattainable in the short term. Relations with Poland were a first step on this journey.

Following independence, Poland was certainly allocated a primary role in Ukraine's strategic planning. Leonid Kravchuk, Ukraine's first president, suggested that co-operation with Poland was to be closer than with any country of the CIS, including Russia, a revealing statement in the light of the strength of economic, political and security ties between Ukraine and Russia. The ostensibly pro-Russian Prime Minister, Leonid Kuchma, endorsed this view in 1993 when he named Poland Ukraine's 'number one state'.

The signing of the Treaty on Good Neighbourly and Friendly Relations and Co-operation in 1992 and the Treaty on the Legal Regime on the Ukrainian-Polish National Boundaries, Co-operation and Mutual Support on Border Issues in 1993 evidenced an apparently more than satisfactory rate of progress and augured well for the future on important issues for both parties. This was especially so in the light of a history of relations throughout the first half of the 20th century which was disfigured by an ugly mutual detestation expressed in reciprocated atrocities. The Treaty on Good Neighbourly and Friendly Relations addressed these issues directly. In renouncing mutual territorial claims, recognising the inviolability of borders, and guaranteeing the rights of each other's national minorities, both sides made a significant move in the direction of resolving mutual and deeply held grievances.

And yet, aside from declarations and adherence to protocol, relations were not developing as expected. By 1993 the glaring gap between word and deed was such that the normally diplomatic Ukrainian ambassador to Poland, Hennadiy Udovenko, was compelled to admit that economic relations between the two states had not developed to the extent desired by the Ukrainians or to the extent necessary if Ukraine's economic dependence on Russia was to be reduced. Ukraine's expectations were not being met by Poland.

The main reason relations between the two states at least up until 1994 had not gone beyond the minimum was the fundamental incongruence between policy objectives. Ukraine wanted closer ties in order to 'return to Europe'. In contrast Poland was wary of closer ties because firstly, they might exacerbate relations with Russia, and secondly, they might prejudice Poland's own 'return to Europe,' i.e. its chances of membership of Western institutions. By examining the Polish perspective in greater detail, the reasons behind this incongruence become clearer.

An impediment to progress: Poland's caution in the East and hopes in the West

By prioritising relations with Russia over those with Ukraine in 1991-1994, Poland exposed the lack of a coherent long-term policy on relations with Ukraine. Working within a framework that presupposed that Russia was the dominant feature in Western strategic planning and therefore that Poland's chances of joining Nato were minimal, during that period Polish strategists pursued four objectives, which entailed close ties with Russia often to the detriment of Ukraine's position. Firstly, while keen to remove foreign troops from Polish soil, Warsaw was also cognisant of the need to guarantee supplies and maintain access to spare parts for the Soviet-era technology used by Polish forces. Secondly, it was deemed important to support Russia in its purchases of Polish military hardware. Thirdly, the need to ensure a constant supply of Russian raw materials, on which Poland was reliant, was regarded as paramount. Fourthly, Poland wished to benefit from the transportation of gas from the huge Russian fields which met approximately 25 per cent of Western Europe's energy needs. All of these objectives required close co-operation with Russia often directly contrary to Ukraine's interests (as in the case of energy transportation for example), the net result of which was that Ukraine was effectively marginalised in Poland's foreign policy in the East.

However, Poland was not just concerned about the damage that too close ties with Ukraine would do to its relations with Moscow. It was also concerned that ties with Ukraine might damage its own prospects for subregional and regional integration. For these reasons Poland was not keen to support Ukraine's efforts to join the Central European Initiative and the Visegrad group prior to 1994.

1994 – a watershed year in Poland-Ukraine relations

A number of factors combined in 1994 to improve prospects for Polish-Ukrainian relations. Above all a series of events in and around Russia set off reverberations around the continent. Firstly, the Yeltsin-sponsored attack by the military on the parliament in Moscow demonstrated that democracy had not taken root as deeply as had been believed. Secondly, the re-warming of ties between Russia and Belarus suggested that Sovietesque ambitions lingered in Minsk as least. Finally, the ongoing conflict in Chechnya revealed that military power continued to figure prominently as a means of resolving problems in Russia. For these reasons, both Poland and Ukraine started to rise up the political agenda not only in Western capitals but also each other's.

The first evidence of Poland's promotion was Bill Clinton's proclamation in Warsaw in July 1994 that Nato expansion was 'no longer a question of whether, but when and how'. This was bolstered at a meeting of Nato defence ministers in September, when the German Minister of Defence argued that 'We must at last say who is welcome to join Nato and who is not. I believe that the countries of the Visegrad Group should be the leading candidates for membership of the European Union and Nato.' The impact on Poland was immediate, as evidenced by Kwasniewski's statement that 'Decisions will be made about the widening of Nato, therefore Poland needs to demonstrate a lot of activity not only in the European Union and Nato but also regionally' i.e. towards Ukraine. In sum, following the scares in Russia and Poland's brightening prospects of membership of Western institutions, Warsaw started to develop a more coherent policy towards Ukraine. More specifically, in pursuit of a secure and stable Eastern border, Poland took on the responsibility of 'europeanising' Ukraine.

Polish attempts to 'europeanise' Ukraine

In the first instance, the 'europeanising' of Ukraine involved furthering Kiev's interests within Western institutions. The most tangible evidence of this new positive strategy was the vigour with which Poland supported Ukraine's entry into subregional institutions such as the Central European Initiative, which Ukraine finally joined in 1996. Poland has similarly tried to defend Ukraine's interests within the European Union acting as its 'ambassador in Brussels'. Indeed, so vigorous was Poland in this regard that it was warned that such a strategy might be detrimental to its own interests.

The second means by which Warsaw hoped to bring Ukraine closer to Europe was by closely co-ordinating its position with Kiev in dealings with regional institutions. When in 1997 Ukraine dropped its objections to Poland's entry into Nato, it was in direct response to Warsaw's active campaign for a Charter on a Distinctive Partnership between Ukraine and Nato. The two parties achieved their respective goals in the summer of 1997.

The third strand to Warsaw's strategy of 'europeanising' Ukraine was the establishment of closer state-level working relations with Kiev. The signing of a series of important documents in 1997 such as the Memorandum on the Liberalisation of Trade were more than symbolic gestures. The Memorandum was a breakthrough, an important first step toward creating a free trade area with Poland. The signature of the Declaration on Agreement and Unity the same year was another milestone and was designed to draw a line under the unfortunate past the two states shared.

Above all, Poland tried to export its experience of systemic transformation to Ukraine by establishing a series of institutional platforms for co-operation including the Consultative Committee of the Presidents of Poland and Ukraine and a series of specialised bodies dealing with economic co-operation and trade, local government, inter-regional co-operation, parliamentary relations, and European integration. Although most of these bodies met with limited success, the most important, the Presidential Consultative Committee, has gone from strength to strength after an inauspicious start. It has met extremely regularly and provided an opportunity for the two leaders to become well acquainted. In addition, using Poland as a mouthpiece, the West has been able to use it as a forum to transmit messages to which Kiev may not otherwise have been receptive. On the other hand, the Inter-Governmental Co-ordinating Council has been overwhelmed by the task of co-ordinating the activities of 9 Polish and 17 Ukrainian groups concerned with border issues. Especially high hopes were held out for the Polish-Ukrainian Standing Conference on European Integration, within which Warsaw sought to familiarise Kiev with European values. From Warsaw's point of view, the conference failed to achieve its most important, albeit implicit goal, namely persuading Kiev that what happens *within* Ukraine is more important to the West than its geopolitical role.

Poland has also been very active in terms of involving Ukraine in 'European' processes, for example by trying to incorporate Ukraine in CFSP activities. At Warsaw's insistence, Poland's joint battalion with Ukraine (POLUKRBAT), established on the basis of Nato standards and interoperability with the alliance, may eventually form an important component of the European capability for out of area operations (within the scope of Petersburg missions - tasks adopted by the WEU in 1992 comprising humanitarian and rescue tasks, crisis management, peacekeeping and peacemaking). Indeed the battalion has already served in KFOR in Kosovo. In May 2001, Bronislaw Komorowski, the Polish Defense Minister, suggested to the EU that the Polish brigade which will serve in the EU's rapid deployment force (to be operational in 2003) might include a Ukrainian military battalion.

A stalling partnership

Despite the above successes Ukraine has proved to be a difficult partner. While, following independence, Ukraine could reasonably be said to be democratising, a path along which its was proceeding more or less successfully, a number of events since 1999 have demonstrated that Poland's self-proclaimed goal of 'europeanising' Ukraine has not been attained. Firstly, the corrupt presidential election campaign run by the incumbent, Leonid Kuchma, alienated the West and demonstrated that democracy had not taken root there. Secondly, the Gongadze affair exposed the unreformed nature of the state machinery, which suppresses freedom of the press and political opponents. Thirdly, the Ukrainian Parliament's dismissal of the reformist government of Prime Minister Yushchenko in April 2001, despite the fact that his government had turned round Ukraine's economic performance within one year, was interpreted in Western capitals as a distinctly retrograde step motivated by an unholy alliance of communists and oligarchs in parliament.

Thus, as of autumn 2001, Poland's strategic partnership with Ukraine can be deemed to be stalling if not failing. 10 years after independence it is clear that Ukraine is increasingly either unable or unwilling to abide by the democratic and economic regime that the EU demands as a precondition for closer ties despite its avowed intention, announced in 1996, to join the European Union. Poland just has not got the capacity to 'europeanise' Ukraine single-handedly and it is clear that Poland's self-imposed role is more challenging that anticipated in the early 1990s.

Poland's task has been made considerably harder by the EU itself, which has not shared Warsaw's belief that Russia will step into any vacuum in Ukraine that the West fails to fill. Poland has in effect been trying to 'europeanise' Ukraine without Europe itself being very interested. Arguably, the EU has in fact placed impediments in the way of Poland's relations with Ukraine such as Brussels' inflexible insistence on the imposition of a visa regime between the neighbours. There is evidence that following Yushchenko's dismissal, the EU is changing its stance towards Ukraine, something which may alleviate Poland's predicament. In May 2001 and in direct response to Yushchenko's dismissal, Romano Prodi and Goran Persson wrote that the EU would enable EU Member States to develop trilateral co-operation with individual candidate countries in joint projects involving Ukraine. Exactly what Prodi and Persson were hinting at is still unclear, though Poland will obviously be among the most important of the above-mentioned candidate countries. The move suggests that as Polish membership of the EU looms, and Ukraine becomes a direct neighbour of the EU, Brussels is finally beginning to take a more active stance on Ukraine. Warsaw-Kiev relations will come to be replaced by Warsaw-

Kiev-Brussels relations – bilateral relations will become more multilateral. Increasingly Poland is pinning its hopes on being able, once in the EU, to shape the EU's Eastern policy around Poland's interests in the East. Following membership, Poland should be better able to influence decisions. Poland is also likely to enjoy the support of other, smaller CEE states which also have an interest in closer ties with Ukraine.

Yet there is no suggestion that the EU is going to do anything about the single biggest problem facing Ukraine-Poland relations following enlargement, the erection of a Schengen border between the two neighbours. (It would be politically unacceptable for Poland to have a Schengen border with Germany in order to maintain ties with Ukraine). Poland is just not in a position to demand exclusions from the non-negotiable Schengen regulation of the border with Ukraine, especially in the light of Ukraine's porous borders with CIS states. Yet an open border is critical for both Poland and Ukraine. For example, there were 10 million border crossings in 2001, with Ukrainian 'tourists' spending on average $400 dollars in the impoverished Eastern Polish regions. It has been estimated that a collapse in this shuttle-trade could lead to a loss of 60 per cent of jobs in border towns. Proposals to soften the impact of the border regime include improving staffing levels in consulates, the introduction of long-term multi-entry visas valid only in issuing states, and cheap, short-term, single entry visas, though as ever these proposals must meet with the approval of Brussels. Inevitably the imposition of custom duties, trade tariffs and commercial regulations will also have a deleterious impact on economic relations between Ukraine and Poland.

Any amelioration of the situation hinges on Ukraine having a tighter border with Russia. (It has been estimated that 60-70 per cent of the 500,000 illegal immigrants arriving in Western Europe in 2000 came through the CIS via the porous borders with Ukraine). To this end Poland and Ukraine signed an agreement in 2001 designed to encourage co-operation between their respective border guards. This is intended to allow Ukraine to reduce the number of guards on its Western border and bolster the numbers on the border with Russia.

It has however to be acknowledged that there are advantages accruing from the imposition of the Schengen regime. The current Polish-Ukrainian border is benefiting from massive investment in border control and management, which will benefit the population at large given the current chaotic state of affairs on the border.

Conclusion

From the mid-1990s, Poland embarked almost single-handedly on a process of dragging Ukraine westward, despite the problems put in its way by Brussels, Moscow and indeed Kiev itself. However, the task is beyond Poland, as has been acknowledged in the domestic debate in Poland on its strategy vis-à-vis Ukraine. This is despite the long-standing fear that any deterioration in relations will inevitably result in Ukraine drifting back towards Russia. Indeed, in 2000 it was evident that this drift was already taking place despite the best efforts of Poland.

So far Brussels has not been supportive of Warsaw in its endeavours. The demands of Poland's EU membership are such that a symbolic barrier between Poland and Ukraine will be erected which will demarcate areas of increasingly different political and economic systems. Ukraine is likely to pose a considerable challenge for both Poland and the EU.

Much depends on the Ukrainians themselves, perhaps more than they have hitherto realised. By overestimating its own geopolitical importance and underestimating the need for economic reform and certain minimum political standards, Kiev has itself contributed to the West's exasperation and highlighted Warsaw's apparent ineffectiveness in its 'europeanising' role and impotence in bringing about meaningful change within Ukraine.

5

The EU and Ukraine

UKRAINE AND THE EU
WHAT PROSPECTS FOR INTEGRATION

Inna Pidluska

In April 2000, the German Foreign Minister, Joschka Fischer, announced that Europe should be moving towards full integration and finally forming a single federal state with common legislation, common executive bodies, and a common foreign and security policy. His plans for building a common European home captured the minds of politicians and put onto the agenda the question 'What is Europe?' As the word Europe has often been used to refer to 27 states (current members of the EU plus countries in the process of accession negotiations), in Ukrainian political circles there has been increasingly frequent criticism of the EU for 'privatising the notion of Europe'.

In Ukraine's case, the question is not limited to 'geographical' and 'culturological' discussions on whether or not Ukraine is a part of Europe. Rather, the question is whether Ukraine has a realistic chance of claiming membership of the EU in the foreseeable future, what real steps are being made towards it, and what alternative there may be, if any, to the membership *vs.* exclusion dichotomy.

Until recently, the EU's decision to continue dialogue with Ukraine along the lines of the Partnership and Co-operation Agreement (PCA), rather than start talking about an association agreement, was reflected in the much-quoted comment by EU Commissioner Guenther Verheugen that any discussions about Ukraine's potential candidacy for membership were 'irresponsible', adding: 'I think that anybody who thinks that Ukraine should be taken into the EU should perhaps come along with the argument that

Mexico should be taken into the USA.' It is not just that Ukraine's per capita GDP is only a quarter of Slovakia's and less than a fifth of Hungary's – some candidate states, like Romania and Bulgaria, are doing rather modestly in terms of their economic progress. The problem with Ukraine is that it has been too slow in transforming its institutions, economy and society to be a credible applicant. The other side of the coin is that the EU, having made a political decision to include CEE countries in the EU enlargement process and facilitate the development of institutions that would allow those countries to be fully compatible with EU institutions and practices, has refrained from making a similar decision concerning Ukraine.

A balance sheet

Ukraine was the first CIS country to sign a Partnership and Co-operation Agreement (PCA) with the EU, in 1994, and to join the Council of Europe. European integration (and Euro-Atlantic integration too, though this was later quietly dropped from Ukraine's official language) was declared to be the government's strategic goal. However, the PCA was ratified by the EU states only in 1998, when other CEE countries had already moved far ahead with their associate membership. While implementation of the PCA had a long way to go, on June 11 1998 the Ukrainian President approved the Strategy of Integration of Ukraine to the European Union, stating that 'national interests of Ukraine require the identification of Ukraine as an influential European country, full-fledged EU member'. Particular emphasis was laid on the fact that as a result of the EU's eastward enlargement, Ukraine would have a common border with the EU, which 'would create a principally new geopolitical situation' that required a 'clear and comprehensive definition of the foreign policy strategy concerning Ukraine's integration to the European political, economic and legal space'. The Strategy defined the principal requirements of the integration process as approximation of Ukrainian legislation to EU legislation, political consolidation and democracy, economic integration and the development of trade, and co-operation in the field of justice and home affairs, and set out the main priorities for state executive bodies for the period up to 2007, when Ukraine was expected to meet the conditions for full EU membership. The main medium-term foreign policy priority was defined as acquiring the status of an associated member of the EU.

Approximation of legislation was seen as a way to 'ensure development of the political, business, social and cultural activities of Ukraine's nationals, economic growth of the country within the EU framework as well as facilitating gradual improvement of their well-being, making it closer to the level existing in the EU Member States'. The development of economic integration was expected to involve liberalisation and synchronisation in the opening up of markets in the EU and Ukraine, the achievement of a trade balance, creation of a favourable investment climate in Ukraine, facilitation of access of Ukrainian goods to the EU market, and measures to enhance competition and counter state protectionism. The Strategy envisaged sectoral co-operation primarily in the fields of trans-European transportation routes, energy generation, and information networks, and stressed co-operation in justice and home affairs (JHA), particularly the prevention of and fight against organised crime and drug trafficking, customs co-operation, science and research. The security dimension of integration was covered: 'Recognition by the European Union of considerable importance of Ukraine in creation of a new European security architecture may and shall be utilised as an important tool of realisation of Ukrainian interests in relations with the EU.' It envisaged 'comprehensive integration of Ukraine into the European political, legal, economic, information and cultural environment' and 'identification of the EU policy towards Ukraine, its separation from the EU policy towards Russia, and support of the European countries and the world community of the strategy of integration of Ukraine with the EU.' However, so far the EU has not shown much enthusiasm for Ukraine's integration initiative, explicitly indicating that Ukraine should meet its obligations under the PCA first. Direct contacts between Ukrainian ministries and other executive bodies and relevant Directorates of the European Commission remain scarce, and meetings of the Ukraine-EU Co-operation Council mostly produce only declarations of intent to continue discussion.

This lukewarm response did not discourage the Ukrainian leadership. In his inaugural speech on 30 November 1999 Ukraine's newly re-elected president Leonid Kuchma announced: 'Reaffirming our European choice, we define joining the European Union as our strategic goal.' The Strategy of integration into the EU was developed into an ambitious Programme of Integration of Ukraine to the European Union, introduced by presidential decree on 14 September 2000. A number of decrees and resolutions were adopted to facilitate approximation of Ukrainian legislation to that of the EU, and a substantial volume of reports emerged describing the technical assistance and advice given to the Ukrainian government. However, prospects for making practical steps have been largely affected by the lack of adequate institutions capable of producing the desired change.

Nowadays, key themes related to integration, in addition to prospects for EU-Ukraine co-operation in the field of JHA, include: further implementation of the PCA, financing of safety measures at the Chernobyl nuclear power plant, closed down as part of Ukraine's commitments to the EU in December 2000, the construction of compensating nuclear reactors at Rivne and Khmelnytsky nuclear power plants, EU technical assistance to Ukraine in aligning its legislation to EU standards, prospects for Ukrainian membership of the WTO and recognition of Ukraine's status as a market economy.

At the end of 1999 official Kiev, represented by then Foreign Minister Borys Tarasyuk, claimed that up to 70 per cent of Ukrainians supported its pro-European course and emphasised the need for a 'political signal' to give new strength to Ukraine's striving for European integration. The Ukrainian leadership wanted to see words confirming the country's right to join the EU in the future in the text of the EU's Common Strategy on Ukraine, approved at the Helsinki summit in December 1999. EU officials diplomatically responded that there was no need to include the phrase in the official document as any European state had the right to appeal for EU membership, at the same time hinting that Ukraine should first complete the transition to democracy and a free market. Of about 10 thousand pieces of Ukrainian legislation, only about 400 actually meet European standards. By the end of 1999, Ukraine had failed to meet 22 provisions of the PCA and was too far from meeting the requirements for joining the WTO to proceed to the creation of a free trade area with the EU. While the EU is Ukraine's main trading partner except the CIS states, and its share in Ukraine's total trade is 22.5 per cent (15.4 per cent of imports, 14.8 per cent of exports), Ukraine's share in EU trade is negligible. In 1995 Ukraine accounted for 0.4 per cent of EU exports and 0.3 per cent of imports. By 1999 the former had declined to 0.3 per cent, with the share of imports remaining unchanged at 0.3 per cent. Yet discussions between the Ukrainian leadership and EU officials within the Ukraine-EU committee in charge of monitoring implementation of the PCA have apparently been limited to declarations that the EU supports Ukraine's striving for European integration and welcomes closer ties with Ukraine.

At the end of 1999, the appointment of the pro-reform Yushchenko government, which was prepared to take international advice on improving the quality of the policy process in Ukraine, making it more transparent and the government more accountable, showed new promise for supporters of Ukraine's pro-European aspirations, particularly after the launch of structural reforms and improvements in the tax collection and energy sectors resulted in substantial economic growth. At the end of May 2000 then Prime Minister Victor Yushchenko announced that his government 'has in fact removed 50 per cent of [the reasons for] criticism made by the EU and blocking co-operation.' He referred to the favourable comments made by Jaime Gama, Foreign Minister of Portugal, then holder of the EU Presidency – 'The EU is satisfied with recent changes in reform of the Ukrainian economy' – and by the EC Commissioner for Foreign Affairs, Chris Patten, who was quoted as saying 'The Ukrainian colleagues are making substantial efforts to resolve all questions that have complicated our co-operation.' The common statement issued by participants in the third meeting of the Ukraine-EU Co-operation Council also referred to 'a quality rise' in bilateral relations.

Commenting on the results of Victor Yushchenko's official visit to Brussels in May 2000, the then head of the government's group of advisors, Valery Lytvytsky, announced that the EU had demanded clear identification of specific forms and ways of assisting the Ukrainian government in implementing reforms. He referred to Romano Prodi's reported promise that the discussion about granting Ukraine associated and, in due course, full membership in the EU, might be realistic after Ukraine fulfilled the PCA. Although Ukraine remained rather slow in implementing the PCA, recognition of its aspirations for membership was reconfirmed in the European Commission's resolution of 15 March 2001.

'Agenda – Ukraine': progress report

While emphasising its 'European choice', the Ukrainian leadership repeatedly expressed concerns over the reluctance of the EU to include Ukraine in the enlargement process and called for consultations on ways of minimising the potential negative impact of EU enlargement on Ukraine, formalising and institutionalising Ukraine-EU relations in the field of JHA, foreign and security policy, military and military-technical co-operation and, finally, reforming the system of Ukraine-EC bodies in order to enhance the effectiveness of all existing instruments in relations between Ukraine and the EU. The proposals were formally presented as position papers and memoranda to relevant EU bodies: 'Position paper for negotiations between Ukraine and the EU on minimising the negative impact of EU enlargement' (early 2001), 'Memorandum of Ukraine on concluding an agreement [on co-operation] between Ukraine and the EU in the field of the fight against organised crime' and the Memorandum of Ukraine on 'Strengthening co-operation between Ukraine and the European Union in the sphere of Foreign and Security Policy, Military and Military-Technical Co-operation' (at the Paris Ukraine-EU Summit on 15 September 2000), a position paper on 'Reflection of the Ukrainian side on a Joint Action Plan on Common Action between Ukraine and the EU in the Area of Justice and Home Affairs' (at the third meeting of the Co-operation Committee between Ukraine and the EC on 18 December 2000), and the Memorandum of Ukraine on 'Reforming joint bodies that have been set up by Ukraine and the EU in accordance with the provisions of the Partnership and Co-operation Agreement between European Communities and their Member States, of the one part, and Ukraine, of the other part, of 14 June 1994.'

Some practical results have been achieved. The issue of major concern for the EU, the closure of the Chernobyl nuclear power plant (NPP), has been settled. In 2000, the EU committed 430 million Euros as a contribution to the Chornobyl shelter fund. Ukraine fulfilled its part of the Memorandum of Understanding and now expects the funding committed by the EU for the construction of compensating capacities at the Rivne and Khmelnytsky NPPs. Progress in Ukraine-EU relations includes new bilateral co-operation agreements in the spheres of trade in textiles, opening access to the Ukrainian market for EU pharmaceutical products, liberalising exports of scrap metal and introducing legislation for the protection of intellectual property rights. The security aspect of Ukraine-EU relations has developed dynamically, as Ukraine remains an important stability factor in the Baltic Black Sea region and contributes to the settlement of the Balkan crisis by taking part in peacekeeping operations.

Ukraine has repeatedly stressed the potential benefits for the EU of using Ukraine's gas transportation system and electricity transportation capacities. In April 2001 Foreign Minister Anatoliy Zlenko called on the EU to involve Ukraine more actively as 'an equal participant' in projects that are designed to expand the European energy supply network. The offer has not however had an enthusiastic response so far, given the plans for construction of a major gas transportation pipeline bypassing Ukraine, through Belarus and Poland, by the Russian Gazprom and a group of European corporations.

A number of questions in Ukraine-EU relations remain open. Why did Ukraine from the very start take an option that was not meant to bring it any closer to the EU – the PCA – while all the other countries of Central and Eastern Europe succeeded in making 'Europe agreements' and taking the path of associate membership? Was there any other choice? To what extend were Ukraine's European integration prospects influenced by the different goals and scope of the two assistance programmes, Tacis and Phare? How realistic is it to make a connection between implementation of the PCA and passing on to an association agreement? No clear answers to these questions have been given so far.

Ukraine – EU relations: perceptions

While the policy of European integration has been promoted as a foreign policy priority by the Ukrainian leadership and supported (mostly declaratively) by a part of the political elite, it remains far from being understood and approved by the general population. The high reported percent of support for EU integration as a preferred course for Ukraine, in the absence of any public debate on the issue, may indicate a lack of understanding of the nature and implications of EU enlargement for Ukraine.

At the level of Ukraine's business and administrative-political elites, the idea of Ukraine's European integration does not enjoy broad support because many representatives of that segment of the Ukrainian elite have their key business and financial interests outside the EU. Moreover, many of them are not prepared to comply with a number of EU guiding principles and EU membership criteria such as competition policy. The overall awareness of EU issues, the enlargement process and cost/benefits of integration remains critically low and has a negative impact on policy-making in the field.

According to an opinion poll carried out in July 2000 by the Ukrainian Center for Economic and Political Studies (UCEPS) to survey perceptions, among the general public and experts, of the EU enlargement process and its likely impact on Ukraine, the national decision-making elite was the strongest supporter of the idea of European integration (48 per cent). The advocates of this course were more numerous than advocates of integration with Russia, the CIS or the USA taken together (39 per cent). However, the Ukrainian population seemed to be more supportive of the idea of integration with the CIS and, primarily, Russia (57 per cent support, 31 per cent and 26 per cent respectively), while only 29 per cent saw relations with the EU as the top priority. Another major difference in perceptions between experts and the general population was that while 49 per cent of 'ordinary' respondents believed the EU was interested in Ukraine's accession, and 31 per cent believed it was not, the predominant majority of experts (84 per cent) agreed that the EU was increasingly sceptical about Ukraine's prospects for full membership. According to experts, reasons for the EU's lack of interest in Ukraine's accession included the slow pace of democratisation and economic, legal, institutional and administrative reform in Ukraine, the low quality and, hence, low competitiveness of the bulk of Ukraine-made goods and, finally, the fact that Ukraine's share in EU's foreign trade was very low. According to a survey conducted by the UCEPS shortly before the September 2001 Yalta summit, 32 per cent of Ukrainians believed that European integration was a priority for Ukraine, while 41 per cent chose ever-closer co-operation with Russia.

What are the reasons for this disparity in attitudes between the elite and the general population? First, it reflects the fact that European integration remains a matter of government-sponsored discussion within a limited group of experts but not a matter of everyday life visible to the population. Second, general information about the EU is lacking, and a targeted information campaign about European integration has yet to be developed. According to the 2000 UCEPS study, 74 per cent of representatives of the decision-making elite who took part in the poll described the level of information provided to support the course of European integration as totally inadequate. About one third of the general population had no information about European integration processes at all. Meanwhile, both the elites and the general population operate on myths rather than facts. The elites also appear to be reserved about the prospect of opening EU markets to Ukrainian goods and services, particularly referring to politically-motivated rejections of Ukraine's projects (like the Antonov-7X cargo aircraft) and a number of anti-dumping investigations.

Experts are almost unanimous in seeing key points that weaken Ukraine's quest for EU accession as poor economic performance and slow reform (92 per cent); rampant corruption (90 per cent) and flawed taxation policy, lack of transparency and instability of economic legislation (90 per cent). Far fewer are concerned with lack of democracy (54 per cent) and lack of respect for intellectual property rights (41 per cent). Interestingly, only one third of the experts surveyed by UCEPS (33 per cent) pointed to Ukraine's excessive dependence on Russia for energy sources, and very few believed that Ukraine's prospects for EU integration were hindered by Ukraine's membership of the CIS. The reasons for this view may be the reluctance of Ukraine's business-political elite to see the CIS, and primarily Russia, where most of their business interests lie, as a challenge to Ukraine's EU integration course, which most of them, in their turn, see as something abstract.

Many Ukrainian analysts seem to share the view that Ukraine's weak position in promoting her European integration aspirations results from inconsistent and slow domestic reform; domination of political declarations over practical implementation of Ukraine-EU documents; weakness of administrative and institutional support for Ukraine's European integration ambitions and lack of expertise on European integration processes in the government. Key challenges are seen as a lack of co-ordination and coherence in the actions of state institutions with regard to European integration efforts and lack of institutional capacity, as well as lack of public interest, awareness and support and demand for European integration.

'Two to Tango'

During the Paris Ukraine-EU summit in September 2000 the EU agreed that Ukraine had made some progress in the pursuit of reforms and officially stated that establishment of a free trade area between Ukraine and the EU was a priority not only for Kiev but also for Brussels. Since then Ukraine has made some significant steps in the right direction. While EU officials still argue that the PCA and the EU's Common Strategy on Ukraine offer ample opportunities for co-operation that should be explored to the maximum and are in no hurry to make any promises concerning potential changes of Ukraine's status vis-à-vis the EU, developments since mid-2000 appear to suggest that hope for EU integration can be a stimulating factor for Ukraine's stability, democratisation and reform. In a comment to the International Herald Tribune on 22 May 2001 the President of the European Commission, Romano Prodi, and the Prime Minister of Sweden, Goran Persson, argued that 'Ukraine's progress should be a priority for all Europe', routinely expressed their regret about the fall of the Yushchenko government and called on the Ukrainian leadership to continue the pursuit of reform while warning that 'the EU has been closely monitoring developments in Ukraine.' Following the traditional reference to Ukraine being 'a key factor in the development and maintenance of stability in the whole of Europe', a compliment on the closure of Chernobyl, a mention of Ukraine's 'geographically strategic position' and reassurance that 'closer co-operation with the EU is in no way an obstacle to close, fruitful relations between Ukraine and Russia' the two EU men summed up by stating: '[It] is in the EU's interest to ensure Ukraine's favourable development' and 'there is no reason at this stage to limit further rapprochement.' Nothing, however, has been said about what exactly the EU would do to ensure that: 'The speed with which we can intensify co-operation is dictated by the pace of reform.'

Relations between Ukraine and the EU are believed to have reached a new stage after the Gothenburg summit, where Ukraine was mentioned for the first time in the section on the 'future of the EU' instead of in the 'External Affairs' part of the presidency conclusions, and the subsequent visit by Goran Persson to Kiev, marked by the declaration that the EU invited Ukraine to closer political co-operation. The EU-Ukraine Yalta summit on 11 September 2001, described by Javier Solana as a 'signal of friendship', did not bring significant progress to the EU-Ukraine dialogue in terms of outlining new prospects, but referred to major issues of concern in the field of 'political criteria' – free and fair elections, freedom of the press, fighting corruption – and emphasised continued assistance within the Tacis programmes and the potential for co-operation in the fields of approximation of the Ukrainian legislation to that of the EU, and in the field of JHA.

Ukraine (as well as Russia and Moldova) were invited to take part in an autumn 2001 European Conference in Brussels for the first time, to join in the discussions between EU member and candidate states on international terrorism, border controls and countering illegal migration and drugs trafficking. The invitation to take part in the conference was interpreted in Ukraine as a signal of understanding of Ukraine's major role in countering those challenges and an invitation to closer co-operation. According to Ukraine's Foreign Minister, Anatoliy Zlenko, the invitation to participate in the conference represented *de facto* recognition of Ukraine's right to claim membership by the EU. European integration and eventual EU membership for Ukraine was not just a foreign policy priority, but a 'vitally important prerequisite for the development of our state.' The question, however, is Ukraine's ability to make credible proposals that would enhance the EU's interest in involving it more closely in co-operative projects, and the EU's willingness to assist Ukraine in developing the institutional capacity for making declared co-operative projects work.

A window of opportunity?

It is conventionally argued that EU enlargement opens up new opportunities in various fields of Ukraine-EU co-operation, but there is no clear answer to the question as to what exactly Ukraine will gain from EU enlargement. The

Joint Statement of the September 2001 Ukraine–EU summit in Yalta defined those opportunities as aligning Ukraine's legislation, norms and standards as far as possible to the EU model. According to Messrs Prodi and Persson, CEE candidate countries, especially those with a common border with Ukraine, are a valuable resource for further co-operation, due to their experience of fast and radical transformation and the substantial progress they have made in meeting the membership criteria. These countries may be involved in EU-Ukraine projects and trilateral initiatives between Member States, candidate states and Ukraine. 'The EU initiative will convey an important message to candidate countries, to the effect that greater involvement in Ukraine will be an important asset in the accession process.' Indirectly admitting that so far the EU has lacked a coherent far-sighted vision of the development of its relations with Ukraine and shown reluctance to search for effective ways of moving the relationship on, the EU representatives noted that 'it takes two to tango' and that 'while the EU and Ukraine may be out on the dance floor, both have to know the steps.'

An effort to improve the implementation of the PCA and to move towards practical steps was made with the adoption of the Ukrainian Government's 'Priorities for stimulating economic activity, savings and investment, creation of conditions for sustainable economic growth in 2002-2004.' Specific tasks for the Ukraine-EU rapprochement include 'continuing work on harmonising provisions of national legislation in order to contribute to the free movement of people, goods, services and capital between Ukraine and the EU in accordance with the Partnership and Co-operation Agreement', 'implementing institutional measures in every branch, improving the legal basis in accordance with provisions of the Programme of Integration of Ukraine into the EU [...] and sectoral programmes in order to approach EU standards', and 'improving working conditions for [...] exporters by means of further liberalisation of the foreign economic regime with the EU.' Individual ministries and departments were given specific tasks in the area of European integration, and some have already been carried out. Seeking to streamline its European integration efforts, the government transformed the Ministry of Economy into the Ministry of Economy and European Integration and established a special European Integration Department in the Ministry of Foreign Affairs. But there is still a long way to go.

What more can Ukraine do to make its European aspirations a reality? First of all, pursue domestic structural, administrative and political transformation, continue harmonising its legislation with that of the EU (which may prove a challenge indeed, given the EU's massive 20,000 plus pieces of legislation, the fact that many of Ukraine's laws were initially built on different principles and the slow pace of approximation), make its policies consistent, abide by existing agreements and implement current programmes, build up its GDP (which today amounts to only 2.5 per cent of that of the EU) and work for integration as the national strategic goal. Ukraine should also seek to develop tripartite co-operation within the 'Ukraine – accession state – EU member state' framework, keeping in mind that its integration initiatives should also be of interest to the EU and the candidate states with which it intends to co-operate. Most significantly, the EU could contribute substantially to building EU-compatible institutions in Ukraine and introducing procedures that will facilitate co-operation.

In addition to expanding co-operation in the field of Justice and Home Affairs and devising compatible policies on countering illegal migration and organised crime and common foreign and security policy, co-operation in the area of environmental protection is necessary because environmental pollution knows no state borders, and the effects of environmental (and, particularly, technogenic) disasters in some countries in the immediate proximity of an enlarged EU will inevitably be felt in neighbouring countries and beyond. Therefore, Ukraine – EU co-operation in setting and maintaining common environmental protection and nuclear safety standards will be both unavoidable and mutually beneficial. The same is true of Ukraine-EU co-operation in maintaining quality and safety standards for food and other consumer products – a necessary condition for any expansion of the scope and size of trade.

About 90 per cent of the structural changes Ukraine has to accomplish to comply with EU membership criteria do not have to be linked to accession, as they need to be pursued in any case if the state's goal is to overcome the economic crisis and build a functioning market economy. While the economic dimension of integration can be relatively clearly expressed in the form of quantitative and qualitative indicators, and claims of political rapprochement may be supported by exchanges of official visits and the adoption of documents, the real challenge is to ensure that the whole of society (the political and civil service elite included) shares common European values and works to make them a reality in Ukraine. European integration efforts would be incomplete without measures taken to promote cultural, educational, scientific and technical rapprochement by raising awareness of Ukraine's European cultural identity through introduction of European standards in education, science and technology, the dissemination of Ukraine's own cultural achievement in the EU, and the implementation of joint cultural, research and educational projects.

In lieu of conclusions

Having many foreign policy priorities looks like having none of them clearly defined and followed. So far Ukrainian officials have been arguing in a number of European fora that integration mechanisms should be used more actively to involve countries that share European principles but, for some reason, are not yet ready for membership, and that the EU should be more explicit in responding to Ukraine's quest for a place in the enlargement process. However, calls for welcoming signs from the EU in response to Ukraine's 'demonstration of its political course towards European integration' have proved to be insufficient to transform declared intentions into a coherent policy of co-operation.

The EU seems to be clear about what it does not want from Ukraine – it does not want Ukraine to turn into an unreformed black hole of insecurity and instability, or an integral part of a new Russia-led pact. Yet, the EU is not entirely clear about what it wants Ukraine to become, and has not been explicit enough in separating its policies towards Russia and Ukraine, and considering Ukraine outside Russia's sphere of influence.

When visiting Kiev in the last days of July 2001, the EU's High Commissioner for Common Foreign and Security Policy, Javier Solana, announced that Brussels was 'satisfied' with Ukraine's pursuit of reform, but that there was still a long road ahead. In Kiev, however, routine praise for the pace of reform (which is, presumably, more evident from the outside than from the inside) and compliments on the Ukrainian government's success in re-scheduling payments to the Paris Club and reaching agreement with the

World Bank and the IMF, do not sound convincing as long as the critical questions – what can be done to 'soften' the new dividing lines in Europe and how can the desired outcome be achieved – remain unanswered.

UKRAINE'S RELATIONS WITH EUROPE

A BRITISH PERSPECTIVE

Roger Liddle

The European Union is on the brink of one of the most important steps in its history – enlargement. Enlargement to the East may be the EU's greatest challenge, but it is also its greatest opportunity. Nobody who considers how the European Union has underpinned peace and democracy in the reconstruction of post-war Western Europe can doubt the benefits that enlargement will bring post-Cold War Europe and the Balkans. But EU enlargement also creates fears – unfounded fears, I believe, but important to address nonetheless. Enlargement, rightly managed, will not create new divisions on the continent, but will open up new opportunities

Ukraine is central to the EU. Its stability and prosperity are vital to the EU's own security and this is enhanced by EU enlargement, not diminished. Ukraine enjoys a pivotal position between Central Europe and Eastern Europe making it a vital partner for the EU. It is clear to me from my many meetings with the Government of Ukraine that there is a strong desire to further relations with the EU. But I believe that Ukraine now has a framework in the shape of the Partnership and Co-operation Agreement (PCA) and the EU Common Strategy in which it can pursue existing commitments to move towards EU standards in the economic, social and political spheres.

The route via the PCA and the Common Strategy is the best way forward for EU-Ukraine relations. It is the best way to avoid new barriers, not just physical barriers, but barriers between those who have successfully transformed their societies and economies and those who have not. This is the greatest danger – a barrier between reform and stagnation. The EU's structure with Ukraine goes far in ensuring that there will not be a barrier between the EU and Ukraine, but a bridge. In Britain we recognise and support Ukraine's European vocation.

Ukraine will be the EU's neighbour, and in this ever more interdependent world, neighbours are no long strangers, but friends. Ukraine is a member of the European family. The EU has shown its commitment time and time again and will continue to do so. Enlargement makes Ukraine more central, not less, and the lessons of the last decade show that more is achieved when we work together.

Without enlargement, Western Europe will always be faced with the threat of instability, conflict and mass migration on its borders. And the countries on the Union's borders will share in that increased threat. The legacy of the Balkans reminds us all how vital regional co-operation is in today's world. The enlargement process not only induces the candidate countries to reform economically and politically, but also encourages neighbouring countries to participate in that reform process, and to take, and adhere to, some difficult decisions. Interdependence calls for unprecedented levels of co-operation, and instability in any country makes us all lose. That is why Britain supports enlargement not only in principle, but in practice. Tony Blair, the British Prime Minister, called on Europe's political leaders to commit themselves to a specific framework leading to an early end of the enlargement negotiations and accession. Specifically, he asked that the new Member States should be able to participate in the European Parliament elections in 2004 and have a seat at the table at the next Inter Governmental Council.

Ukraine is part of the European family and the PCA allows Ukraine to grow even closer to the EU. Ukraine is now able to engage in real dialogue and to bring its legislation closer to that of the Union. The reality is that Ukraine will border a Europe with a single market and a single currency and there will inevitably be a need for closer economic co-ordination and co-operation.

It is also a reality that in other areas such as trade there will be much for us to co-operate on. Already Ukraine is pursuing its application for WTO membership with vigour. Britain is encouraging that application not only in sentiment, but in practice. Our Department for International Development is funding projects to help Ukraine with WTO accession.

In areas like the environment, organised crime and in policing, Europe needs to work together. In foreign and security policy, though nations will guard jealously their own national interests, there are times when it will be of clear benefit to all of us that Europe acts in unison. And Ukraine has already shown a keenness to co-operate with the EU as it develops its European Security and Defence Policy. The EU is not just about free trade. It is about prosperity, security and strength, and Ukraine is central to the achievement of these objectives.

Ukraine has real fears that enlargement will increase trade barriers between itself and the EU. But I believe that enlargement is more likely to result in increased trade, not increased trade barriers. Demand for exports will rise due to increased economic growth in the candidate countries. The Community's external tariff is low, and that, coupled with increased demand, means that Ukraine will have a real opportunity to be one of Europe's most competitive economies.

But on a global level, in a world with the power of the USA; with new alliances to be made with Russia; developing nations with vast populations like India and China; Japan, not just an economic power but a country that will rightly increase its political might too; with the world increasingly forming powerful regional blocs like ASEAN and Mercosur; Europe needs to be strong and united. Europe needs to be a power in the world and the European family needs to co-operate.

But in this inter-dependent world – nations and identities remain important. The EU's enlargement process for instance is not about robbing peoples and nations of their hard-won sovereignty. Those citizens who struggled so hard to achieve statehood, many of whose citizens shed their blood in that cause, are not going to give it up lightly. Europe is about celebrating our diverse cultures and identities, our distinctive attributes as nations. The EU is a Europe of free, independent sovereign nations who choose to pool that sovereignty in pursuit of their own interests and the common good, achieving more together than we can achieve alone. The EU will remain a unique combination of the intergovernmental and the supranational. Evidence of that is clear even from among the candidates.

But with the EU, Ukraine is making real progress and I have no doubt that the momentum of reform will increase as we move closer to the EU's Eastern enlargement. The EU serves as a catalyst for reform. We are no longer just neighbours, but family.

A stable Ukraine is in the interests of the EU. Enlargement to encompass Central Europe will not weaken our relations with Ukraine; it will strengthen them. The EU and Ukraine will share a border, and co-operation will be essential. Poland already recognises that, and is actively engaged with Ukraine on discussing the border with Ukraine and other accession states. Enlargement will bring the borders of the European Union to the doorstep of Ukraine.

The Partnership and Co-operation Agreement, which lies at the heart of EU/Ukraine relations, has far-reaching implications. The primary task is to work together to realise the full potential of this agreement. This will take time, but the potential mutual benefit, both political and economic, is great.

The EU appreciates Ukraine's efforts to implement the relevant provisions of the Partnership and Co-operation Agreement and its commitment to fight organised crime including drug trafficking, trafficking in women and money laundering. Ukraine faces significant difficulties on its Eastern frontier as it attempts to control better the influx of migrants who seek to enter the Union illegally. Ukraine has specific problems as a transit country between East and West.

Ukraine's continued engagement with the EU is to be welcomed and, as noted below, we are continually improving our proposals for practical co-operation.

A landmark was reached in December 1999 when the Helsinki European Council adopted the EU Common Strategy on Ukraine. It was only the second EU Common Strategy to be adopted (the one on Russia was the first, adopted in June 1999).

I say that the strategy was a landmark because for the first time it set out clearly the EU's overall objectives for dealing with Ukraine over a four year period. It imposed a discipline on the EU to pursue its objectives collectively. And it recognised Ukraine's long term EU aspirations and welcomed its pro-European choice. As with any multilateral organisation there is scope to have multiple interfaces with third countries. The Common Strategy goes far in bringing the different interfaces under one umbrella, thereby ensuring that the EU has a coherent cross-pillar strategy towards Ukraine.

But what specifically does the Common Strategy deliver? What is its focus? Primarily it ensures that each in-coming Presidency maintains a focus and produces a plan of action for EU-Ukraine relations. This, I believe, ensures that Ukraine remains at the top of the EU's agenda. The Common Strategy's Article 46 could not be clearer when it calls on the incoming Presidency to present to the Council a Workplan setting out its stall on how it intends to take forward the implementation of the Common Strategy.

The Common Strategy also focuses other Member States in a coherent manner. It has three very broad objectives:

- to encourage the democratic and economic reform process in Ukraine;
- meeting common challenges on the European continent (stability and security, environment, energy and nuclear safety);
- strengthening co-operation between the EU and Ukraine (support for WTO accession, investment protection, co-operation in justice and home affairs, encouragement for the development of cross border infrastructure networks).

The Common Strategy mandates us all, Commission and Member States, to be guided by its principles. Britain believes the Common Strategy is a valuable instrument and also a significant development of the EU's Common Foreign and Security Policy. I believe that the EU's relationship with Ukraine is stronger because of the Common Strategy – already policies are more coherent and their effectiveness enhanced.

The EU-Ukraine Co-operation Council held in June 2001 is indicative of how our relationship is improving and becoming more concrete. Six areas were targeted for further work.

Energy – to include energy reform, including cash collection, follow-up to privatisation and reform of the gas market; renewable energy and energy efficiency; energy transportation, especially transit of gas; nuclear safety and related issues.

Trade – here it will concentrate on accelerating the negotiating process for Ukraine's accession to the WTO, including the introduction of international standards and technical regulations, and improved protection of intellectual property rights as foreseen in the PCA and the WTO rules.

Justice and Home Affairs – here it is intended to strengthen the management of borders, including development of border infrastructure; immigration questions; judicial reform and combating organised crime in all its forms. The aim is to complete the Action Plan by the end of 2001.

Approximation of Ukraine's legislation to the norms and standards of the EU – a key objective

Environmental Protection – in addition to nuclear safety it is intended to concentrate primarily on the implementation of the Kyoto protocol.

Transport – in this sphere it is intended to include further integration of Ukraine's transport infrastructure, in particular ports, into the European transport network along Pan-European Transport Corridors.

But this is not a one-way street. Ukraine has much to offer the EU. Ukraine has shown a keen interest in European Security and Defence Policy. There is, I believe, scope in the future to have fruitful discussions in the area of, example, military capabilities. In Central and Eastern Europe, Ukraine has a vital role in continuing to provide security and encouraging stability in the region.

On the economic front, Ukraine is also vital to the EU. Ukraine is a bridge between Eastern and Western Europe. It is crucial to Europe's future energy needs in terms of oil and gas supply. Its potential as a transit country delivering much needed energy to Western Europe will become increasingly apparent. It is also very important not to overlook Ukraine's highly skilled workforce. Ukraine has strong scientific and research foundations that in the right economic climate can deliver tremendous economic growth. This economic climate is essential to Ukraine's future and also to Europe's. The right economic climate attracts much foreign direct investment; which improves industry; which brings greater growth; which delivers prosperity.

Ukraine borders the world's biggest single economic and political partnership of democratic states. This represents a huge opportunity for Europe and the peoples of Ukraine. The Union of democracies has the capacity to sustain peace in our continent, to deliver unprecedented prosperity and to be a powerful force for democratic values in the rest of the world. Ukraine shares in that capacity. Our task in the EU, with the help of the new democracies about to join, is to shape a responsive European Union - in touch with the people, transparent and easier to understand, strengthened by its nations and regions; a European Union whose vision of peace is matched by its vision of prosperity. A civilised continent united in defeating brutality and violence. A prosperous continent united in extending opportunities to all. A continent joined together in its belief in social justice. An economic powerhouse through the completion of the world's biggest single market, the extension of competition, an adaptable and well educated workforce, support for businesses large and small. A civilised continent through common defence, the strength of our values, the pursuit of social justice, the rich diversity of our cultures.

Ukraine, as a country that in the future will share one of the longest frontiers with the EU, is central to that goal. On the Justice and Home Affairs dossier, encouraging progress is being made, and further efforts are needed to enhance JHA co-operation. For example on people trafficking we need to work together to combat one of the great evils of our time.

As with all previous enlargements, concerns are raised about tariffs, visas, etc. These concerns are not unique to Ukraine. As I said earlier the trade issues have been over-stated and I believe that the EU's Eastern enlargement will actually bring increased trading benefits, not less, as demand increases in the candidate countries. Ukraine's real concern is on its Western frontier where upwards of 20 million crossings per year are made on the Polish-Ukraine border. Poland and Ukraine are working together on this issue and more importantly many regional governments are now engaged in fruitful discussions. Strong borders result in strong security and a strong prosperous relationship between the Union and its neighbours.

Ukraine's transition will be more difficult than that in some other countries in the region which enjoyed longer periods of independence prior to World War II. But with continued faithfulness to the challenges of economic and political reform, progress will be achieved and a rich dividend reaped. Enlargement offers Ukraine a great opportunity to develop a new partnership with the EU; a unique partnership. Enlargement cannot, and will not, create a new dividing line in Europe. In an enlarged EU, Ukraine will not only be closer, physically, socially, politically and economically, but also culturally. Ukraine is as much part of Europe as Britain or Greece. It is a valued member of the European family with much to contribute to the common future of Europe.

EU-UKRAINE RELATIONS
A VIEW FROM THE EUROPEAN PARLIAMENT

Christopher Beazley

The Pan-European vision of a United Europe from the Atlantic to the Urals would only twelve years ago have appeared as improbable as today's borders of France to Thomas à Becket. Twelfth century France was divided into a patchwork of principalities, dukedoms and fiefs, one of the largest territories, the Angevin Empire, being ruled over by the King of England and one of the smallest by the King of France. Different languages abounded, different cultures and different mentalities.

The Europe of 1989 was similarly divided most graphically and symbolically by the Berlin Wall. President Gorbachev's reform programme indicated to the peoples of Central and Eastern Europe that the brutal Soviet repression of East Germany in 1953, Hungary in 1956, Czechoslovakia in 1968 and Poland in 1980 would not be repeated. As he stood with Eric Honecker, the East German Communist leader, at the official celebrations of forty years of GDR statehood, Gorbachev had already told him that Soviet tanks would stay 'confined to barracks' in the face of the developing demands of the reform movement.

The Velvet and Singing Revolutions of 1989-90, bloodless except for the unseemly end of Ceaucescu in Romania, brought back into being pre-Yalta Europe. The unnatural East-West divide hermetically sealed by the Iron Curtain on which the global strategies of both sides had been predicated for forty years was gone.

Although many of us had yearned to see the day, what very few people including President Gorbachev could have foreseen was the implosion of the Soviet Union under the weight of its own internal contradictions.

The Lonely Planet Travel Survival Kit records the event aptly: 'Shortly after the failed coup in August 1991, the Communist Party of Ukraine (CPU) was barred from power and on 24 August 1991, the Supreme Rada (Parliament) adopted a declaration of independence pending a nation-wide referendum. In December of that year some 84 per cent of the population voted overwhelmingly (90 per cent) in favour of independence. Leonid Kravchuk, former Chairman of the CPU, was elected first President of Ukraine.'

The European Parliament had always taken a close interest in Central and Eastern Europe but developing close ties between Brussels and Kiev was naturally going to be harder than for example with the Baltic States, with whom we had been working directly for some time. Before the EU-Ukraine relationship could be brought into being there had to be an understanding in the EU of the nature of Ukraine, her historical background, her cultural heritage, her regional diversity. The monstrous legacy of the Soviet period of cultural amnesia lingers with us today. The propaganda, as it was intended to do, worked its trick with those indirectly affected. The incorporation of Ukraine into the USSR so brilliantly encapsulated in Michael Bulgarkov's book 'The White Guard' was to have cruel consequences. The famine of 1932-33, whose very existence the Soviet authorities denied, claimed between 5 and 7 million lives. This deliberate genocide stands alongside the Nazis' holocaust against Europe's Jewish people in the annals of infamy.

But to be fair it was not only the Soviets who claimed Ukraine as their own. The Polish-Lithuanian Commonwealth ruled Ukraine during the Middle Ages and into the 16th Century, the Crimea was the homeland of Tartars, while Imperial Russia described Ukraine as 'Little Russia'. Most histories of Ukraine have therefore portrayed it as part of someone else's history. Only since independence has the origin of Ukraine been revisited, Kievan Rus in the 10th Century, and the exercise undertaken of seeing succeeding developments through Ukrainian eyes. The national anthem 'Ukraine has not yet died' mirrors the Polish experience of seeing their country fought over, the spoils divided and the country expunged from the maps of political geography.

Many authors, notably Anne Apelbaum, have drawn attention to Europe's borderlands and of course, as the Lonely Planet guide reminds us, the word Ukraine means Borderland. The European Union was established to prevent borders becoming barriers to trade and from dividing Europe's people into rival camps. This must be the first lesson which the European Parliament draws. With the enlargement process we would have failed in our enterprise if we erected new barriers where today there are none, whether between first and second wave entrants or between Poland and Ukraine, whose ultimate relationship with the EU remain undetermined.

The essence of the European Parliament's considered opinion on EU/ Ukraine relations is summarised in the Report 'On the Common Strategy of the European Union on Ukraine' (C5-0208/2000-2000/2116 (cos)) drawn up by Rapporteur Paavo Vayrynen and adopted by Parliament on 28 February 2001.

The European Parliament has been the motor for enlargement. Facing down obstruction from the French Presidency of the Council under Ministers Vedrine and Muscovici, the Parliament successfully advocated the target date of 2004 for first-wave accession.

It was acknowledged that Poland is the cardinal factor, with a population approximately equivalent to that of Spain and with a third living in rural areas. Politically Germany places great store on Poland being included in the first wave alongside Hungary, the Czech Republic, Estonia and Slovenia and possibly others.

However, we are all conscious that the creation of new barriers between Poland and Ukraine would be counter-productive. Historically, culturally and economically there are enduring ties between Eastern Poland and Western Ukraine, centred on Lviv.

Ukraine's strategic position and agrarian potential is also acknowledged as pivotal to the success of the enlarged EU.

Genuine concerns remain however, notably in the domains of representative democracy, the separation of powers, and, perhaps most significantly, a free media and press guaranteeing human rights.

The energy programme for Chernobyl is important. The trans-Ukraine gas pipeline must be sustained free from allegations of interference so that Russian suppliers and EU consumers are not subject to unwarranted transit costs or disruption.

The EU should improve its investment portfolio in Ukraine and be allowed to operate in an environment where the legal and administrative infrastructure permits conventional commercial relations. The conclusion of a Free Trade Agreement would be propitious.

Enhanced university and school exchanges, the development of joint and Pan-European research programmes are to be encouraged. Examples to be built upon include the twinning of Shrewsbury School with its opposite number in Kharkiv. Aerospace projects promise mutual benefit.

Security co-operation based on the Peace through Nato organisation should be developed, notably in the restoration of harmony in the Balkans.

Respect for human rights based on an independent judiciary is crucial. Concern in the EU about the murder of the journalist Gongadze must be allayed. The abolition of the death penalty in Ukraine is welcomed. A genuinely free press is a *sine qua non* for EU membership.

Exchange of cultural contacts will facilitate a growing together of the EU and Ukraine. To this end a welcome step would be the broadcasting of Euronews and other EU media outlets throughout Ukraine. The EU should ensure a Ukrainian language service of Euronews.

The EU should continue to ensure that available structural funds, notably the Tacis (Tempus and Democracy) programmes are wisely and successfully implemented.

The free movement of people is one of the four freedoms of the EU Single Market. Accordingly a responsible and flexible visa policy is envisaged between the EU and Ukraine. It remains essential that the trafficking of women be classified as a crime and the practice be stamped out through co-operation between Europol and the Ukraine police authorities. Article 31e of the EU Treaty is explicit.

Above all the EU-Ukraine relationship must be based on mutual understanding of the difficulties inherent in the transition from the Soviet experience to independence.

The European Parliament has affirmed that all necessary steps should be taken to enable Ukraine to move expeditiously to the point where she may apply for full membership of the enlarged EU. This has been resisted in certain quarters, notably the European Council.

President Prodi, representing the European Commission, has taken a personal interest in encouraging ever-closer EU relations with Ukraine.

If we are to make a success of restoring harmonious relations throughout Europe in the post-Soviet period Ukraine has a key role to play. The EU was established to abolish the barriers to trade and to cultural understanding in order to prevent war in Europe following the three wars of 1870, 1914-18, 1939-45.

The 'road map' to Ukraine's EU membership includes:

i) The full restoration of pluralist democracy.

ii) EU investment.

iii) Improved working relations between educational establishments.

iv) Sustainable energy programmes.

v) The political will to prevent the creation of new borders between the enlarged EU and Ukraine.

vi) Harmony and mutual respect between the Catholic and Orthodox denominations of the Christian faith.

The European Parliament in its dealings with the Ukrainian Rada and with Ukrainian interests at large will continue to play a constructive role in improving the EU-Ukraine relationship. Most important of all is the fact that any country which conforms to the three basic qualities of being European, democratic in the accepted sense of the word, and able to implement the *acquis communautaire* is *ipso facto* entitled to apply for EU membership if its government, supported by the population, so decides.

THE EU COMMON STRATEGY ON UKRAINE

A RESPONSE TO UKRAINE'S 'PRO-EUROPEAN CHOICE'?

Gwendolyn Sasse

By now the Common Strategy (CS) on Ukraine – and its counterpart: the CS on Russia – have become a standard point of reference in the discussion about the EU's relations with the East European 'outsiders', but there has been surprisingly little discussion of the CSs as such.[1] While the CS is only one part of the institutional framework shaping the interaction between the EU and Ukraine, it is a prism through which EU-Ukrainian relations can be analysed. Its language and content reveal some of the problems and characteristics of EU foreign policy.

A history of the common strategy

Ukraine was the first post-Soviet state to sign a Partnership and Co-operation Agreement (PCA) with the EU (June 1994), although it only came into force on 1 March 1998 after Ukraine, the EU and the EU Member States had ratified it. The PCAs are binding treaties regulating relations with the EU and institutionalising a regular multi-level political dialogue. The PCAs cover trade, investment, competition and regulation issues and, to a lesser extent, political and security questions. The ratification of the PCA with Ukraine was followed by President Kuchma's decree on 'The Strategy of Ukraine's

Integration into the EU' (June 1998). EU membership was singled out as Ukraine's strategic goal, and associate membership as the mid-term foreign policy objective. It mapped the key actions to be taken by Ukraine's executive in order to meet the preconditions for EU membership by 2007. This general foreign policy direction was reinforced by Ukraine's National Programme on Integration into the European Union, approved by presidential decree on 14 September 2000.

One of the areas in which the shortcomings of the Maastricht Treaty had been most obvious was CFSP. The Amsterdam Treaty of 1997 introduced the CS as a new CFSP tool alongside the Secretary General of the Council/High Representative for CFSP and the Policy Planning and Early Warning Unit. The CSs emerged as a compromise solution at the deadlocked IGC in 1997. They are agreements between the EU Member States and the European Council which are meant to streamline the Union's CFSP mechanisms, integrate the activities of individual Member States and introduce Qualified Majority Voting (QMV) on CFSP issues in the Council. The shift away from consensus-driven unanimity has remained a bone of contention: so far QMV has not been applied, a fact which calls the whole institutional package of the CSs into question. The CSs are both a part of the EU's external relations and an internal institutional innovation, although the latter aspect is often overlooked in the discussion about the EU's relations with Ukraine or Russia.

The text of the Amsterdam Treaty (article 13) is extremely brief on the content and implementation of the new foreign policy instrument, but it highlights that the drafting process is based on a common denominator derived from the national interests of the Member States:

> The European Council shall decide on common strategies to be implemented by the Union in areas where the Member states have important interests in common. Common strategies shall set out their objectives, duration and means to be made available by the Union and the Member States. The Council shall recommend common strategies to the European Council and shall implement them, in particular by adopting joint actions and common positions.

At the Vienna Summit 1998 the Council decided to devise CSs on Russia, Ukraine, the Mediterranean and the Balkans - the geographical borderlands of the Union. The CS on Russia was adopted on 4 June 1999; the CS on Ukraine followed on 11 December 1999. Both were adopted for an initial period of four years. They declare that the EU and the member States have to develop 'co-ordination, coherence and complementarity of all aspects of their policy' towards Russia and Ukraine, and the Member States are reminded that they are obliged to co-operate with other international organisations. The implementation of the CSs is left to the individual EU presidencies: their work plans have to be presented to the Council. The structure and wording of the CS on Ukraine mirrors that on Russia, although the 'Christmas tree method' shines through even more clearly. A minimum consensus on the need for a common foreign policy position was broadened out by individual Member States adding more and more 'decoration' according to their own national interests, thereby blurring the priorities.

The CS on Ukraine begins with a carefully worded and watered down mission statement which 'acknowledges Ukraine's European aspirations and welcomes Ukraine's pro-European choice' and emphasises that 'the EU remains firmly committed to working with Ukraine at national, regional and local levels in order to support a successful political and economic transformation in Ukraine, which will facilitate Ukraine's further *rapprochement* with the EU'. It defines a basic strategic partnership 'based on shared values and common interests' as 'a vital factor enhancing peace, stability and prosperity in Europe', but also adds a forceful reminder that 'the main responsibility for Ukraine's future lies with Ukraine itself'.

The CS on Ukraine identifies three principal objectives: 1) support for the democratic and economic transition process in Ukraine; 2) ensuring stability and security and meeting common challenges on the European continent; 3) support for strengthened co-operation between the EU and Ukraine within the context of EU enlargement. There are few references to concrete actions and resources. Instead, implementation is explicitly tied to the pre-existing structures of Tacis, the PCAs, other initiatives and bilateral programmes, leaving the distinct contribution of the CS unspecified. Within itself the CS is imprecise and inconsistent, and there is considerable overlap with the PCA. It is unclear how the different objectives (visions, principal objectives, specific initiatives) are ranked and how they relate to each other.

How common? How much of a strategy?

As internal EU documents, the CSs do not allow for any formal input by the external country in question. The current Member States had different views about the need for CSs in general, the mission statements and, most importantly, on QMV in the Council. The introduction of QMV through the CSs aimed to decouple broad strategic decisions based on unanimity and smaller tactical steps approved by QMV. This logic brought about extremely vague strategic documents in order to avoid QMV. The so-called 'strategic goals' are essentially a shopping list of problems and existing activities rather than a forward-looking strategy.

The gist of the 'strategy' on Ukraine is the signal that the EU will not close the door on Ukraine, while not locking the EU into any premature commitments. For the EU Ukraine represents, above all, a number of problems and soft security risks. The mismatch between the objectives of the EU and Ukraine's membership aspirations have left a clear imprint on the CS. Nevertheless, the CS started an interesting process, as the question of Ukraine's EU membership had not been officially addressed before.

The status of the common strategy

The CS reinforces the importance of the PCA as the basis of EU-Ukrainian relations. There is, however, an inherent tension between the PCA and the CS, which has not only impaired the successful implementation of the CS, but is also indicative of a key contradiction inscribed in the EU: the tension between consensus-driven EU integration and intergovernmentalism. The CS is essentially an intergovernmental framework by means of which individual Member States are reasserting their say in EU foreign policy.

The practical value of the CS in the Commission's daily work is limited: the emphasis has remained on the implementation of the PCA.[2] There are a few Home and Justice Affairs on which the CS is more specific than the PCA, but it is unclear whether follow-up initiatives in this area were instigated by the CS as such. Each EU presidency is obliged to draw up a six-month work plan on how to implement the CS. This stop-go mechanism suffers from a built-in tendency to replicate the CSs every six months. Although Tacis is one of the main instruments for the implementation of the CS, the Tacis regulations for the period 2000-2006 only mention that 'applicable provisions of assistance ... should take due account of the Common Strategies adopted by the European Council'.[3] The Tacis Indicative Programme 2000-2003 focuses on three key areas: 1) institutional, legal and administrative reform; 2) the private sector and assistance for economic development, and 3) the social consequences of transition. There is some overlap with CS objectives, but there is no specific reason to believe that the CS actively shaped the formulation of these Tacis priorities. Tacis programming operates on 4-7 year cycles, whereas the EU presidency changes every six months. Moreover, presidencies have their own national priorities. The extent to which Ukraine belongs to this set of priorities varies, as does the capacity of individual presidencies to leave a mark on the CS work plans and the degree of transparency with which they are drawn up, implemented and monitored. The country desk at the Commission has to ensure that the presidencies do not commit the Commission to unrealistic goals, while presidencies tend to include ongoing bilateral activities in their final report on their implementation of the CSs.

On 9 October 2000 the General Affairs Council called on the High Representative for CFSP, Javier Solana, to submit an evaluation report on the operation and possible improvement of the existing CSs. Solana's report starts with the realisation that the CSs have 'not yet contributed to a stronger and more effective EU in international affairs'.[4] It clearly identifies the gap between poor effectiveness on the one hand and the expectations raised by the CSs on the other hand. The report criticises the limited value of the CS as an internal working tool, in particular in sensitive crisis situations, and the uncertainty as to how the CSs relate to the already existing instruments, most notably the PCAs. The prospect of QMV decisions is singled out as a reason for making Member States more reluctant to engage with the CSs. The presidencies' work plans are referred to as 'routine exercises' and 'inventories of existing policies and activities'. Solana's report asks for the CSs to be turned into primarily internal EU policy documents, to be more selective in scope and contain 'verifiable objectives' against which progress can be measured and on the basis of which Member States could promote the CSs in other international institutions. The European Parliament expressed its support for both the CSs and Solana's conclusions about the need to make the document more credible and ensure realistic means for its implementation.[5]

A view from Ukraine

The former Foreign Minister Borys Tarasyuk commented positively on the CS: 'This document refutes forever the ungrounded assertions of some domestic isolationists who claim that we are not noticed, nor wanted, nor expected in Europe'.[6] Prominent Ukrainian analysts adopted an equally optimistic tone.[7] However, the initial optimism was bound to fade. While the CS is still being referred to in high-profile speeches as short-hand for the importance of Ukraine's stability, it does not represent a breakthrough in EU-Ukrainian relations.

There is a key difference between Ukraine's and Russia's position vis-à-vis the EU. Ukraine had chosen a pro-active approach, explicitly putting the membership issue on the agenda and thereby forcing the EU to respond via the CS. Conversely, Russia had never asked for membership, which made general engagement with Russia the driving force behind the CS on Russia. Ukraine's strategic document on EU integration, which had been approved by a wide range of political institutions in Ukraine prior to the drafting of the CS, was not immediately acknowledged by the EU. Later the EU chose not to engage with it in detail. Russia continuously focused on alternative foreign policy channels: its Mid-Term Strategy 2000-2010, presented in October 1999, goes far beyond the CS and clearly stipulates Russia's national interests. While the timing of this document appears to be prompted by the CS, President Putin's foreign policy concept of July 2000 does not even refer to the CS.

While Russia has repeatedly tried to gain some leverage over the EU enlargement process, Ukraine's position sends out a different signal: the end goal of membership has been stated publicly, but the request for a consultative role has been more modest, engaging with EU instruments such as the CS. Ukrainian diplomats in Brussels and Kiev have actively tried to shape the EU presidencies' work plans. Only a few of their detailed suggestions, referred to as 'wish lists' on the EU side, have been taken up. Ukraine's continual attempts to gain the EU's attention has led to a degree of 'Ukraine fatigue' in the Commission, which is met by a similar sense of frustration on the Ukrainian side.

Conclusions

It is clear that Ukraine's closer integration with the EU depends primarily on Ukraine's internal structural reforms. While a number of official documents demonstrate a degree of political will at the top level of decision-making in Ukraine, the implementation of these decisions is still lagging behind. Foreign policy, domestic politics and public awareness are still rather separate domains, in particular with regard to Ukraine's westward orientation towards the EU.

The EU's need to engage more systematically with Ukraine is apparent. The need for a common position on the future neighbours to the East entered the EU agenda rather late. The CSs signalled one step in this direction and an official recognition of the need to look beyond the accession negotiations as an intrinsic part of both the enlargement process and CFSP. The CS may have helped Ukraine to regain some international credibility, it may have facilitated additional dialogue and inserted a new reference about the EU's commitment to Ukraine into bilateral relations and EU policy, but it is difficult to link any specific initiative to the CS alone. At this point three outcomes seem possible: firstly, the CS may simply not be renewed when its current lease of life comes to an end in 2003. Secondly, a committed reform along the lines of Solana's critique would start almost from scratch in order to devise a more specific and workable strategy. The non-committal status-quo, however, suits many Member States. Thirdly, incrementalism and a lack of alternative ideas may well lock the EU and Ukraine into a formalised unproductive relationship that lacks an inherent source of momentum.

For the time being, Ukraine speaks about closer integration with the EU in very general terms, while the EU focuses on the implementation of the PCA. The CSs were born out of frustration about the underdeveloped CFSP and the slow progress of transition in countries like Russia and Ukraine. They are both an external and internal experiment for the EU. In the end, their main contribution may lie in pushing along internal EU reforms. At present, the CS on Ukraine is a misnomer, as it is neither 'common' nor 'strategic'. It sent out ambiguous signals, as it is situated in the underdefined space between internal EU policy and interaction with Ukraine. It has only been a limited interim response to both Ukraine's 'pro-European choice' and the EU's need for internal institutional reform. It marked the beginning of a gradual rethinking but has so far not achieved tangible results.

NOTES

[1] The CS on the Mediterranean region is the third CS of its kind and was adopted on 19 June 2000. It suffers from similar general problems to the other two CSs, but the concrete issues at stake are different and will not be addressed in this article.

[2] Author's interviews with Commission officials, Brussels, 27-29 March 2001.

[3] Council Regulation No. 99/2000, 29 December 1999, *Official Journal of the European Communities*, 18 January 2000.

[4] Secretary General/High Representative: Common Strategies report, Brussels 21 December 2000, declassified 30 January 2001, 14871/00, CAB 21.

[5] European Parliament Resolution on the Common Strategy of the European Union on Ukraine (C5-0208/2000-2000/2116 (COS)), 28 February 2001.

[6] Borys Tarasyuk, 'Foreword', in *Roadway Into the Future – Roadway to Europe. Ukraine's European Integration*, Centre for European and International Studies: Kiev 2000, p. 4.

[7] Ihor Burakovsky, Hryhoriy Nemyria, Oleksandr Pavliuk, 'Ukraine and European Integration', *Politics and the Times, No. 1-2*, 2000, p. 10.

This paper draws on work for the project 'Elites and Institutions in Regional and Local Governance in Eastern Europe' funded by the ESRC 'One Europe or Several?' Programme, award number L213252030.

UKRAINE-EU ECONOMIC CO-OPERATION

THE SOVIET LEGACY STRIKES BACK

Igor V. Burakovsky

The development of economic co-operation between Ukraine and the EU is based upon the Partnership and Co-operation Agreement (PCA) and a number of agreements between Ukraine and EU Member States. Ukraine's aspirations to membership of the WTO must also be taken into account.

Economic co-operation between Ukraine and EU at present is limited to technical assistance, trade and investment.

Over the period 1991-1999, total assistance amounted to 4 billion Euros: 1.5 billion from the EU and 2.5 billion from the Member States. Currently the top priorities are institutional and administrative reform as tools for strengthening the rule of law, nuclear safety and environmental protection, state enterprises restructuring and private sector development. EU technical assistance plays an important role in Ukraine's implementation of the provisions of the PCA, approximation of legislation and Ukraine's bid for accession to the WTO.

Trade and investment

In bilateral trade, the share of Ukraine's commodity exports going to the EU rose from 11.1 per cent in 1996 to 16.2 per cent in 2000 (and for imports from 14.9 per cent to 20.6 per cent). However, CIS countries in general and Russia in particular dominate Ukrainian commodity flows (accounting for 30.9 per cent of Ukraine's exports and 57.6 per cent of imports), while the EU ranks second as a trading partner. (Tables 1 and 2)

Table 1. Ukraine's foreign trade in goods (mn USD).

	Export				
	1996	1997	1998	1999	2000
Total	14400.8	14231.9	12637.4	11581.6	14572.5
CIS countries	7405.2	5585.7	4202.3	3252.2	4497.5
Rest of the world	6995.6	8646.2	8435.1	8329.4	10075.0
Including					
EU countries	1596.4	1757.1	2119.3	2118.6	2354.4
	Import				
	1996	1997	1998	1999	2000
Total	17603.4	17128.0	14675.6	11846.1	13956.0
CIS countries	11175.9	9879.4	7897.0	6743.2	8039.9
Rest of the world	6427.5	7248.6	6778.6	5102.9	5916.1
Including					
EU countries	2769.0	3379.3	3170.5	2398.9	2881.2

Source: State Statistics Committee of Ukraine

Table 2. Ukraine's foreign trade in goods (per cent).

	Export				
	1996	1997	1998	1999	2000
Total	100	100	100	100	100
CIS countries	51.4	39.2	33.3	28.1	30.9
Rest of the world	48.5	60.8	66.7	71.9	69.1
Including					
EU countries	11.1	12.3	16.8	18.3	16.2
	Import				
	1996	1997	1998	1999	2000
Total	100	100	100	100	100
CIS countries	63.5	57.7	53.8	56.9	57.6
Rest of the world	36.5	42.3	46.3	43.1	42.4
Including					
EU countries	15.7	19.7	21.6	20.3	20.6

* Author's calculations

Source: State Statistics Committee of Ukraine

Ukrainian exports have traditionally been dominated by base metals and base metal products (44.4 per cent in 2000), chemical (10.6 per cent) and mineral products (9.6 per cent) while machinery and equipment made up 9.3 per cent. Among imports, mineral products ranked first in 2000 at 46.9 per cent (due above all to gas and oil supplies from Russia). Machinery and equipment ranked second at 13.9 per cent.

The commodity structure of Ukraine's exports to the EU is very similar (Table 3). Base metals and base metal products amounted to 32.5 per cent (machinery and equipment – 5.2 per cent). In imports from the EU, machinery and equipment ranked first at 28.3 per cent followed by chemical products (13.7 per cent).

Table 3. Ukraine-EU Trade Commodity Structure (mn USD, per cent).

	Export			
	1999 mn USD	1999 per cent	2000 mn USD	2000 per cent
Total	2118.2	100	2340.3	100
Including				
Plant products	121.6	5.8	114.2	4.9
Food industry products	26.5	1.3	26.8	1.1
Mineral products	457.8	21.7	259.6	11.1
Chemical products	194.3	9.2	275.3	11.8
Plastic materials and cauotchouc	5.6	0.3	6.9	0.3
Pulp	2.6	0.1	2.2	0.1
Textile and textile articles	312.6	14.8	360.4	15.4
Base metals and base metals products	573.7	27.2	760.8	32.5
Machinery, equipment and appliances	99.4	4.7	120.5	5.2
Means of transport	56.7	2.7	23.5	1.0
	Import			
	1999 mn USD	1999 per cent	2000 mn USD	2000 per cent
Total	2398.9	100	2881,2	100
Including				
Plant products	33.0	1.6	47.8	1.7
Food industry products	77.7	3.7	115.8	4.1
Mineral products	152.5	7.2	131.3	4.6
Chemical products	333.1	15.7	387.2	13.7
Plastic materials and cauotchouc	136.8	6.4	190.0	6.7
Pulp	97.6	4.6	129.6	4.6
Textile and textile articles	189.0	8.9	305.6	10.8
Base metals and base metals products	95.5	4.5	212.9	7.5
Machinery, equipment and appliances	640.0	30.1	799.6	28.3
Means of transport	96.3	4.5	68.0	2.4

* The most important ones

Source: State Customs Services of Ukraine. Some figures may be slightly different from data provided by the State Statistics Committee of Ukraine.

There are a number of factors hampering Ukraine's exports to the EU:

- the weak competitiveness of Ukrainian goods (especially industrial goods), above all in terms of quality;
- the slow restructuring of enterprises in terms of both technical modernisation and corporate governance;
- tough competition in certain sectors of the EU market, etc.

EU quotas are not at present a major problem for Ukraine's exporters. In 2000 Ukraine exported to the EU 242 861 tonnes of metal products, 91.9 per cent of its export quota (263 339 tonnes) for that year. The shortfall is indicative of Ukrainian producers' inability to expand production in order to utilise the quota. At the same time, export quotas may shortly limit Ukraine's exports to the EU, especially in these areas: coiled rolled metal (99.8 per cent of export quota utilised), thick sheet rolled metal (99.7 per cent), other flat rolled metal (95.4 per cent), beams (85.8 per cent), rolled wire (99.9 per cent) and other rolled shapes (71.2 per cent).

Ukraine has undertaken a number of steps to liberalise its foreign trade regime. The average customs tariff fell from 7.49 per cent in 1998 to 7.05 per cent at the beginning of 2001. This was done to meet the needs of Ukraine's internal market as well as commitments resulting from negotiations with WTO member countries on the harmonisation of tariff levels, the requirements of the PCA, and obligations to the IFIs. But the business environment still needs serious improvement.

Ukraine has not been successful so far in attracting foreign investment. As of 1 January 2001 the cumulative inflow of foreign direct investment (FDI) into Ukraine since 1991 was 3.865 billion USD from 110 countries. (Over the same period Poland received FDI of around 40 billion USD). The main sectors to benefit from FDI were the food industry (20.1 per cent of cumulative FDI), domestic trade (18.8 per cent), machine-building and metal-working (9 per cent), financial sector (6.4 per cent) and fuel industry (5.9 per cent). By origin of investment the United States has dominated – 635.8 million USD (or 16.4 per cent). US companies are followed by Cyprus (9.6 per cent), Netherlands (9.4 per cent), Russia (8.1 per cent), UK (7.7 per cent), Germany (6.2 per cent), British Virgin Islands (4.6 per cent), Republic of

Korea (4.4 per cent), Switzerland (4.4 per cent), Ireland (2.4 per cent), Austria (3.3 per cent), Sweden (1.9 per cent), Liechtenstein (1.9 per cent), Italy (1.9 per cent), Poland (1.5 per cent), Canada (1.5 per cent), Hungary (1.3 per cent), other countries (13.3 per cent). According to a number of surveys the dominant motive for investment in Ukraine is the search for markets, with efficiency and resources of only secondary significance.

Legal framework

The current legal regime for foreign investors is governed by Ukrainian legislation and a number of international treaties signed by Ukraine.

The first foreign investment law addressing the status of foreign ventures (companies with 10 per cent or more foreign investment in their statutory funds) was adopted in early 1992. This law granted a range of privileges to foreign investors. It provided, for example, guarantees against changes in Ukrainian legislation and expropriation, guarantees of compensation for damage caused by illicit acts of state bodies, and guarantees on the withdrawal of investment and the transfer of profit and income. 'Qualified' investors were granted a number of special privileges such as exemption from import and/or export duties, customs and internal tax concessions, and privileges regarding land and corporate income taxes.

The scope of such privileges has been constantly declining, however. On 29 January 2000, parliament passed a law which cancelled all existing privileges and introduced a single regulatory regime for all companies operating in Ukraine. (This law also confirmed the unconditional application of national treatment for all enterprises.) However, guarantees generally accepted in international practice – to repatriate profits, withdraw investment, etc. – remained intact.

At the same time foreign investors can enjoy a number of preferences granted to companies located in the 12 special economic zones and 8 areas with a special investment regime. Companies operating in special economic zones are exempt from import duty and VAT on imported goods, and in some zones from mandatory sale of currency proceeds. A special investment regime provides inter alia exemption from import duty for goods imported for investment purposes until the project comes into operation. In addition, equipment, fittings and components are exempt from value-added tax.

Today Ukraine is a party to more than 20 bilateral treaties on the promotion and protection of investment. Ukraine is also a party to the New York Convention on the Recognition and Enforcement of Foreign Arbitral Awards and the Washington Convention (the Convention on the Settlement of Investment Disputes between States and Nationals of Other Countries).

Current Ukrainian legislation puts no restrictions on the share of overseas participation in Ukrainian enterprises (up to 100 per cent) or the form of the investor's contribution (in cash or in kind). Foreign investment in armaments, explosives, drugs production and some sectors 'of strategic importance' are forbidden.

To meet PCA provisions on financial market liberalisation the January 2001 Law on Banks and Banking Activities eliminated discrimination against foreign banks. Earlier regulations limited foreign banks' share to 15 per cent of the aggregate capital of the Ukrainian banking system. The Cabinet of Ministers has also submitted a draft law to liberalise the insurance market. Currently Ukrainian legislation restricts foreign participation to 49 per cent of the chapter capital of insurance companies.

Despite attempts to improve the legal environment for business (domestic as well as foreign) a number of fundamental drawbacks remain:

- administrative procedures (customs clearance, licensing and certification) remains slow, complex and unpredictable;
- the state has limited administrative capacity resulting in weak application and enforcement of the law;
- the professional level of legislative and judicial personnel needs serious improvement;
- foreign investors have been discouraged by the weaknesses and ambiguities in the copyright, bankruptcy and taxation regimes.

Model of co-operation

Perhaps the best description for current economic relations between Ukraine and the EU is the 'trade model of co-operation'. This has several important features:

- Co-operation between Ukraine and the EU is limited in its export and import assortment, forms of economic ties and level of reciprocal influence.
- Ukraine, like other economies in transition, receives credits and other financial resources provided on a bilateral and multilateral basis to carry out certain projects aimed at developing market infrastructure and financing critical imports.
- Economic ties between Ukrainian and European companies are predominantly based on simple export-import transactions, though there are also outward processing schemes in which EU partners supply products for processing at Ukrainian plants and take away processed products. As a rule, European investors refrain from large-scale investment in the Ukrainian economy though in certain cases (tobacco, manufacturing) the investment is quite substantial by Ukrainian standards.
- The structure of Ukraine's trade with EU countries does not significantly differ from that of Ukraine's overall exports and imports (exports of low-processed commodities and imports of machinery and equipment, industrial consumer goods and foodstuffs), while the structure of the EU's trade with Ukraine to a certain extent resembles EU trade with developing countries.

Clearly there are a number of reasons, objective and subjective, for the emergence of this model. In my opinion Ukraine's integration into the European economy is to a large extent hampered by a production structure inherited from the USSR.

The Soviet legacy

Ukraine's foreign trade problems, like other social and economic difficulties, are strongly influenced by the legacy of the USSR. Before independence in 1991 Ukraine had for decades been an integral part of the Soviet system's 'economic complex' both in terms of its management (Soviet-type command economy) and geography.

This system was not based on the administrative and territorial divisions of the USSR but governed in an extremely centralised fashion from Moscow. Ukraine had no experience of making and implementing state policy or any clear idea of liberal economic development, because in the former Soviet Union the state was the one and only rule-setting institution determining the behaviour of all economic agents.

Ukraine inherited significant industrial facilities with extremely high energy consumption. Over the last ten years the problem of excessive energy consumption has remained unresolved. This leads to another problem – increased sensitivity of the economy to any fluctuation on the energy market. Also, many if not most industries had developed as part of the Soviet economic complex, with its distorted prices (extremely cheap resources as compared with international prices), attempts to create universal patterns of production without taking into account the long-term effects, stress on economies of scale etc. Under the new conditions these sectors turned out to be internationally non-competitive.

Ukrainian economic policy-makers have lacked a deep analysis of international experience and of their own mistakes as well as adequate assessments of present and potential opportunities and trends. Some strategic decisions seem to have been made by intuition or under the influence of external factors such as the advice of the IFIs or the 1998 crisis in Russia.

The recession in Ukraine has been deeper and more prolonged than in most post-Communist states (except for the former Soviet republics of Tajikistan, Georgia and Armenia, plagued by civil unrest and hostilities). The Ukrainian recession, like its counterparts in the other former Soviet republics, was brought about principally by internal factors. This is reflected in the lack of correlation between national and international, particularly European, economic trends.

Ukrainian enterprises had neither experience of working on external markets nor the necessary infrastructure (information services, expertise, data banks) for companies operating abroad. In the USSR all foreign economic activities were conducted by 'foreign-economic associations' (nearly all in Moscow), and only a limited number of producers were allowed to participate in foreign trade directly. After the collapse of the USSR Russia inherited all these associations, so Ukraine and the other former Soviet republics had to start developing external economic activities from scratch.

Ukraine's enterprises have traditionally had considerable production and commercial ties with enterprises in the former USSR. In the past Ukraine specialised chiefly in manufacturing intermediate products. The factories making end products were usually located elsewhere. As a result, Ukraine's foreign economic policy-making is influenced by the ties which still exist within the framework of the former single market. This forces Ukraine to take part in economic integration with the former Soviet republics at bilateral and multilateral level.

The archaic structure of Ukrainian industry has continued unchanged. It is dominated by metal- and energy-intensive industries such as heavy and power engineering, chemical and construction engineering, agricultural machinery and tractor production. High-tech industries have not yet developed to any significant extent (with very few exceptions). Furthermore, the technical level and quality of engineering products are extremely low.

Ukrainian industry requires large-scale restructuring and modernisation. It is currently envisaged that this will be carried out through a new industrial policy. The strategy, methods and instruments to be used to implement this policy have yet to be defined, but in Ukraine it will undoubtedly involve large-scale state intervention in the economy in general and in foreign economic activities in particular. It should be noted that the acute shortage of financial resources poses a strong temptation for policy-makers to resort to administrative measures and protectionist instruments in order to solve Ukraine's fiscal problems.

WTO membership

Today there is a growing understanding in Ukraine of the need to join the WTO. To this end the President of Ukraine issued a special decree 'On Additional Measures Aimed at Accelerating Ukraine's WTO Accession' (5 September 2001).

The process of Ukraine's accession to the GATT/WTO system began on 17 December 1993, when the Government of Ukraine submitted an official application to the WTO Secretariat notifying it of its intent to join the WTO. In November 1994 Ukraine submitted a Memorandum on the Foreign Trade Regime of Ukraine for consideration by a WTO Working Party.

Since then, a number of bilateral negotiations and Working Party meetings have taken place. Ukraine has already submitted practically all the documents required for the accession procedure – memorandum on its trade regime, agricultural data, tariff offer, schedule on goods and services – as well as answers to questions raised by Working Party members. As of autumn 2001 Ukraine was conducting active bilateral negotiations with almost 30 countries, including Australia, Bulgaria, Canada, Poland, Romania, Slovenia, Slovakia, the USA, Hungary, the Czech Republic and Japan, as well as the EU.

Since submitting its official application Ukraine has done much to improve its trade regime in accordance with WTO norms and principles. Today there is a growing understanding in Ukraine that WTO membership is important not only in terms of integration into the world trade system but as a means of pushing forward and locking in economic reforms.

Nevertheless there are a number of fields where negotiations are proceeding with difficulty, such as market access (tariff rates and technical barriers to trade), intellectual property rights, customs clearance procedures, and harmonisation of legislation and its application according to the norms and principles of the WTO (especially taxation).

WTO accession must be a political commitment of the government based not only on legislative authority but a consensus involving the industrial, agricultural and banking private sectors as well. Such a consensus can be reached through dialogue between the executive power and private business, but at present the dialogue is rather weak and the executive is hampered by the lack of an unbiased analysis of foreign trade liberalisation and the impact of implementation of WTO principles on the national economy and specific sectors.

New direction

An analysis of the problems of and prospects for co-operation between Ukraine and the EU points to the need to look again for an answer to the fundamental question of self-determination, broadly defined.

Internal self-determination consists in choosing and carrying out a particular strategy for economic development. Naturally, in many aspects such a strategy is shaped (in conceptual terms) retroactively. Trying to follow the road of market transformation, Ukraine has declared building a market economy as its strategic course. However, so far its economic system can only be described as transitional: it has ceased to be strictly an administrative and command economy but at the same time it does not have many market mechanisms. Nor is there any clear plan for building and implementing a market strategy in terms of economic policy priorities.

External self-determination means choosing to target certain markets and regions to strengthen the country's position in the modern global economy and ensure its stable economic development.

In the case of Ukraine and other post-communist countries, our choice of the European option reflects our commitment to introduce rules and standards that have already been implemented in the region in which we wish to integrate rather than any geographical orientation of policy. In other words, the European option signifies Ukraine's desire and willingness to develop its economic system according to EU rules.

It should be noted that in certain circumstances even rapprochement with the CIS could be regarded as a movement towards the EU – for instance if universally recognised WTO rules and regulations were to be introduced within the CIS, with the latter becoming a place of civilised economic policy and standards.

Adoption of EU membership as a strategic priority means Ukraine must face a number of questions regarding its further strategy for reforming its national economy. And to answer these questions Ukraine must have the political will to engage in real and not just declaratory large-scale economic transformations.

Integration into the world economy, including the EU, is rather a complicated matter for any state. However, with political will, social consensus and a well-defined strategy Ukraine has an excellent chance to become a welcome economic partner and fully-fledged member of the great European family and in doing so to promote its own further development.

This paper draws on official statistical data issued by the EU, State Customs Services of Ukraine and State Statistics Committee of Ukraine.

BARRIERS TO EUROPEAN INVESTMENT IN UKRAINE

Yuriy Petrus

The European Business Association (EBA), of which I am Executive Director, is a non-profit organisation serving the needs of the European business community in Ukraine. It provides support to its members through collective advocacy of common interests, information support, serving as a strong voice in the EU-Ukraine relationship and in developments affecting business in Ukraine.

In February 2001 the Association, at the request of the Swedish Presidency of the European Union and the European Commission, prepared a review of the barriers to investment in Ukraine. The aim of the report was to review some of the barriers to the investment process identified by members of the Association, and consider some ways forward based on practices adopted in many other parts of the world.

A focus on barriers to investment necessarily gives the report an emphasis on negative features of the Ukrainian business environment. This does not mean that the Association fails to recognise the progress that has been achieved in Ukraine, the continued stability of the currency and the stabilisation of government finances being good examples. Nor should it imply that the Ukrainian authorities themselves are unaware of the problems; in many cases, resolution of these problems is a central part of current policy.

Nonetheless, it is important to acknowledge that many difficulties with the investment process are longstanding and tenacious, and are reflected in consistently low levels of foreign direct investment. Ukraine has received, as of October 2000, only $3.7 billion in foreign investment since independence in 1991; Ukraine's own estimate of its investment needs in the five-year period from 1996 was $40 billion.

Working in Ukraine over many years, EBA members are aware of the potential of a large and resource-rich country. Those with whom they work, and those that they employ, have also become aware of the benefits that foreign investment can bring in terms of new technologies, expertise and capital.

A critical challenge for Ukraine is the attraction of significant new capital investment. International investment flows are huge, yet investors still face a choice about which opportunities to pursue and which to postpone or delay. In evaluating these options, a company must be confident of its ability to generate a return commensurate with the risks taken. Availability of natural and human resources are key criteria in this decision-making process. However, most important is a stable, clear and predictable business environment, where the legal, fiscal and commercial terms under which the investments are made are clearly defined, and consistently and fairly applied.

The report notes some specific problems related to the business environment, and puts forward the Association's own suggestions on ways in which these might be resolved. However, the specific points are secondary to two fundamental categories of risk associated with doing business in Ukraine. The Association considers that a concentration on these two areas is a necessary condition for the creation of an internationally competitive investment climate:

- Decreasing intervention in the operation of private businesses. Excessive state presence, intervention and regulation is a pervasive encumbrance on the operation of private businesses, and market mechanisms in general. While many Western European countries have significant levels of public ownership, nowhere is this incompatible with a flourishing private sector. In Ukraine the private sector contributes less than a quarter of GDP; it needs to be given at least the chance to develop. To illustrate part of the problem: an EBRD survey in 1999 suggested that enterprise management in Ukraine spends up to 17 per cent of overall management time in complying with government regulatory requirements; this finding coincides with the experience of EBA members.

• Increasing consistency, stability and uniform application of legislation. Ukraine has a vast body of legislation and regulation, some of which is contradictory, some on occasion introduced retroactively, without any clear hierarchy of legislative acts to establish precedence. Interpretation, enforcement and execution of legal acts is far from predictable across the country.

The often discussed issue of corruption in Ukraine is a symptom of the failure to make adequate progress on these two problems. To assist with their resolution, the EBA has urged the Ukrainian authorities to pursue a consistent objective of increasing regulatory transparency and business liberalisation. Where possible, Ukraine should look to adopt international standards on a whole host of issues from accounting and banking through to health, safety and the environment. If such measures can be introduced, rigorously applied and enforced, Ukraine can do much to gain the confidence of both foreign and domestic investors.

Ukraine also maintains some significant barriers to import, not only through high tariffs on certain goods (insulin is a case in point), but mainly through some formidable non-tariff barriers. Chief among these is the existing system of standards and certification, which is both complex, expensive, and out of line with EU and international standards. The Association understands that reform measures are included in three new pieces of legislation being considered by parliament, and welcomes the willingness of the current leadership of the State Committee on Standards and Certification to discuss the substantive measures proposed. Nonetheless, companies believe that more can be done in the interim to improve procedures and fee structures for receiving Ukrainian certificates.

Alongside standards and certification, the Ukrainian sanitary, phytosanitary, ecological and veterinary controls are also opaque and inconsistent. A current example is the fact that hygiene certificates (as well as certificates of conformity) are often, but not always, required for motor vehicles and certain building materials. In many cases, evaluation and registration are managed by state enterprises granted monopoly power to charge for their services.

Imported products supplied to Ukrainian and foreign businesses in Ukraine require maintenance to maximise uptime. However, the import of spare parts can be at least as complex as the import of the equipment itself, if not more so, and this means that foreign suppliers cannot meet their own targets for a high level and speed of service. In addition, for instance where an entire piece of equipment needs to be removed to Western Europe for repair, there is no workable procedure for temporary export.

Fees for services related to the import of goods are high, and often not related to the service provided. Port fees in Ukraine are the highest on the Black Sea, fees for evaluation and registration of other goods (pharmaceuticals, crop protection products) are also expensive. Even where such fees are nominally equal for all market participants, there is some evidence that individual local applicants can enjoy significant discounts (and even exemptions from registration requirements through devices such as one-time allowances).

The EBA nonetheless welcomes progress in 2000 in adopting new and more transparent procedures for the registration of pharmaceutical and crop protection products. These, as well as many other decisions of the new Ukrainian Government, sent a clear signal to the private sector about its willingness to co-operate and to resolve the problems of foreign investors in a constructive way.

In preparing this report, the EBA was trying not only to identify the scope of problems, but, based on international expertise and experience, to offer some creative approaches to their solution. Only through an open dialogue with the Ukrainian Government can we count on further positive changes in the Ukrainian economy, which are a prerequisite for sustainable growth and stability.

The complete text of the EBA report 'Barriers to Investment in Ukraine' can be found on the EBA website: www.eba.com.ua

A SUCCESS STORY
UKRAINE INTERNATIONAL AIRLINES

Richard Creagh

To avid readers of the international business press, the expression 'success in Ukraine' must appear a bit of an oxymoron. For those who have lived through the re-birth of this nation, Ukrainian success is to be applauded and supported. One such success is Ukraine International Airlines. This is its story.

When it became independent in 1991 Ukraine inherited a share of the old Soviet airline Aeroflot, which became and remains Air Ukraine. Some in the airline business however thought that the fleet, standards and image were not sufficient to service the needs of the newly emerging democracy, and that there was room in the market for a wholly new and independent national airline.

Ukraine International Airlines (UIA) was founded in 1992 as an independent closed joint stock company whose shares were held by the Ukrainian Government (87 per cent) and GPA Group (13 per cent).

The objectives set out for the company were to

- create a modern, competitive international Ukrainian airline;
- extend Ukraine's international, economic, cultural and tourist relations;
- introduce advanced technology and management methods;
- integrate Ukraine's air transport into the international network;

- attract foreign investment;
- earn profits.

The original capital came from GPA Group PLC, an Irish company, from whom the airline leased its first aircraft. The new company had a mixed management team, with Ukrainians from the Ukrainian Association of Civil Aviation and a group of Western experts as part of an initial investment by GPA of $6.5 million equity plus loans. The Ukrainian Government shareholding was transferred to the State Property Fund to facilitate further privatisation.

The company took delivery of two new Boeing 737s and celebrated its first flight, to London, in November 1992. These were the first new Boeings to appear in the former Soviet Union. From the outset the airline aimed to be one of the most professional airlines in the region in terms of service, reliability and efficiency, with all its staff trained to the highest standards by Western airlines. In 1996, when UIA was already established in the market and had made operating and net profits, Austrian Airlines and Swiss Air saw its potential and bought 18 per cent of the equity. This was not just an injection of capital; it provided additional expertise that enabled the company to develop even faster and gave the fledgling airline a new credibility in the aviation industry. The relationship is managed through an Alliance Steering Committee composed of senior management from the three airlines. This forum provides extensive support for UIA in all aspects of the business.

In 2000 the European Bank for Reconstruction and Development became a ten per cent shareholder in UIA, investing new equity and adding new expertise. The two airlines, the EBRD and debis AirFinance (GPA's successor) have seats on the Board of UIA and have the right to appoint the Deputy President and Financial Controller; but the day-to-day management is left in the hands of the UIA team.

Today UIA is arguably the leading East European airline. Customer feedback ranks its service better than that of most of its Western competitors. The company has 126 interline agreements and has code sharing arrangements with Austrian Airlines, Finnair, KLM, Iberia, Sabena and Swiss Air, operating 88 flights a week to 13 destinations. Over 50 per cent of the passengers then fly on to some 2,300 destinations worldwide. UIA is one of the few East European airlines to operate same-day interconnect services to almost anywhere on the globe. In 2000 UIA moved just under half a million passengers.

In 1999 UIA achieved another advance in being the first East European airline to buy its own aircraft. The new Boeing 737-300, named after the Kipling character Mowgli (MAU being the Ukrainian for UIA), has become a bit of a national celebrity and was recently used to transport the Pope on his visit to Ukraine. Two additional aircraft are to be added to the fleet in 2002. In 1998 UIA's engineering department was the first in the former Soviet Union to be awarded JAR145 status by Bureau Veritas, showing UIA's maintenance standards to be no less than those of many of the world's leading carriers and dispelling the myth that all East European airlines are unreliable. UIA's reliability and punctuality are on a par with the world's best.

As described above, UIA's ownership structure has changed since it was set up. It remains 63 per cent owned by the State Property Fund (though it operates on a wholly commercial basis with no state subsidy or support), with the balance of the shares owned by the Western investors including partner airlines and the EBRD. UIA has to compete on a level basis in the maelstrom that is world air travel. Yet it has succeeded in the marketplace; it is the only East European airline with quality Western airline and EBRD investment; has run an operating profit for 8 out of its 9 years; is unique in code-sharing with 6 of the big names in European aviation; attracts a large proportion of choosy Western passengers; and is not supported by state handouts. How has it managed not only to survive but to flourish in what is agreed to be a difficult investment climate in Ukraine?

Part of the answer lies in top class management: customer focus and a corporate philosophy of striving for excellence; training and good management throughout the chain of command; success in attracting foreign investment and loan funding; good marketing, distribution and sales; good cost control; excellence in operations, maintenance and resource management.

Beyond that, UIA works because the management are a team ready to be flexible and adapt to both ex-Soviet bureaucratic cultures and Western business philosophies. We aim to combine best Western business practice with the reality of life in Ukraine. In the same way that the Ukrainian management has had to learn Western business techniques, so the Western team members have had to learn how to do business in Kiev. It is a two-way street where both parties recognise the skills of the other. UIA had to learn very quickly that if you want to compete successfully you have to be better than your competitors, and that means training, professionalism, understanding, patience, a long term outlook and above all the will to succeed.

Even with the difficult problems that all airlines face today Ukraine International is confident in its ability to cope and grow stronger.

On this basis UIA has confounded the pundits, overcome negative perceptions and become a real example of what is possible in the region if opportunity is combined with best business practice.

JUSTICE AND HOME AFFAIRS BEYOND ENLARGEMENT

WHAT KIND OF BORDER?

Inna Pidluska

Ukraine, while seeing the European Union as an area of freedom, security and prosperity and seeking integration into the European Community, has been too slow in transforming itself to be a credible applicant for EU membership. The EU, for its part, has taken a wait-and-see position on Ukraine. Yet, issues of immediate concern and practical significance for both Ukraine and the EU demand a new quality of dialogue and interaction. Foremost among those issues is justice and home affairs (JHA).

The conclusions of the June 2001 Gothenburg summit suggest that Ukraine will become closer to the European Union shortly – at least geographically, with Ukraine's Western border becoming the Eastern border of the enlarged EU. And yet, neither Ukraine, nor its immediate neighbours to the West who are likely to join the EU in the near future, nor the EU itself appear to be fully prepared for the new situation or to have a clear understanding of how to put into practice their declared determination to prevent the emergence of new dividing lines in Europe. While both sides have stated their intention to develop a working relationship, Ukraine and the EU need to produce effective solutions to the challenges linked to enlargement, and to involve Ukraine in the European integration process.

The 1998 Strategy of Integration of Ukraine to the European Union laid particular emphasis on the fact that as a result of enlargement Ukraine would have a common border with the EU, which 'would create a principally new geopolitical situation' that required a 'clear and comprehensive definition of the foreign policy strategy concerning Ukraine's integration to the European political, economic and legal space'. The Strategy, modelled closely on Poland's EU accession strategy, defined co-operation in JHA, as one of the principal guidelines of the integration process. The Ukrainian leadership has repeatedly expressed concern over the reluctance of the EU to include Ukraine in the enlargement process and called for consultations on ways of minimising the potential negative impact of EU enlargement on Ukraine, formalising and institutionalising Ukraine-EU co-operation in the field of JHA in order to enhance the effectiveness of all existing instruments in relations between Ukraine and the EU. The proposals were formally presented as a series of position papers and memoranda to relevant EU bodies. While the EU has shown limited enthusiasm for Ukraine's initiatives, some practical results have been achieved.

While the policy of European integration has been promoted as a foreign policy priority by the Ukrainian leadership and supported by a part of the political elite, it still enjoys limited understanding and support from the general population. Overall awareness of EU issues, the enlargement process and the costs/benefits of integration remains critically low and this has a negative impact on policy-making. This is particularly true in the field of JHA. The complexity of the challenges faced by Ukraine, the lack of unbiased information and capacity to counter the challenges effectively, have provoked – amid increasingly frequent warnings that Ukraine risks becoming a centre for illegal migration and organised crime, and growing resentment among Ukrainians at being treated as potential illegal migrants by EU consular officials – a specific 'side effect'. While accurate data on the correlation between illegal migration, organised crime and drug trafficking are not available, Ukrainian law enforcement agencies tend to link the three phenomena in their public statements, thus adding to prejudice against 'other' ethnic groups and countries in Ukrainian society. Ukrainians themselves are affected by the growing xenophobia in EU member and candidate states, where public fear of an influx of cheap labour, potential instability and dilution of national identity are on the rise. It is estimated that some 500,000 illegal immigrants arrived in the EU in 2000, compared with about 40,000 in 1993. The influx of immigrants into Western Europe, both legal and illegal, has increased 20-fold in the last decade, and Ukraine is seen as one of the key transit countries. Some 60-70 per cent of illegal migrants are reported to arrive in Western Europe via Ukraine. As the Western border of Ukraine becomes 'harder', with the adoption of Schengen rules by candidate countries, and so long as Ukraine's Eastern and Northern borders remain 'porous', thousands of illegal migrants are likely to stay in Ukraine. Since the situation in the main countries of origin is unlikely to improve fast, the challenge of illegal migration, as well as the related challenges of organised crime, trafficking in human beings and drugs, are likely to remain among the main points of concern for Ukraine as well as for the EU.

The pursuit of European integration in general, and co-operation in JHA between Ukraine and the EU, have been substantially hindered by Ukraine's lack of a specialised agency to formulate, co-ordinate, implement and monitor European integration efforts. There is now a Ministry of Economy and European Integration, and a special Department of European Integration within the MFA to co-ordinate diplomatic efforts aiming at rapprochement with Europe – but no single body or integrated strategy for dealing with JHA. JHA issues are dealt with by at least 8 government bodies. As a result, steps taken may be inconsistent and even contradictory due to the lack of joint policy planning, co-ordination and information sharing.

An effort to improve the situation was made with the adoption of the Government's 'Priorities for stimulating economic activity, savings and investment, and the creation of conditions for sustainable economic growth in 2002-2004'. Specific tasks in the area of JHA included the order to the Ministry of the Interior to implement a Complex Programme for Preventing Crime in 2001-2005 and to draft a National Programme for Preventing the Spread of Drugs and Reducing Demand for them for the period up to 2005. The MFA was ordered to increase inter-departmental co-ordination to try to minimise any negative consequences of EU enlargement, primarily the introduction of the 'hard border regime'. Some of the steps set out in the programmes and initiatives have already been taken, but overall success will depend on consistent and sustained effort.

The challenge

Presenting a draft law on immigration to parliament in November 2000, the President's official representative argued that both immigration to and migration through Ukraine had been growing rapidly. The estimated number of illegal migrants from countries of Asia and Africa in Ukraine currently exceeds 100,000, but this only reflects the number of those detained. Applications for Ukrainian citizenship increased from 5,763 in 1994 to 72,797 in 1999. To date, only about 3,000 people, over 1,600 of them from Afghanistan, have formal refugee status. However, the number of people claiming citizenship, asylum or permanent residence is not the principal matter of concern. The problem is that while in 1991 only 148 illegal migrants were detained in Ukraine, by the end of 2000 the figure had reached 15,000 a year. At least 1.6 million illegal migrants had stayed in Ukraine, and more than 80,000 had been detained in 1991-1999, at a cost to the Ukrainian budget of at least US$ 300 million a year – a substantial sum for a country like Ukraine. In 2001, however, the number of illegal migrants detained in Ukraine has been reduced by about 30 percent – presumably due to improved border management and migration control. In 1999-2000, illegal migrants in Ukraine were reportedly victims of 4,742 crimes and committed 1,240 crimes. Trafficking in human beings has grown into a leading 'specialisation' for Ukrainian organised crime and the third most profitable activity after drug dealing and sales of stolen cars.

Illegal migration through Ukraine is not the only reason why Ukraine is included in the 'black list' of countries for which EU visa procedures are particularly strict. There is also a problem of illegal labour migration from Ukraine itself to EU and CEE countries. It is estimated that 60-100,000 Ukrainians work illegally in Poland, over 40,000 in the Czech Republic and about 10,000 in Hungary. In addition to 8,000 Ukrainians who hold formal permits to work in Italy, over 120,000 are there illegally. Currently diplomats are negotiating the possible 'legalising' of some of these as a part of Italy's annual 185,000 immigration quota in exchange for an agreement to return illegal migrants to Ukraine. Of 303,000 registered immigrants in Portugal, there are at least 80,000 Ukrainians. The real figure, however, is believed to be about three times as high.

In response, Ukraine has adopted a number of legal measures designed to help improve the situation. At present Ukraine has a broad (though still inadequate) legal framework for countering illegal migration and organised crime under a series of presidential decrees. Ukraine has ratified the European Convention on money laundering and a number of other conventions on fighting organised crime, and signed bilateral agreements on mutual legal assistance in combating crime with Hungary, Finland, Poland, Cyprus, Lithuania, Estonia, and Latvia. However, Ukraine's efforts to counter illegal migration are hindered by the lack of readmission agreements with countries of origin of illegal migrants and transit states. To help cope, in mid-February 2001 the Ukrainian parliament passed a law introducing criminal liability for repeated illegal border crossing. In June 2001, 351 out of 450 members of parliament voted in favour of a law introducing an annual immigration quota (to be specified by the government) and establishing a single national executive agency for migration. The new law will allow legalisation of immigration status for a number of foreigners and stateless persons, for instance those who came to Ukraine before March 1998 under a 1981 USSR/Vietnam agreement on professional training and work, or refugees from Abkhazia (Georgia) who have lived in Ukraine for at least five years. Immigration will also be open to officially registered refugees and their dependents who have lived in Ukraine for at least three years. However, the potential benefits from these measures may be limited by the scope of the problem as well as by the lack of an adequate response to related challenges.

'Why bother?'

Ukraine - EU relations are not limited to the issues of borders, visas, countering illegal migration, trafficking, drugs and organised crime. However, co-operation in JHA is urgent, and critical to countering the threats to stability and security and to mitigating insecurity, xenophobia and fear in Europe. Co-operation in this field could be one of the most effective and realistic aspects of the much-discussed Ukraine-EU 'strategic partnership'. The alternative, since candidate states must comply fully with the Schengen regime before they actually join the EU, would be a prominent 'Schengen wall' between the enlarged EU and Ukraine.

Currently Ukrainian citizens can travel visa-free to 15 countries: ten countries of the CIS (all except Turkmenistan), Mongolia and four EU candidate states: Poland, Hungary, Bulgaria and Romania. Although both Poland and Hungary have officially announced their decision to refrain from imposing visas on Ukrainians as long as possible, the requirement to comply with the Schengen regime and the desire of the candidate states to join the EU even with 'second-class membership,' with delayed freedom of movement of labour, have prompted some of the candidate states to end previous visa-free arrangements with Ukraine. The visa regime introduced by the Czech Republic and Slovakia in the summer of 2000 showed the potential for damage to exchanges between those countries and Ukraine and led to steps to mitigate this. On 1 March 2001 Ukraine and Slovakia introduced a simplified visa regime involving free visas for certain professionals, children and students, and half-price visas for those travelling under bilateral cultural exchange programmes. An increase in consular staff also had a positive effect. Similarly, when the EU moved Bulgaria to the 'white list', Bulgaria announced it would impose visas on Ukrainians from June 2001, but then chose to postpone the step to October and make the visa regime as liberal and efficient as possible, to prevent the loss of Ukrainian tourists damaging the country's tourist industry.

The visa issue is particularly important in Ukrainian-Polish relations. Poland is keen to minimise the negative effects of its future EU membership not only because of the countries' strong historical and cultural ties but also the intensive contacts at the micro level between Eastern Polish and Western Ukrainian regions, amounting to more than 10 million border crossings a year and nourishing a substantial part of the economy on both sides of the border. The introduction of visas – even with new consulates and buildings, advanced equipment, and a selection of affordable long-term visas – will inevitably reduce this bilateral exchange and could cost up to 60 percent of jobs in some towns. Poland is therefore actively seeking ways to optimise visa procedures for Ukraine and co-operate in managing their common border. Recommendations offered by the Institute of Public Affairs (Poland) include modernising border checkpoints and improving the staffing and performance of consulates to enable them to issue about 5,000 visas a day in Eastern Europe, and introducing a variety of visas to simplify travel for individuals. The options suggested include the introduction – prior to EU accession and for the transition period between accession and the imposition of the Schengen regime for citizens of the new Member States – of a national long-term, probably multiple-entry visa valid only for entry to the candidate state that issued it, and low-cost short-term single-entry visas. Multiple Schengen visas for frequent travellers, businessmen, academics, professionals and residents of the border regions are also seen as a way of maintaining intensive cross-border exchange.

Poland is also assisting Ukraine to manage its borders better. On 25 June 2001 Ukraine and Poland signed an agreement on joint control of the border designed to facilitate co-operation between borderguards and the sharing of checkpoints, enabling Ukraine to reduce personnel on its Western border while strengthening the Ukrainian-Russian border in order to combat illegal entry. Ukrainian border guards have been dismantling the remaining Soviet-era barbed wire barriers on the Western border and introducing new 'border rangers' – inspectors who will live near the border and prevent the use of local paths and residents for illegal migration. Ukraine is also preparing to reduce the number of border guards on the Western border while tripling it on the Eastern border. However, it is unlikely that a simple increase in numbers will make much difference.

Ukraine's Eastern border: a 'Sister Nation' dilemma

In June 2001 the Ukrainian government adopted a resolution under which citizens of all CIS states need valid foreign passports to enter Ukraine. (Previously travel was regulated by the 1992 CIS Convention, which Ukraine never signed but de facto observed, and citizens of any CIS state could enter Ukraine with any identity document.) However the resolution does not apply to citizens of Russia and Belarus, though it is believed that a substantial proportion – up to 90 percent, according to some estimates – of illegal migrants who enter Ukraine and stay or head further West come from or through Russia, Belarus and South-Eastern parts of the CIS. Building 'proper' borders with Russia is problematic at least as long as Ukraine is dependent on and heavily indebted to Russia for energy supplies. The EU has expressed its readiness to earmark some funding to strengthen Ukraine's Eastern border.

However, enthusiastic hopes that the burden of illegal migration on Ukraine would be reduced through strong Eastern borders vanished when an MFA official told the press that no demarcation of the Ukrainian-Russian border was envisaged, both because it was 'not on the agenda' and 'technically impossible to do'. This statement caused such a vivid reaction in the media and opinion-forming circles that a day later the First Deputy Foreign Minister had to clarify that although for the time being the Ukrainian-Russian negotiations focused on delimitation of the border, Ukraine was determined to have proper borders with all its neighbouring states. Foreign Minister Zlenko subsequently explained that delimitation of the Ukrainian-Russian border, '97 per cent agreed', would be completed by the end of 2001 and that both delimitation and demarcation were national security issues. Given the presence of up to 2 million illegal migrants in Russia, likely to increase to some 3 million shortly unless adequate measures are taken, Ukraine's desire to establish proper border management arrangements is natural, as it affects Ukraine's security as well as its prospects for integration into the EU.

Trying to cope

Seeking to respond adequately to the challenge of illegal migration, Ukraine introduced into its Criminal Code from 1 September 2001 criminal liability for organising illegal migration and trafficking in human beings. From early 2000 to mid-2001, the authorities claim to have 'terminated' more than 90 illegal migration and trafficking channels and detained more than 400 organised groups of illegal migrants. At least 1300 foreigners involved in organising trafficking in human beings have been deported from Ukraine. In the first eight months of 2001 Ukrainian border guards detained 3542 illegal migrants, 7905 individuals were denied permission to enter Ukraine, and over 1300 illegal migrants were handed over to border guards of neighbouring states. The media regularly publish information from law enforcement agencies about the detention of groups of illegal migrants and arrests of (mostly transnational) organised criminal gangs involved in trafficking hard drugs from Pakistan, India and Thailand through Russia and Ukraine to the EU. In 2000, for instance, the media were invited to view a demonstrative burning of 624 kilos of cocaine captured in transit through Ukraine to Belgium. In

2000 alone, Ukraine signed 28 legal documents on international terrorism, illicit drug trafficking and illegal migration, but Ukrainian efforts in these fields are unlikely to be effective until corruption and involvement in illegal migration and trafficking among border guards and police officers, readily admitted by the law-enforcement agencies, is eliminated.

As fighting illegal migration was identified as a key national security concern, in 2000 the number of visas issued by Ukraine to citizens of countries regarded as potential sources of illegal migrants was radically reduced. About 149,000 Ukrainian visas were issued in January-June 2000, almost 90 per cent of them to citizens of European countries, the USA and Canada. In the same period in 2001, the number of foreigners arriving in Ukraine was up to 6 times as high. This rapid increase led to the introduction from 1 July 2001 of new streamlined rules for the registration of foreigners in Ukraine. Previously it took up to several days and cost $30 for a foreigner to register with a local agency of the Ministry of the Interior, causing massive dissatisfaction to visiting foreigners. Under the new arrangements, registration at the border will take about 2 minutes and be free of charge. It is expected that all border checkpoints will be fully equipped with the relevant IT by 2003.

Another project, 'The Common Border', involves joint policing of the Ukrainian-Russian, Ukrainian-Moldovan and the Ukrainian-Belarusian borders, improvement in the border infrastructure and equipment for document checks, and maintenance of a common database. The aim is to make border crossing more civilised while reducing the porosity that has made Ukraine an attractive transit state. A number of immigrants enter Ukraine legally, e.g. to study, but then head West as illegal migrants to Western Europe. For instance, in 2000 alone two thirds of foreigners officially arriving in Ukraine to study in Kharkiv were later detained when attempting to cross Ukraine's Western border. In order to reduce the scope for illegal transit, from 25 July 2001 all foreigners are required to fill out an immigration form, part of which is kept at the point of entry and the other part attached to the passport. This procedure, similar to Schengen practice, should help combat illegal migration.

How can Ukraine – EU co-operation be further enhanced?

Even though the EU does not regard Ukraine as a suitable candidate for accession at present, there are areas in which closer co-operation is possible, mutually beneficial and thus highly desirable. These include common policies on countering organised crime, a common asylum and immigration policy, and a common foreign and security policy. Ukraine will soon border the EU, and it would be sensible, as long as European integration remains Ukraine's strategic goal, for it to shape its JHA policies and practices to be compatible with those of the EU. Co-operation in these fields is being established, and may develop successfully with more co-ordination and compatibility. Expert-level talks should continue on visa policies and ways of preventing negative consequences from the imposition of a visa regime on Ukraine by the EU candidate states.

A new quality of dialogue may be reached with the Belgian Presidency's efforts to develop a network of Member States and candidates to counter organised crime and trafficking in human beings and to regulate migration. In this context, the EC's prospective Action Plan for JHA for Ukraine, announced by Chris Patten in March 2001, can contribute substantially to increasing the efficacy of Ukraine's border control and customs services and reducing the flow of illegal migrants through Ukraine. Initial EC funding for improving border controls in Ukraine (and Moldova) – 3.9 million Euros – will be made available through Tacis, but it remains to be seen how effectively it will be used. The lack of a coherent integrated border management strategy and a single body responsible for coordinating JHA activities in Ukraine may have a dramatic effect on the whole effort.

Co-operation with the EU and the candidate states in the field of JHA gives Ukraine an important role in the integration process that does not need to be limited to (and perceived as) that of a buffer zone, a cordon sanitaire or 'the last barrier'. Priorities for Ukraine in this field are completing demarcation of the Eastern border, finding financial resources for the construction of temporary detention facilities and deporting illegal immigrants, and establishing a single executive entity to deal with migration issues. When asked what help is needed, Ukrainian officials routinely ask for money for detention centres and deportations. Such funds may help deal with the consequences of illegal migration but cannot remedy the cause. Opportunities for Ukraine-EU co-operation include creation of a common information environment and information-sharing on organised crime, corruption and money laundering, transfer of practical experience and skills, and EU support for the development of Ukraine's border management and control infrastructure. Those steps will require a substantial increase in technical and financial assistance from the EU, but the benefits of successful co-operation will greatly exceed the costs.

It is generally accepted that a visa regime alone is not an effective barrier to illegal migration, drugs and organised crime. In order to maintain the integration processes in Europe and transform it into a single security area, flexible and innovative approaches are needed in responding to common challenges. In the early 1990s, new opportunities for free movement in Central and Eastern Europe contributed substantially to overcoming historic grievances and mutual prejudice. Regional exchange and co-operation should not vanish after EU enlargement.

Objectively, burdened with enlargement and stressed by the newly-found need to become more comprehensible and closer to its own citizens, the EU is unlikely to change its vision of Ukraine from a 'strategic partner' to a candidate state until after the first wave of enlargement – and until Ukraine is ready to accept that change. The EU seems to be clear about what it does not want – it does not want Ukraine to turn into an unreformed source of insecurity, instability, organised crime and illegal migration, or an integral part of an unfriendly Russia-led pact. Yet the EU is not entirely clear about what it does want Ukraine to become, and has not been explicit enough in separating its policies towards Russia and Ukraine, or considering Ukraine other than as part of Russia's sphere of influence. Co-operation in JHA may be an answer to the insecurity challenge and an indicator of Ukraine's readiness for a broader dialogue with the EU.

NOTES

Facts and figures in this paper are taken from official and other public sources. Particularly useful references are

Ukrainian news agencies 'Interfax-Ukraina' (www.interfax.com) and UNIAN

www.liga.kiev.ua

www.mignews.com.ua

Ukrainian government websites:

Ministry of Foreign Affairs (www.mfa.gov.ua)

Ministry of Justice (www.minjust.gov.ua)

Security Service (www.ssu.gov.ua)

Further reading:

Oleksandr Pavliuk: 'Ukraine and the EU: the Risk of being Excluded' in Iris Kempe (ed.) *'Beyond EU Enlargement'*, volume 1, Bertelsmann Foundation Publishers, 2001.

This paper was produced within the International Policy Fellowship awarded by the Centre for Policy Studies of the Open Society Institute as part of a research monograph on relations between Ukraine and the EU within and beyond the enlargement process.

EU AID POLICY
MORE COMMITMENT REQUIRED

Andre Vanhaeverbeke

Introduction

It is in the EU's strategic interest that Ukraine should be able to maintain a real independence, become a prosperous economic partner integrated into the market economy and, on these bases, consolidate its democracy (respect for human rights and minorities, development of the rule of law, civil society etc.).

Ukraine's main interest in developing closer relations with the EU is to benefit from its economic dynamism but also to some extent to help the transformation of its own society into a Western-style democracy. For Ukraine it is also a matter of counterbalancing the influence of its Eastern neighbour in both the economic and political field.

This convergence of interests formed the basis for the Partnership and Co-operation Agreement (PCA) which was ratified at the beginning of 1998 and is the legal basis for co-operation between the EU and Ukraine. This Agreement above all institutes a permanent 'political dialogue' through regular meetings (summits at Head of State level, Council of Ministers, co-operation with the European Parliament etc.) with two key objectives: the consolidation of democracy and the creation of a market economy open to the world. There is also a specific objective in the nuclear field aimed at resolving the problem of Chernobyl and improving nuclear safety in the country's other reactors.

Various financial instruments were put in place to underpin these policies: Tacis for support for policy reforms, including nuclear safety issues; a system of long-term loans to support the balance of payments, and Euratom loans to assist with Chernobyl. To these should be added some contributions to emergency humanitarian aid financed by ECHO (European Community Humanitarian Organisation).

It should be noted that neither the PCA nor later the EU Common Strategy on Ukraine mention Ukraine's future integration into the EU, the fundamental driver of Ukrainian policy. For the EU, discussion of this issue is premature. The immediate priority now should be implementation of the PCA, which will itself create the basic prerequisites for accession. On the other hand, a 'road map' is referred to here and there, and one of its first steps, the creation of a free trade area, is explicitly mentioned as an objective of the PCA. A further step could be the establishment of a Common Economic Space similar in conception to the European Economic Space.

The Ukrainians realise that there is still a long way to go before they are able to fulfil the entry requirements (the Copenhagen criteria). But nevertheless, they would like to be recognised as eligible for membership. This eligibility should be taken as a valuable psychological signal giving direction to their reforms. That political signal can also be seen as a non-military element of security guaranteeing Ukraine's independence.

Financial elements of European co-operation

EU support is not limited to financial assistance. In addition to political support for Ukraine's integration into the Western Euro-Atlantic structures, one should also note Europe's willingness to take account of Ukraine's difficulties with transition in its opening to international trade, whether in the commercial part of the PCA, in negotiating sectoral trade agreements (for example the recent textiles agreement), or in negotiations on accession to the WTO.

But in a country like Ukraine, facing grave problems of public sector finance, funding in support of policy reforms can play a key role. The following are the main areas of EU activity:

1. Tacis, the chief financial instrument of EU aid, was renewed in 2000 for 4 years. Run by the European Commission, it commits on average about 100 million Euros per year to Ukraine in the form of grants. These allocations are distributed under an annual national Action Plan, regional programmes covering problems of regional or cross-border interest, and, in the case of Ukraine, a nuclear safety programme.

1.1. The current (1999-2002) national Action Plan addresses 4 major priority areas:

- Legal and institutional reforms;

- Support for economic reforms (small and medium enterprises, enterprise restructuring, privatisation, banking reform, etc.);

- Energy: reform of the electricity and coal sector, energy efficiency and conservation;

- More recently, facilitating co-operation on border crossing and border management with front-line candidate states (Poland, Hungary).

Another interesting development is the gradual inclusion of help with the social consequences of transition, especially aspects of public health (the fight against tuberculosis and Aids). In this context, one important area of the programme relates to the reform of Ukrainian university education.

1.2. The regional and cross-border programmes deal mainly with protection of the environment, border crossing, the organisation and management of energy transit (oil and gas) and the creation of major international transport routes.

1.3. The nuclear safety programmes, including the closure and dismantling of Chernobyl, occupy a major place in European co-operation. Within the framework of the G7 Memorandum, the Commission has committed more than 1200 million Euros to nuclear safety, to be allocated as follows:

- 600 million in the form of a grant for the decommissioning of Chernobyl's reactors, reconstruction of the shelter, and the treatment of waste;

- Since the closure of the last reactor the Commission has in addition promised 65 million Euros over 3 years for the purchase of fuel to compensate for the loss of electricity output;

- Above all the Commission has decided to grant a $585 million Euratom loan to complete the two reactors whose output will compensate for the closure of Chernobyl. This loan will, it is hoped, become operational at the end of 2001 when the conditions to be fulfilled by Ukraine (including reform of the electricity sector) are met and all the funds required ($1.4 million) are in place;

- Finally, part of the Tacis funding is used to improve safety in the reactors which are operational.

This is therefore an area where EU action has been important in financial terms and will have a decisive impact on nuclear safety to the benefit not only of Ukraine but of the whole of Europe.

2. Balance of payment loans (around 400 million Euros so far) are granted on a long-term basis on international market terms, and hence very advantageous for Ukraine. They are disbursed basically in accordance with IMF conditionality plus some commercial conditions linked to PCA implementation.

3. Lastly Ukraine has also benefited from the emergency humanitarian programme (ECHO). This is financially limited but has been able to play an important role at the local level in mitigating the social consequences of Chernobyl and natural disasters (floods etc.).

Impact of the EU Programme: neither visible nor concrete

To assess its impact, one must consider EU aid as part of Western aid as a whole. This involves a division of labour: the international financial institutions (IFIs) deal with macroeconomic reforms supported by balance of payments assistance, and the World Bank and EBRD with sectoral and investment support, while the EU and US aid concentrate essentially on policy advice and technical assistance. It is the IFIs which, having the financial clout, have the real leverage in terms of reform.

For sure, the EU is listened to by Ukraine, whose primary goal is to join one day, but its direct impact on policy choices is not as great as its political attraction for lack of adequate financial instruments to assist implementation of changes and reforms. Actually, set against the massive need for public funding to support industrial restructuring and mitigate the social consequences of transition, Tacis's 100 million Euros per year (equivalent to approximately the cost of an Airbus A 340) seems derisory. Even the totality of Western financial help seems tiny in comparison with the scale of the problems.

As President Clinton once said speaking of Russia, but it is even more true for Ukraine, this country will require a Marshall Plan to recover. Obviously, massive external public sector funding can be justified only as a support to profound reform. The problem therefore is establishing a confidence-building process between the partners.

The domestic and foreign private sector should of course progressively play their part, but this can only complement action on restructuring and reform requiring external public sector funding.

Towards a more visible, identifiable and concrete European co-operation

Tacis is a valuable tool which has been effective in certain areas. But in comparison with the role the EU could play in a Ukraine with a European vocation, it is grossly inadequate. It should be accompanied by instruments of public investment supporting the effective implementation of reforms, as in Central and Eastern Europe, where Phare and the European Investment Bank play a major role.

If the EU is to acquire greater legitimacy vis-à-vis public opinion both at home and in Ukraine, it must – in addition to providing funding, advice and technical assistance – help to resolve concrete problems of direct relevance to the lives of citizens and give priority to areas where important common interests are involved.

For example, Ukraine plays an important role in the transit of Russian gas to the EU, and will do so in future for Caspian oil. These are major EU interests. There is potential to establish a 'strategic partnership' between producers, consumers and transit countries, with the European Commission acting as facilitator, helping Ukraine to manage its pipeline network on the basis of purely professional and commercial criteria with an essential role for the private sector.

There are many other examples of common interests, like public health, the fight against tuberculosis and Aids, and facilitating border crossing between Ukraine and candidate members of the EU to compensate for Schengen controls. So we have to get away from the present image of the EU as a man who, seeing someone drowning, advises him to learn to swim! For the future, the EU must create for itself an identity which provides a model for development, but also contributes to the pragmatic resolution of concrete problems, making transition sustainable in political and social terms.

Given that the success of the PCA and Ukraine's rapprochement with the EU are essentially European problems, the EU must play a leadership role, relying not only on policy advice and political dialogue but also on substantial financial contributions managed by its own structures, as in the candidate countries. The EU has to do its utmost in a visible and concrete way to avoid Ukraine sinking into despair, or being driven to choose options other than democracy and the market economy.

UKRAINE
WHERE NEXT?

Ann Lewis

It would be rash to draw any very sweeping conclusions from the diverse contributions to this book, but it is worth trying to pull together some of the main threads by looking at possible answers to some of the most obvious questions.

Is Ukraine serious about seeking European integration?

Ukraine proclaims European integration as its strategic foreign policy goal. But what is meant by 'integration' is sometimes unclear – perhaps deliberately so. Ukraine's most insistent demand is to be acknowledged as a fully European country, a member of the European family. This is not problematic, now that Ukraine is clearly established as a stable, secure and independent state – not something that could be taken for granted on independence. This in itself is a major achievement and a measure of how far Ukraine has progressed in a single decade.

Beyond that, Ukraine aspires to European integration in the sense of membership of the EU – at its most ambitious, full membership by 2007. It says it accepts the Copenhagen criteria, and has taken steps towards meeting them. But whether it has the political will to adopt and carry through all the necessary changes is less clear. Contributors to this book suggest that while some in the Ukrainian leadership understand and accept what is required, there is less understanding, let alone acceptance, in the middle layers of government, and even less among the general population. A major information programme is perhaps needed.

The desire for integration no doubt stems from a wish to join the most successful and prosperous club on the continent. The leadership's pressure on the EU to acknowledge that it can in principle join may additionally stem from amour-propre; a wish to be recognised as at least as advanced on the road to democracy as some of those already in the membership queue; and a desire for endorsement of the leadership's credentials.

Nevertheless it is doubtful whether anyone in Ukraine sees full membership of the EU as a realistic option in the near future. A more realistic option is associate membership, or joining the long queue of those whose right to join is recognised by the EU as and when the country meets the relevant criteria. So far the EU has withheld any undertaking to admit Ukraine as an accession country (though the European Parliament has taken a slightly more positive view).

Does Ukraine matter to the EU?

The answer to this would superficially seem obvious: a huge and potentially powerful country, strategically located on the EU's post-enlargement Eastern border, must matter. But Ukraine does not at present pose any great security threat. It is quiet, has maintained ethnic peace at home and causes no problems internationally. Some might argue (though not in public) that for it to be a client state of Russia, forming a buffer zone on the frontier of the EU, would suit Western interests well. Some in Ukraine so interpret the EU's caution, and in particular the way the EU has, as they perceive it, treated Ukraine as an element in its Russia policy rather than as a country in its own right.

At all events, this kind of attitude, if it ever existed in the EU, has faded into the background. Ukraine has clearly been rising up the EU agenda recently. This seems to be for both positive and negative reasons. The positive is a recognition that Ukraine has made some progress in reform and can play a useful role on the international scene; the negative that, if the wrong policies are pursued, Ukraine could be a major liability in relation to issues of increasing importance, such as illegal migration, drugs and organised crime, terrorism, and strategic energy supplies.

Why is the EU playing hard to get?

There is some truth in the Ukrainian assertion that the EU is treating Ukraine less favourably than certain countries which have been admitted to the membership queue although they are no further ahead with reform than Ukraine. The EU is charged with double standards.

All EU contributors to this book steer well clear of addressing this issue, and any comment can only be speculative. But a number of factors may apply:

- Ukraine is a large country with powerful industrial and agricultural potential; it is not a country that could easily be absorbed into the EU, unlike many of the smaller candidates;
- It has not engaged in wholehearted, rapid and radical transformation such as would make its candidacy difficult to refuse; but neither is it a major headache for the EU;
- It was late in coming to the table; by the time its approach came up for serious consideration, the EU was preoccupied with internal development and some EU governments (and their publics) were becoming increasingly concerned about the implications of enlargement and loath to make further commitments.

In short, Ukraine's approach was too little, too late. The EU's position would however look more untenable if Ukraine were clearly on a par with those accession countries likely to be first to join the EU.

How far is Ukraine from meeting the criteria?

This is one is the recurrent themes of this book, with many writers, both Ukrainian and Western, pointing to what might be called the 'unfinished business' of democratic transition. Alongside Ukraine's achievements, they point to a number of problem areas:

- A tendency to mistake the theoretical for the real, the declaration for action. Ukraine has an excellent constitutional and legal framework, and has signed many documents on human rights and other matters, but that does not help if commitments are not met in practice.

• The leadership's penchant for the 'administrative methods' of the communist state (like the traditional 'phonecall from the top'), coupled with a desire to have centralised control of the body politic. This denotes both a lack of respect for due process and a lack of trust in the individual citizen. One damaging result is a deep cynicism in the population, a lack of faith in democratic processes, and a turning away from civic involvement.

• The pervasive corruption, personal and systemic, which warps many aspects of life. Corruption in the judicial and law enforcement agencies, whose job is to uphold the rule of law, is particularly damaging. Equally pernicious is the influence of the oligarchs or clans, who support their business interests through puppet political parties, control of the media, shady dealings and private bank accounts overseas.

Ukraine has also been hampered by the lack of any strong individual or movement dedicated to real democracy, like those who inspired and led democratic reform in the most successful Central European countries. The reasons for this are not clear, but perhaps include a disaffection with politics in the corrupt environment or an inability to work together for a common good.

Is anything changing in Ukraine?

There are some signs of movement on the political scene, with the left no longer monolithic, the oligarchic parties liable to fall out when there is no common enemy to defeat, and signs at last of more reform-minded individuals entering the political scene. While it may be too late now for any radical change before the March 2002 parliamentary elections, there is scope for political realignment in time for the 2004 presidential election. These elections also provide Ukraine with an opportunity to demonstrate its democratic credentials. Observers will be looking not just at the conduct of the vote itself but at other aspects of the elections: whether parties have reasonable access to the media; whether the main TV channels provide balanced reportage; whether candidates and electoral officials are free from intimidation.

The growth in power of the oligarchs may have been slowed recently thanks to reforms which have increased the use of cash instead of barter in payment for energy supplies and introduced stricter tax-collection and budget management. Any decline in the power of the oligarchs would make more space for legitimate business, and if that could thrive there would be less temptation for others to go down the corrupt route. A desire for acceptance and international respectability has been an important factor in other countries in encouraging entrepreneurs down the straight and narrow. Legitimate business needs the rule of law for its own protection, thus increasing pressure for a law-based state.

The economic turnaround in 2000-2001 is the brightest spot on the Ukrainian scene, though growth can only be sustained if further reforms are carried out quickly. If they are, the strengthening of market mechanisms and fairer competition should encourage overseas investors, and overseas investment must be one of the keys to the modernisation of Ukraine's outmoded industries, including the crucial energy sector, and the establishment of new businesses more attuned to the needs of the twenty-first century. A substantial body of foreign investors would also give Ukraine a powerful lobby vis-à-vis Western governments.

There is hope that with economic growth permitting an improvement in living standards and welfare provision, the hard-pressed Ukrainian citizen will become more active in supporting democratic reform and participating in public life.

This may be too optimistic. It is not impossible that we shall see a stagnation in the reforms and a further strengthening of the oligarchs, or even a Ukraine retreating again into a Soviet-style society. But that would be a major set-back to Ukraine's European ambitions.

Can Ukraine achieve a foreign policy balance?

Externally, the main challenge for Ukraine is likely to be the balance between its relations with Russia and those with the EU and the USA – the country's three foreign policy priorities.

It is on Russian/Ukrainian relations that contributors to this book differ most widely. Given the two countries' shared past, common culture and extensive links at many levels, relations are and will inevitably remain close. But is Russia to be seen as a benevolent neighbour, happy to have equal relations with Ukraine and to see it form strong links with the West, perhaps using these to its own benefit? Or is Russia intent on preserving its traditional influence in Ukraine, by threats or coercion if necessary, exploiting the relationship for political and economic reasons, and anxious to disrupt any closer links with the West? Russia has not hesitated to exploit Ukraine's dependence in the past, though scope for this may become less with the recent movement on the debt problem.

Views no doubt differ within both leaderships about how to handle the other country. If Ukraine can be viewed as a child who has reached maturity and left home, the wise parent knows that the best way to preserve a strong relationship is to let the child go, establish its independence and form new relationships. The wise young adult knows that unpaid obligations can distort and sour a relationship.

What is clear is that the EU and the West in general have no interest in forcing Ukraine to make a choice: a strong Ukraine with good relations with all its neighbours can contribute best to European and regional stability.

It is too soon to judge how far the recent coming together of Russia and the West in the campaign against terrorism, and Russia's new interest in strengthening its own relationship with the EU, will affect Ukraine. On the one hand it could help ease some of the tensions in Ukraine's balancing act; but equally it could reduce interest in Ukraine from both sides. At all events Ukraine was quick to express solidarity with the anti-terrorism campaign and to permit use of its airspace. Given that Ukraine is one of the main routes for smuggling from Afghanistan via Russia to Western Europe, it has the potential to play a significant role in certain aspects of the anti-terrorism campaign, and may be able to use the situation to consolidate its relations with both East and West.

What can the EU do to encourage and support Ukraine on the path of reform?

There are many suggestions scattered throughout this book. The most sweeping proposes a hugely increased level of support on the lines of the Marshall Plan. This seems unlikely given the current focus on other priorities in the Middle East and elsewhere. But some re-focusing of current policies and programmes should be possible and in some cases is already in hand.

The EU's Tacis programme is widely criticised on grounds of both focus (or lack of it) and efficiency. EU countries' technical assistance is considered inadequate, in quality as much as quantity. Ukrainians cast an envious eye at the democracy programmes offered to Central European countries under the EU's Phare programme and bilateral schemes such as the UK's Know How Fund, and at the transition programmes offered to accession countries. Contributors to this book plead especially for a sharing of expertise, information, best practice and skills-based training, especially in the fields of structural reform, capacity-building, the strengthening of NGOs and civil society, and media development. There is a real hunger for bilateral, regional and twinning links between organisations of all kinds.

Several authors press the need for a more concerted effort by interested governments, multilateral organisations and multinational companies to look at possible solutions to oil and gas transportation issues in order, among other things, to make effective use of Ukraine's (cheaper) systems and reduce the need for investment in (more expensive) alternatives.

There is also a strong case for increased assistance in areas where Ukraine's needs coincide with the EU's interests, such as improving Ukrainian capability in law enforcement and border control. Such programmes should not only be mutually beneficial but more than repay their costs.

The way ahead

What seems to be on offer to Ukraine for now is a kind of privileged partnership with the EU going beyond that with other non-accession states but falling short of even associate membership, at least for the time being. The main elements of such a relationship appear to be enhanced dialogue and co-operation on foreign and security policy; membership of the European Conference; practical co-operation on issues such as transportation, energy, the environment, justice and home affairs; WTO membership and a free trade agreement; regional programmes with neighbouring EU states; strengthened bilateral relations with some EU members; and, in a different context, a consolidation of Ukraine's already fruitful relations with Nato. All of this can be developed further in line with internal developments in Ukraine.

Ukraine could content itself with exploiting what is on offer in this relationship to secure many of the practical benefits of EU membership. If, on the other hand, it is really serious about going for associate status and then full membership, it needs to demonstrate an unmistakable commitment, in deed as well as word, to undertake rapid, radical and wholehearted reform of its political practices and economic mechanisms. So far its attitude has sometimes lacked conviction.

Some in Ukraine maintain that the EU's attitude makes it more difficult to introduce reform, arguing that there needs to be, as an incentive, the prospect of a closer association with the EU. But it is clear from the experience of successful transition countries that the driving force for change must come from within, from a real desire to adopt democratic norms and standards for their own sake, and not as a means to an end.

If Ukraine does take up this challenge, and the Government really demonstrates the political will and the ability to carry through reforms so that it can meet the EU criteria, then the EU will be forced to reconsider its position and is likely to be much more inclined to view with favour the prospect, in due course, of EU membership for Ukraine.

APPENDICES

APPENDIX 1
What is the Agreement on Partnership and Co-operation?

A brief guide to the Agreement signed in Luxembourg on 16 June 1994 between the European Union and Ukraine*

The European Union

The European Union consists of fifteen countries : Austria, Belgium, Denmark, Finland, France, Germany, Greece, Ireland, Italy, Luxembourg, the Netherlands, Portugal, Spain, Sweden and the United Kingdom.

The European Union draws its existence from four treaties which have as their underlying aim the safeguarding of peace and stability in post-war Europe and the joint development of the member countries through economic integration. The first treaty, the Treaty on the European Coal and Steel Community (ECSC), was concluded in 1951 to bring the coal and steel production of the countries that had been at war only a few years earlier under one supranational authority. Its fundamental aim was to restore Europe's industrial capacity without giving any country the possibility to build up an offensive army again.

The success of the ECSC brought the Member States to conclude a similar Treaty on the European Atomic Energy Community (Euratom), and a much wider Treaty on the European Economic Community (EEC), both in 1957. The Treaty on EEC, commonly known as the 'Treaty of Rome', was special in that it was an active, dynamic treaty : it provided a programme for closer economic integration which started with a free trade area, evolved into a customs union and since 1993 – into a single European market with common rules and legislation in many areas of economic life.

In the 1980s, the EEC also developed European Political Co-operation, enshrined in the 1992 Treaty on European Union (TEU), also known as the 'Maastricht Treaty'. The Maastricht

---

* This guide was issued by the Delegation of the European Commission in Ukraine. The full text of the Agreement is available at the Delegation's website: *www.delukr.cec.eu.int*

Treaty takes economic integration a step further by creating an economic and monetary union, and introducing a single European currency, the Euro, in 1999. The TEU also reinforces political integration by instituting EU-wide co-operation in the areas of justice and home affairs, and by transforming the loose European Political Co-operation into a more elaborate Common Foreign and Security Policy (CFSP). In 1997, the European Union drew up a new treaty for Europe, the Treaty of Amsterdam. Its four main objectives are: employment and citizens' rights; freedom of movement; to give Europe a stronger voice in world affairs; and to make the Union's institutional structures more efficient with a view to enlarging the Union, with new Member States joining.

Why the agreement on partnership and co-operation?

The Agreement on Partnership and Co-operation was signed on 16 June 1994 in Luxembourg by the President of Ukraine, the President of the European Commission and the representatives of the European Union Member States. The Agreement with Ukraine was the first such agreement to be signed with a country of the former Soviet Union. Many parts of it are identical with the 'Europe Agreements' the EU has with Central and Eastern European Countries (CEECs).

The Agreement on Partnership and Co-operation results from the desire to establish close relations between the European Union and Ukraine, based on their existing historical links , and the common values they share. It marks an important step forward, superseding the Agreement on Trade and Commercial and Economic Co-operation which the European Community and the Soviet Union signed in 1989. There have been fundamental political and economic changes since the signing of the 1989 Agreement. In 1991, the European Community recognised Ukraine as an independent state, and since that time Ukraine has set up an Embassy to the European Union in Brussels, and thirteen EU Member States as well as the European Commission have established Embassies in Kiev.

The main aims of the PCA are :

- to develop close political relations by starting a regular dialogue on political issues;
- to foster trade and investment and harmonious economic relations;
- to provide the groundwork for mutually beneficial economic, social, financial, scientific, technological and cultural co-operation;
- to support Ukrainian efforts to consolidate its democracy and to complete the transition to a market economy.

The PCA will remain in effect for a period of ten years, after which it will be automatically renewed unless either Ukraine or the European Union wish to terminate it. This does not mean that the Agreement will not change in the meantime. It does not have a rigid framework and can therefore evolve in any direction the European Union and Ukraine want it to, depending on developments in the EU and Ukraine, particularly regarding Ukraine's progress on the road to a market economy. The Agreement will be reviewed after three years or once Ukraine joins the World Trade Organisation (WTO), whichever is sooner. In 1998, the European Union and Ukraine may examine the possibility of establishing a free trade area, to further economic co-operation.

The Agreement on Partnership and Co-operation demonstrates the spirit of mutual commitment to democracy and a market economy in which both parties can strengthen political, commercial and cultural links, pave the way for further economic integration, and set the agenda for future negotiations on a free trade area. In all of those areas it is much wider ranging than the 1989 Agreement and provides the appropriate framework for Ukraine's closer integration with Europe. At the same time, it respects the existing and traditional close links between Ukraine and its immediate neighbours, which the parties consider essential for future prosperity and stability.

The PCA entered into force on 1 March 1998.

Political dialogue

The PCA foresees the development of a strong political dialogue between Ukraine and the European Union. This is done by providing an institutional framework for regular contact; the institutional provisions establish a number of forums between the Governments and Parliaments of the European Union and Ukraine. In addition, consultations will take place at the highest political level, i.e. between Presidents or with the European Union Troika, which consists of representatives of the present, preceding, and following EU Presidencies.

The aim is to strengthen the political links between Ukraine and the European Union, which goes hand in hand with establishing closer economic ties. Those are:

- to support the political and economic changes currently under way in Ukraine.

This dialogue will be guided by the conviction of both sides of the foremost importance of the rule of law, respect for human rights, particularly those of minorities, the establishment of a multi-party system with free and democratic elections and economic, liberalisation aimed at further developing towards a market economy.

- to increase security and stability by helping to harmonise views on international issues of mutual concern.

This dialogue will reflect the commitment of both sides to promote international peace and security, and to observe the principles and provisions of the OSCE (Organisation on Security and Co-operation in Europe). In this context, the European Union recognises that support for the independence, sovereignty and territorial integrity of Ukraine will contribute to the safeguarding of peace and stability in Central and Eastern Europe as well as on the European continent as a whole.

Economic partnership

1. Market Access for Goods

The European Union is one of Ukraine's main trading partners. The PCA grants Ukraine and the European Union better access to each other's markets, principally by not discriminating against each other's goods, i.e. by treating each other on an equal footing with other trading partners and by ensuring free and fair competition between imported and domestic goods. Details on the competition rules are given below. The Agreement also contains rules on trade-related payments.

a. Most-favoured-nation status

The European Union and Ukraine anticipated Ukraine's accession to the World Trade Organisation (WTO) by already applying a wide range of WTO principles to their mutual trade. This has been important for Ukraine, because it takes several years before a country can accede to the WTO.

The European Union and Ukraine have agreed to grant each other most-favoured-nation status for trade in goods. This means that each party cannot apply higher customs duties and levies than those which are applied to any other country. Neither can they apply worse conditions for trade-related payments or more cumbersome customs procedures than to other countries.

In this context, the European Union is treated as one country, and Ukraine does not yet enjoy the duty-free trade regime which European Union Member States grant each other. However, the possibility to include Ukraine may now be examined. Equally, the European Union will not benefit from advantages granted by Ukraine to countries of the former Soviet Union with regard to tariffs or customs procedures until Ukraine joins the WTO, or until the end of 1998 at the latest. In any case, neither Ukraine nor the European Union will benefit from advantages granted to third countries with the expressed aim of creating a free-trade area or a customs union. An example are the relations between the European Union and a number of Central European countries that will eventually become full members of the European Union. In accordance with WTO rules, the parties further do not benefit from advantages granted to neighbouring countries in order to facilitate trade in border regions.

In fact, Ukraine will pay even lower duties on the export of certain products to the European Union, namely those products which come under the Generalised Scheme of Preferences (GSP), the benefits of which were granted to Ukraine in 1993.

b. No quantitative restrictions

The PCA forbids the use of quotas (quantitative restrictions) on imports.

Nonetheless, Ukraine may temporarily impose quantitative restrictions in two cases:

- to protect infant industries, i.e. those industries that have not yet sufficiently developed to be able to compete with imports from abroad without being swept from the market;
- to protect certain industries facing serious difficulties, particularly where these difficulties produce significant social problems.

There are a number of conditions Ukraine needs to respect when it imposes import quotas :

- Ukraine must inform the European Union of any new quotas before they are introduced and hold consultations on them;
- the amount of imports hit by such quotas must not make up more than 15% of total imports from the European Union;
- any quota restrictions must be applied to all of Ukraine's trading partners and not only to the European Union, i.e. the restrictions must be non-discriminatory;
- also, Ukraine can only make use of these exceptions until it accedes to the WTO or until the end of 1998 at the latest. It should be added that, when Ukraine accedes to the WTO, it will be able to invoke similar exceptions foreseen in the WTO.

The European Union may also apply quotas on the import of textiles and steel products, which are two industries facing difficulties in the European Union. These quotas are contained in special sectoral agreements. These agreements have been in operation since 1 January 1993 for textiles and since 1 January 1995 for steel products. In addition, discussions have taken place on a separate agreement on trade in nuclear materials.

c. Transit is free

The Parties grant each other the freedom of transit over their territories of goods which are destined for third countries. In this context, the provisions of the WTO apply: among other rules, goods in transit must not be subjected to customs duties or be unnecessarily delayed. Also, Ukraine and the European Union treat the transit of each other's goods no less favourably than the transit of goods from third countries.

Equally, goods which are admitted temporarily into Ukraine or the European Union, i.e. which are imported to be re-exported afterwards, are not subject to import charges and duties.

Here again, the European Union does not benefit from advantages granted by Ukraine to countries of the former Soviet Union until Ukraine joins the WTO or until the end of 1998 at the latest.

2. Business and Investment

The PCA contains important provisions which encompass the will to create a favourable and stable climate for investment as well as for the provision of services. In particular, it aims to improve the conditions for the establishment and the operating conditions of Ukrainian companies and subsidiaries in the European Union and vice versa. The Agreement also contains related provisions on payments and the movement of investment capital, on competition and on conditions for employees and business people.

In addition, Ukraine and the individual Member States of the European Union have concluded or will conclude further agreements governing:

- investment protection and promotion.

In this context, they may regularly exchange information on laws, regulations and administrative practises in the investment field, and publicise investment opportunities through trade fairs, exhibitions, trade weeks and other events.

- the avoidance of double taxation.

It should be noted that advantages granted in such separate bilateral tax agreements do not apply to other countries; they are an exception to the most-favoured-nation principle.

a. Establishing and running companies (including joint ventures)

Ukrainian companies in the European Union

The European Union grants most-favoured-nation treatment for the establishment of Ukrainian companies on its territory; it is as easy for an Ukrainian company to establish itself in the European Union as it is for a company from most other countries.

Once a Ukrainian company has established itself, it is granted national treatment for its operation; it is subject to the same operating regulations as European Union companies. Nevertheless, national treatment for operations is not always granted in certain sectors such as mining, fishing, real estate, audio-visual services, telecommunications, certain professional services, agriculture and news agencies. In these sectors specific restrictions exist in some parts of the European Union, but the operating regulations for Ukrainian companies are never more restrictive than for any other foreign company. National treatment is not granted to branches of Ukrainian companies which have no legal personality. Most-favoured-nation treatment is applied to them.

European Union companies in Ukraine

Ukraine applies somewhat different rules with respect to European Union companies. When these companies wish to establish a business in Ukraine they may choose between national treatment (the rules applied to Ukrainian companies) or most-favoured-nation treatment (the best rules applied to foreign companies), depending on which regime is the most favourable. In a number of sectors, however, this choice does not exist and the regime applied to other foreign companies is automatically applied to European Union companies. These sectors are: banking, insurance, real estate, natural resources, fishing, hunting, agriculture, lease of state property, telecommunications, mass media, certain professions and operations affecting historical monuments.

Regarding the operating regulations for European Union companies in Ukraine once they have established themselves, they may choose between national treatment and most-favoured-nation treatment.

Future development of business conditions

Although Ukraine and the European Union grant each other favourable business conditions, some restrictions still exist. The PCA commits Ukraine and the European Union to 'use their best endeavours' so as not to take measures which make the establishment or operation of each other's companies more difficult than they are at present. This means that new restrictions are in principle not allowed from the date of the signing of the Agreement - 23 March 1994 - but may be accepted in certain exceptional cases. In particular, it is agreed that:

- If Ukraine intends to pass legislation which makes business conditions less favourable for European Union companies, Ukraine must make its intentions known. The European Union may request to receive drafts of such legislation and enter into consultations with Ukraine.
- If new restrictions are introduced, they will not apply for a period of three years to those European Union companies which are at that moment already established in Ukraine.

Many of the existing restrictions are in the services sector, even though Ukraine and the European Union undertake, as a principle, to allow on their territories the supply of services by each other's companies. In this area, business conditions will gradually be improved and liberalised. The European Union and Ukraine will consult each other on how this can be done so that a market-oriented services sector continues to develop in Ukraine. The maximum degree of liberalisation to be achieved will be the rules foreseen in the General Agreement on Trade in Services that was concluded in the framework of the WTO.

Approximation of legislation

Ukraine and the European Union recognise that approximation of economic law and related social, environmental and standards law is an important condition for closer economic links. Ukraine will endeavour to gradually make its legislation compatible with that of the European Union, which will make it much easier for companies from the European Union and Ukraine to invest and operate on each other's territory. The European Union, for its part, has started to help Ukraine achieve this by providing assistance.

Special sectoral rules: Transport and Financial Services

> • The provisions governing the establishment and operation of companies do not apply to transport by air, inland waterways or sea. Those should be covered by bilateral agreements between Ukraine and the individual Member States of the European Union.
>
> However, the PCA does specify that, for international transport operations entirely or partly involving transport by sea, Ukrainian and European Union companies offering shipping agency services are entitled to either national treatment or most-favoured-nation treatment (whichever is more favourable), for both their establishment and operations .
>
> All administrative and technical obstacles to free and fair competition between maritime transport companies must be removed. The European Union and Ukraine grant ships that fly each other's flag national treatment in their ports. This will also apply to ships that fly the flag of a third country but are owned by nationals or companies from the European Union or Ukraine.
>
> The PCA explicitly forbids cargo sharing arrangements, even if they are provided for in earlier agreements between a European Union Member State and the former Soviet Union.
>
> • European Union banks, related financial services and insurance companies will not enjoy national treatment when they set up a subsidiary in Ukraine; they will be subject to the existing restrictions on foreign banks and financial institutions. However, these restrictions must not be toughened and Ukraine is committed to abolishing them before 1 March 2003.
>
> The European Union and Ukraine may take measures in the financial sector which run counter to the above principles, but only to protect the integrity of the financial system if investors, depositors, or other persons holding financial assets are at risk and not in order to protect national financial companies from foreign competition.

b. Foreign personnel

Ukrainian companies have the right to send key personnel, such as managers or highly specialised experts, to their branches in the European Union and vice versa, provided they only work for the company that sends them and provided they have been employed by this company for at least one year.

The personnel that Ukrainian companies employ in the European Union and vice versa will, as far as possible, enjoy the same rights as local workers regarding working conditions and rules on remuneration and dismissal. Further separate agreements might be concluded between Ukraine and the individual Member States of the European Union to ensure that they will also be able to accumulate pension rights and other social security benefits, and transfer them to their home country when they return provided they have paid social security contributions during their work period.

The Agreement should not be read as giving the right to any person from the European Union or Ukraine, other than those categories named in the first paragraph of this section, to enter and stay in Ukraine or the European Union respectively; the Agreement does not change immigration rules, and both parties commit themselves to joint efforts to control illegal immigration. At the same time, the European Union and Ukraine will examine how they can improve conditions for Ukrainian business people travelling to the European Union and vice versa.

3. Free and fair competition

The PCA contains a whole series of provisions which serve to advance free and fair competition in the European Union's and in Ukraine's market between companies and between goods.

a. Free and fair competition between companies

The European Union and Ukraine are committed to removing restrictions placed on competition between enterprises. This has three important aspects:

- As regards companies' relations with each other : both the European Union and Ukraine must have adopted and implement laws that force companies to be competitive. Companies must not try to hinder competition, for example by refusing to buy from or sell to a particular company or by agreeing on a fixed selling price with one or two other companies, etc. The European Union is ready to help Ukraine develop such legislation and to discuss with Ukraine possible cases of reduced competition either in the European Union or in Ukraine;

- As regards companies' relations with the state : the state must refrain from reducing competition by granting subsidies to its companies if such subsidies can distort mutual trade, for example export subsidies or subsidies to production which would cause goods to be sold significantly cheaper than imported goods. Subsidies are allowed, however, for the production of primary products (unprocessed agricultural and mineral products). The European Union and Ukraine have the right to ask for information from each other on the subsidies they grant;

- The above rules also apply to state monopolies and to companies, either state-owned or not, which are given exclusive rights by the state to perform certain economic activities. If such monopolies in the European Union or in Ukraine discriminate against companies or nationals from the other party as regards purchases from them or sales to them, then such discrimination needs to be phased out over a four-year period. After four years, the activities of such monopolies must no longer distort trade.

b. Free and fair competition between goods

There must be free and fair competition between domestic goods and imported goods. This applies when imported goods cross the border and when they circulate on the territory, but also as regards their price and the quantity in which they are sold:

• As regards the import of goods, a number of WTO rules are applied for customs valuation, customs fees and formalities, marks of origin, and the publication and administration of trade regulation. For example, the customs services of the European Union and Ukraine must determine the actual market value of imported goods and not administratively fix a higher or lower value; the administrative formalities for goods to enter a country must be reduced to a minimum; fees charged by the customs service and other organisations for services rendered to importers, including those connected with quotas, licensing and exchange control, must reflect the approximate cost of the services and not have the effect of a hidden tax on imports, etc.

• As regards the treatment of goods once they are imported : Ukraine and the European Union grant each other national treatment for goods. This means that, once goods are imported, they are subjected to the same (or possibly even more favourable) treatment as domestically produced goods. In other words, all kinds of taxes and levies (for example excise duties) applied to the goods must not be higher than those for domestic goods, and all regulations affecting the transportation, distribution, purchase, sale or use of the goods must not be less favourable than for domestic goods.

• Regarding the price at which imported goods are sold : both parties must use market-related prices for their exports. If goods are sold at below-market prices, the importing party has the possibility to impose:

* anti-dumping measures, if goods are proven to be sold at prices below their market value, or

* anti-subsidy duties, if goods are sold at low prices because their production or export is subsidised.

Anti-dumping and anti-subsidy procedures and measures must conform to the rules of the WTO. For example, the anti-dumping or anti-subsidy duties imposed must not be higher than the amount needed to reach the market price. In any case, before a party imposes anti-dumping measures it must consult with the other party to try to find a constructive solution to the problem.

• Regarding the quantity of imported goods: when a product is imported in such quantities and under such conditions as to cause or to threaten to cause substantial injury to domestic producers of competing products, the importing country may take 'safeguard measures' to protect its national producers. This means that the importing country imposes temporary quotas on imports of this product. Ukraine and the European Union, however, must first consult each other and try to reach a negotiated settlement before such measures are imposed.

c. Protection of intellectual, industrial and commercial property

Both sides must prevent the illegal importation or sale of intellectual, industrial and commercial property. To this end, Ukraine must improve its protection of intellectual, industrial and commercial property rights, in order to prevent the unauthorised use of designs, trade marks, patents, software, artistic works, etc.

The PCA refers to the obligations arising from multilateral conventions in this field and states that Ukraine should have acceded to an agreed list of these conventions before 1 March 2003. Until then, European Union companies and nationals must be treated at least as well as any other third country and their nationals, except for the countries of the former Soviet Union or those countries which offer more advantageous conditions on a truly reciprocal basis.

4. Payments and capital movements

Ukraine and the European Union must allow their companies and nationals to make payments to each other, if these payments are in a convertible currency and if they are connected with trade in goods, the provision of services or the movement of people.

Moreover, the transfer of capital in connection with the establishment and operation of businesses as described in the above sections (direct investment) is also allowed. Profits stemming from such investments may be freely repatriated and investments may be withdrawn.

The PCA does not lay down rules for payments connected with liquid capital movements such as investments in securities, but Ukraine and the European Union will consult each other on how to facilitate such payments.

The rules and conditions for payments (except liquid capital movements) may be made more favourable but they may in no case be made more restrictive. There are only two exceptions to this 'standstill'. If Ukraine grants or receives short or medium-term loans it may impose exchange restrictions in connection with such a loan, but only if such restrictions are a condition for the loan and if they are permitted by the IMF. Such exchange restrictions must apply to all of Ukraine's trading partners and not only to the European Union. As a second exception, the European Union and Ukraine may restrict capital movements if existing capital movements threaten to cause serious difficulties for exchange rate and monetary policy, but only if such restrictions are strictly necessary and on condition that they are not applied for longer than six months.

Economic co-operation

The PCA specifies a wide range of areas for co-operation between the European Union and Ukraine. The overall aim is to contribute to the process of economic reform and to the recovery and sustainable development of Ukraine's economy, taking into account the need to address social and environmental problems. For this purpose, the PCA identifies twenty-eight areas in which the European Union and Ukraine wish to increase and expand their co-operation :

- industrial co-operation
- investment promotion and protection
- public procurement

- standards and conformity assessment (certification)
- mining and raw materials
- science and technology
- education and training
- agriculture
- energy
- the civil nuclear sector
- the environment
- transport
- the space industry
- postal services and telecommunications
- financial services
- the fight against money laundering
- monetary policy
- regional development, including contacts at regional level
- social co-operation: health and safety, employment and social protection
- tourism
- small and medium-sized enterprises
- information and communication
- consumer protection
- customs
- statistics
- economics
- the fight against drugs
- culture

Co-operation is already under way. In the economy, for example, European experts work with Ukrainian colleagues to transfer know-how in the field of company management and industrial and agricultural technology. In science and education, exchanges of scientists, teachers and students are being organised and joint projects are set up. Administrative co-operation is developing in areas such as customs and the fight against crime, and documentation is exchanged between administrations in technical areas such as standards and statistics. Large amounts of grant finance are devoted to improving nuclear safety and dealing with the consequences of the Chernobyl accident.

Much more can still be done, and the Co-operation Council shall make recommendations as to how co-operation can be further developed in all areas. The European Union and Ukraine agree that special attention will be paid to those measures which also foster co-operation with the neighbouring states of Ukraine.

The main instrument of the European Union to finance economic co-operation is the Tacis technical assistance programme.

Institutions

The PCA requires, as a means of ensuring that its provisions are observed and implemented, that three monitoring committees are set up - the Co-operation Council, the Co-operation Committee and a Parliamentary Co-operation Committee.

5. Co-operation Council

The Co-operation Council meets once a year. It consists of members of the Government of Ukraine on the one hand, and of the members of the Council of the European Union and members of the European Commission on the other.

The Co-operation Council supervises the implementation of the PCA. The Agreement assigns the Co-operation Council a number of specific tasks, but it has the right to discuss any subject of mutual interest and make recommendations.

The explicit tasks include studying immigration control measures, conditions of employment for each other's nationals, conditions for social security transfers, conditions for business people, making recommendations on the opening of the services market, making recommendations concerning the protection of intellectual, industrial and commercial property, making recommendations on sectoral co-operation and on technical assistance, discussing disputes over the Agreement and referring them if necessary to conciliators who can make non-binding recommendations.

The Co-operation Council must be informed about any new foreign exchange restrictions, competition law, existing or planned subsidies, and any existing or planned quantitative restrictions in trade.

6. Co-operation Committee

The Co-operation Committee meets at senior civil servant level. It must prepare the meetings of the Co-operation Council and ensure continuity between its meetings.

The Presidency of both the Council and the Committee is chaired alternately by Ukraine and the European Union.

7. Parliamentary Co-operation Committee

The Parliamentary Co-operation Committee consists of members of the Ukrainian Parliament (Verkhovna Rada) and the European Parliament. It is the forum for political dialogue between parliamentarians from the European Union and Ukraine. The Parliamentary Committee exchanges information with the Co-operation Council and has the authority to make recommendations.

8. Global exceptions and dispute settlement

a. Global exceptions

The provisions of the PCA are binding on the European Union and on Ukraine. There are only a few specified cases when the parties may take measures in the public interest that are not in line with the Agreement :

- measures meant to prevent the disclosure of essential state secrets;
- measures relating to the production and trade of weapons;
- special measures to maintain law and order and to safeguard peace.

In addition, the European Union or Ukraine retain the right to impose limitations on market access and business and investment in the following cases, as long as any prohibitions do not constitute a means of arbitrary discrimination or a disguised restriction on trade :

- to enable public policy and official activities relating to public policy, in order to protect public security, public health, public morality, etc.;
- to protect natural resources including gold and silver, art treasures, intellectual property, etc.

b. Dispute settlement

Between the European Union and Ukraine

In the event of a dispute over the application or implementation of the Agreement, the Co-operation Council will try to find a resolution by making a recommendation. If this fails, the Council, Ukraine, and the European Union may each appoint a conciliator. The latter will make a recommendation by majority vote which will, however, not be binding.

If either party considers that obligations are not being fulfilled, they can take appropriate action but only after notifying the Co-operation Council and giving it sufficient time to find a solution. However, if one of the parties repudiates the Agreement or violates the basic principles of democracy and human rights or those of a market economy, then the other party may immediately suspend the Agreement without prior consultations. In either case, retaliatory action should cause minimum disturbance to the functioning of the Agreement.

Between nationals and companies of the European Union and Ukraine

Individuals and companies from the European Union and Ukraine must have the possibility to effectively defend their rights arising from the Agreement and other agreements and legislation. For this purpose, the European Union and Ukraine guarantee each other's nationals and legal persons the same access to courts and administrative organs as their own nationals and legal persons are entitled to. In commercial disputes, the European Union and Ukraine will encourage the use of arbitration in accordance with international practice and on the basis of international law.

APPENDIX 2
Strategy of Ukraine's integration to the European Union

Approved by Decree of the President of Ukraine. 11 June 1998

This strategy defines principal directions of Ukraine's co-operation with the European Union (EU) – organisation, which in the process of its development has achieved high level of political integration, unification of legislation, economic co-operation, social protection and cultural development.

National interests of Ukraine require identification of Ukraine as an influential European country, full-fledged EU member. In the result of the EU enlargement which is expected in the nearest years – through entering the EU of Poland and Hungary – Ukraine will have a common border with the EU, which would create a principally new geopolitical situation. In connection with this a clear and comprehensive definition of the foreign policy strategy concerning Ukraine's integration to the European political, economic and legal space is necessary.

Strategy of Ukraine's integration to the EU is based upon:

- Constitution of Ukraine, which sets the goals of the Ukrainian foreign policy activity at ensuring its national interests and security through maintaining peaceful and mutually advantageous co-operation with the members of international community according to the universal principles and standards of international law;
- Main Directions of Ukrainian Foreign Policy and Concept (basics of state policy) of the National Security of Ukraine;
- Partnership And Co-operation Agreement, signed between Ukraine and the European Union (PCA), which defines mechanism of interaction between Ukraine and the EU.

Strategy of Ukraine's integration to the EU sets out main priorities in activities of state executive bodies for the periods until 2007 year. During this period there should be created preconditions required for getting by Ukraine of an EU full-pledged member status.

Strategy of Ukraine's integration to the European Union shall ensure involvement of Ukraine into the European political, economic and legal space and acquiring on this basis a status of the EU associated member – that is the main foreign policy priority of Ukraine in the middle-term perspective.

I. Main guidelines of the integration process

1. Approximation of legislation of Ukraine to the legislation of the EU, guarantee of human rights.

Approximation of Ukraine' legislation to the EU legislation means its getting closer to the contemporary European legal system, that would ensure development of political, business, social, cultural activities of Ukraine's nationals, economic growth of the country within the EU framework as well as would facilitate gradual improvement of the well-being, making it closer to the level existing in the EU Member States.

Approximation of Ukraine's legislation stipulates reformation of its legal system and its gradual bringing into line with the requirements of the European standards. It covers private, customs, labour, financial, tax, intellectual property labour protection legislation as well as legislation dealing with protection of life and health, environment, consumer's rights, technical rules and standards, transport and other industries as defined in the PCA. Participation of Ukraine in conventions of the Council of Europe, which set out common for this organisation and the EU standards, should be considered as an important element of reforming the legal system of Ukraine.

The stages of the legal approximation process are: implementation of the Partnership and Co-operation Agreement, signing sectoral agreements, bringing Ukraine's current legislation into correspondence with the EU standards, creation of a mechanism to adapt the draft legislative acts of Ukraine to the existing standards of the EU.

2. Economical integration and development of trade relations between Ukraine and EU.

Major factors of economic integration and development of trade between Ukraine and the EU are globalisation of the world production, unification of national economies on the basis of GATT/ WTO, economic tendencies in the EU Member States related with the consolidation of the EU by common monetary policy and monetary union, potential mutual advantages of the free trade.

The Partnership and Co-operation Agreement represents the basic document which defines the guidelines of economic integration of Ukraine with the EU and development of bilateral trade.

Development of economic integration means liberalisation and synchronisation in the EU and Ukraine markets opening, achievement of harmonised trade balance, granting on the mutual basis of the favourable regime promoting investments from the EU to Ukraine and Ukrainian producers on the EU markets, introduction of common legal environment and unified standards in the spheres of competition and state support of producers. Economic integration is based on co-ordination, synchronisation and adequacy in decision-making in economies of Ukraine and the EU and foresees abolition of competition limitations and limitation of the instruments of protectionism, formation of the major economic prerequisites for full-fledged membership of Ukraine in the EU.

3. Ukraine's integration to the EU within the context of all-European security.

Security of Ukraine within all-European security shall be based on the fact that development and strengthening of the EU shall deepen the all-European security system in all its dimensions.

Principle of indivisibility of the European security is equally important for Ukraine as well as for the EU and its full fledged and associated members. The EU along with other European and transatlantic structures is actively searching for co-operative security which shall be the guarantee of security of Ukraine itself. Development of co-operation between Ukraine and Western European Union (WEU) as a key EU defence and security structure is one of the major components of the Ukraine's integration to the EU.

Recognition by the European Union of considerable importance of Ukraine in creation of a new European security architecture may and shall be utilised as an important tool of realisation of a Ukrainian interests in the relations with the EU. At the same time strengthening of the security of Ukraine is linked with the achievement of the economic security and political stability in the country.

4. Political consolidation and strengthening of democracy.

Political consolidation shall provide persistent deepening of political dialogue and improvement of general environment for relations between Ukraine and the EU (summits, consultations on ministerial level, meetings of experts).

Political consolidation and strengthening of democracy shall be aimed at:

- safeguarding political stability both in Ukraine and on the whole European continent;
- securing the peaceful development and fruitful co-operation of all the European continent;
- strengthening democratic principles in the Ukrainian society.

Political consolidation within the context of the strategy of Ukraine on European integration should be considered on two planes.

Foreign policy consolidation shall be aimed first of all at the strengthening of the European security. From one hand, it includes the comprehensive integration of Ukraine into the European political, legal, economical, informational and cultural environment. From another – it shall be aimed at identification of the EU policy towards Ukraine, its separation from the EU policy towards Russia and support of the European countries and world community of the strategy of integration of Ukraine with the EU. In this context, co-operation with the European Commission, European Parliament and other institutions, as well as deepening of relations with separate EU Member States are of major importance. Gradual involvement of Ukraine into the inter-regional initiatives of the Union should be also regarded as an important part of the mentioned foreign policy consolidation. One of the real steps on the road of rapprochement of the political position of Ukraine and the EU may be an agreement on joint positions in the UN regarding the global international issues.

Consolidation in domestic policies shall be based upon the choice made by Ukrainian society in favour of integration with the EU. This includes first of all strengthening of democracy and rule of law in the state. European integration helps to create civil society in Ukraine and further formation of Ukrainian political nation as full-fledged member of the family of European nations. Important element of the domestic policies' consolidation is formation of the devotion in the society to the idea of acquiring in the future the membership in the EU as a real opportunity to ensure decent future for Ukraine and its citizens.

Political consolidation can hardly be achieved by unilateral steps only. During the period before Ukraine becomes the EU associated member, the principle of equal footing should be persistently observed striving for adequate steps from the EU side.

5. *Adaptation of the Social Policy of Ukraine to the EU standards.*

Adaptation of the Social Policy of Ukraine includes reforming of the systems of insurance, labour protection, public health, pension ensuring, employment policy and other branches of social policy according to the EU standards and gradual achieving of the common European level of social security and protection of population.

This direction of the integration process should be implemented within the framework of the general programme of reforms with active involvement of the EU's and its Member States' institutions and programmes, and first and foremost directing of the EU technical assistance exactly to the adaptation of the Social Policy. It is of great importance in this context the ratification and further implementation by Ukraine of the European Social Charter, as well as concluding of agreements on the co-ordination of the systems of social security of workers, which have Ukrainian citizenship and are working on the EU Member States' territory.

6. *Cultural – educational and scientific and technical integration.*

Along with the mentioned directions of the European integration, cultural – educational and scientific and technical integration directions gave a special place, that stipulated by the potential possibility to achieve weighty successes in the integration process exactly on these directions. They cover the fields of secondary and higher education, training, science, culture, arts, technical and technological spheres.

Integration process in the corresponding directions includes introduction of the European regulation and standards in education, science and technology, distribution of own cultural and scientific and technical achievements in the EU. In the final result such steps will promote upsurge of the European cultural identity in Ukraine and integration to the European intellectual – educational and scientific and technological environment.

Realisation of this task presumes mutual abandoning of any principal, in contrast to technical, restrictions on contacts and exchanges, distribution of information. Especially important is realisation of joint scientific, cultural, educational and other projects, involvement of Ukrainian scientists and specialists in the European programmes of scientific research.

7. Regional integration of Ukraine.

Practical implementation of the integration process is possible only under the condition of complementarity of the common European dimension of co-operation with regional integration and deepening of the sectoral co-operation between Ukraine and the EU. This direction gets special meaning taking into account important for the EU trend expressed in the slogan 'EU: from the Union of states to the Union of regions'.

The basis for regional integration is PCA, European Local Government Charter, other corresponding EU and Council of Europe legislation.

Regional integration foresees launching and deepening of the direct contacts between some regions of Ukraine and Member States and candidate countries, development of these contacts in the directions defined in this Strategy in order to transfer the main weight of the integration process from the central executive bodies to the regions, to the institutions of local government, territorial communities and, finally, to provide as wide as possible involvement of Ukrainian people.

8. Sectoral co-operation.

Sectoral co-operation includes co-ordination and interaction between Ukraine and EU in certain branches and spheres of economic activity. During forthcoming years priority in sectoral co-operation should be given to the sphere of trans-European transport, power industry and information networks, co-operation in the field of justice, prevention and fight against organised crime and drugs distribution, customs co-operation, scientific and research sphere, industrial and agricultural co-operation etc.

The legislation basis for sectoral co-operation is PCA, corresponding legislation acts of the Parties, agreements and protocols concluded between Ukraine and EU and Member States regarding co-operation and interaction in general and in the defined areas.

It is worthwhile to elaborate and approve by the corresponding Ministries and other central bodies of the executive power of Ukraine the programmes of development of relations with the EU, which should be based on the general provisions of the Strategy of Integration and gradually (during 1.5 - 2 years) form the entire package – National Programme of Integration.

Sectoral co-operation provides, along with adoption of the sectoral programmes of co-operation with the EU, elaboration of the list of structures and civil servants in the central bodies of executive power, local power institutions, which are responsible for the formation and implementation of the State policy of Ukraine regarding the EU, getting direct contacts between Ministries and other central bodies of executive power of Ukraine and corresponding Directorates of the European Commission. In the short – and midterm context the utmost responsibility for concordance of the sectoral co-operation is put on the Ukrainian Part of the Ukraine – European Communities (European Union) Co-operation Council, and for its implementation – on the Ukrainian Part of the Ukraine – European Communities (European Union) Co-operation Committee and National Agency of Ukraine for Development and European Integration.

9. Co-operation in the environment protection.

Environment protection shall be recognised as a public policy priority and subject of public elevated heightened attention in the European states, one of the main fields of the EU activity and vital issues for Ukraine, determined not only by consequences of the Chernobyl NPP accident but by general environmental conditions in Ukraine.

The legal framework of co-operation is the PCA as well as international treaties and agreements on environment safety, parties to which are Ukraine and the EU.

As a result, the co-operation in the environmental field should lead to the creation of safe and a man-friendly pan-European ecological space.

II Internal support of the integration process

Internal support of the process of integration to the EU shall be the responsibility of the highest, central and local bodies of the executive power of Ukraine in co-operation with the body of legislative power, relevant local authorities.

The President of Ukraine shall exercise management of Ukraine's integration strategy.

The Cabinet of Ministers shall provide implementation of the Strategy of Ukraine's Integration to the European Union.

The Ministry of Foreign Affairs shall implement measures in the field of political relations of Ukraine with the EU and co-ordination of the activities of executive power bodies in this field.

The National Agency of Ukraine for Development and European Integration shall exercise interagency co-ordination of intersectoral economic and social co-operation between Ukraine and the EU.

Other ministries and central bodies of the executive power shall ensure realisation of sectoral co-operation between Ukraine and the EU, implementation of the Partnership and Co-operation Agreement, shall exercise other measures according to their responsibility and tasks defined by the Strategy in order to deepen the support of Ukraine's integration to the EU.

Integration strategy provides the following fields of internal support for Ukraine's integration to the EU.

1. *Organisational support*

1. Approvement by the President of Ukraine according to the proposals of the Cabinet of Ministers of Ukraine the list of the central bodies of the executive power, organisations, institutions, officials responsible for carrying out the tasks defined by the Strategy of integration.

2. Regular holding of the Ukrainian part of the Ukraine - EU Co-operation Council meetings in order to ensure the fulfilment of the tasks defined by the Strategy of integration.

3. Providing formation and implementation of sectoral and regional programmes of co-operation with the EU according to the responsibility of Ukrainian party.

4. Creation of new programmes in education, employees training and professional qualification development for representatives of legislative, executive power and local authorities in accordance with the main directions of Ukraine's European integration, introduction of specialisation on EU issues within the framework of high institutions training programmes.

5. Creation of the programme of linguistic training for government officials and professionals who implement the integration process, elaboration and realisation of the complex of measures on expanding and upgrading the quality of learning EU languages in secondary and higher education.

2. *Financial support*

1. Elaboration of the programme for financing measures on Ukraine's integration to the EU according to the Strategy of integration.

2. Financing measures aiming Ukraine's integration to the EU for the expense of budget funds with the wide involvement of off-budget funds, funds of private persons and assistance programmes of the EU for Ukraine.

3. *Legal support*

1. Providing adaptation of legislation acts approving by executive power bodies as required by the EU.

2. Revision of training programmes for legal education with the purpose of their adaptation to the EU programmes, research of legal principles for EU institutions

activities, studying processes in the legislation of the EU Member States as well as applicant countries.

4. *Informational support*

1. Realisation of the wide scale of promotional and informational national campaign with the purpose of supporting Ukraine's integration to the EU. Elaboration and implementation of the programme to inform public concerning situation in the EU, problems and progress of Ukraine's integration to the EU.

2. Providing the access to the European legal, reference and other informational databases.

3. Setting-up the National Data Centre (Bank) on the EU.

After creation of the National Programme of the Integration Strategy, the Action Plan on implementation Ukraine's strategic course for integration to the European Union shall be elaborated annually.

APPENDIX 3

European Council Common Strategy on Ukraine

(Adopted by the Helsinki European Council on December 1999)

Part I: Vision of the European Union for its Partnership with Ukraine

1. The strategic partnership between the European Union (EU) and Ukraine, based on shared values and common interests, is a vital factor enhancing peace, stability and prosperity in Europe. The freedom, independence and stability of Ukraine rank among the greatest achievements in the new Europe rid of old dividing lines. Geography as well as size, the resources of its population as well as its location along the North-South and East-West axes give Ukraine a unique position in Europe and makes it a determinant regional actor.

2. Ukraine enjoys today excellent relations with all its neighbours and has taken important steps in nation-building and towards consolidating its democracy. The fact that Ukraine has since independence been a source of regional stability, despite its domestic difficulties and diversities, is a laudable achievement. The EU welcomes the close involvement of Ukraine in the stabilisation of its region and encourages the strengthening of Ukraine's role in regional co-operation fora. The EU also welcomes Ukraine's commitment to nuclear disarmament as well as its co-operation in the maintenance of European and international peace and security, namely through the Organisation for Security and Co-operation in Europe (OSCE) and the United Nations.

3. The strategic partnership between the EU and Ukraine has been continuously reinforced since the independence of Ukraine. In this context, the Partnership and Co-operation Agreement is a significant achievement. Ukraine was the first of the Newly Independent States to sign such an agreement, thus marking the EU's and Ukraine's wish to strengthen co-operation. Through macro-financial assistance, the Tacis-programme, as well as through bilateral programmes, valuable support is provided by the EU to help Ukraine in her transition and reform process.

4. Following the current enlargement process, some future EU Member States will share an external border with Ukraine. The enlargement of the Union will further enhance economic dynamism and political stability in the region, thus increasing the possibilities for co-operation with Ukraine.

5. The European Union has the following strategic goals with regard to Ukraine:

- to contribute to the emergence of a stable, open and pluralistic democracy in Ukraine, governed by the rule of law and underpinning a stable functioning market economy which will benefit all the people of Ukraine;
- to co-operate with Ukraine in the maintenance of stability and security in Europe and the wider world, and in finding effective responses to common challenges facing the continent;
- to increase economic, political and cultural co-operation with Ukraine as well as co-operation in the field of justice and home affairs.

6. The EU acknowledges Ukraine's European aspirations and welcomes Ukraine's pro-European choice. The EU remains firmly committed to working with Ukraine at national, regional and local levels, in order to support a successful political and economic transformation in Ukraine, which will facilitate Ukraine's further rapprochement with the EU. The EU and its Member States offer to share with Ukraine their various experiences in building modern political, economic, social and administrative structures, fully recognising that the main responsibility for Ukraine's future lies with Ukraine itself.

7. The European Council therefore adopts this Common Strategy to strengthen the strategic partnership between the EU and Ukraine. The European Council recognises that a successful, stable and secure Ukraine is in the best of interests of the EU. The legal basis of the relationship between the EU and Ukraine is the Partnership and Co-operation Agreement (PCA). The full implementation of this agreement is a prerequisite for Ukraine's successful integration into the European economy and will also help Ukraine assert its European identity.

8. The EU and its Member States will develop the co-ordination, coherence and complementarity of all aspects of their policy towards Ukraine. The Union, the Community and its Member States will also work together with and within regional and international organisations as well as with like-minded partners to meet the objectives set out in the PCA and this Common Strategy. The positions taken by the Community and its Member States in all relevant fora will conform to this Common Strategy. The European Council invites Ukraine to work with the EU on the basis of this Common Strategy to the benefit of both.

Part II: Principal Objectives

The European Council has identified the following principal objectives:

I. Support for the democratic and economic transition process in Ukraine

II. Ensuring stability and security and meeting common challenges on the European continent

III. Support for strengthened co-operation between the EU and Ukraine within the context of EU enlargement

I. Support for the democratic and economic transition process in Ukraine

The EU and Ukraine have a common interest in accelerating the democratic and economic transition process in Ukraine. The successful transformation in Ukraine will bring prosperity not only to Ukraine but to the entire region. In order for this transition process to be successful, reforms must take place to consolidate democracy and the rule of law as well as economic and social reform in view of establishing a functioning market economy.

The EU proposes to strengthen co-operation with Ukraine in the following priority areas:

I(i) The consolidation of democracy, the rule of law and public institutions in Ukraine

9. The EU welcomes Ukraine's achievements in laying the foundations of a democratic system namely in establishing a multiparty system and adopting a parliamentary constitution. The EU acknowledges Ukraine's achievements in maintaining its unity despite the country's diverse make up.

10. The EU supports Ukraine in all its efforts aiming at the consolidation of democracy and good governance, human rights and the rule of law. The Union considers that the rule of law is a prerequisite for the development of a functioning market economy which offers opportunities and benefits to all the citizens of Ukraine. The EU supports Ukraine's efforts to reform the legal system in the framework of the PCA. A properly functioning independent judiciary, a professional police force, the development of a meritocratic, well-trained public administration at national, regional and local levels are all key elements in the effective implementation of government decisions. The EU encourages Ukraine's efforts to develop the efficiency, transparency and democratic character of its public institutions, including the development of free media. These are prerequisites for economic and social development and contribute to the building of a modern civil society.

11. The EU attaches importance to the development of civil society and a competitive, investor friendly business environment in Ukraine and encourages closer links between the peoples and non-governmental organisations of the Union and Ukraine. The EU welcomes Ukraine's agreement of a Memorandum of Understanding with the OSCE and strongly recommends Ukraine to work in close co-operation with the OSCE project co-ordinator in Ukraine. The EU supports Ukraine's efforts aiming at the protection

and promotion of rights of minorities and calls upon Ukraine to continue its good work in this domain, including in co-operation with the High Commissioner for National Minorities.

12. The EU attaches particular importance to close co-operation with Ukraine in the framework of the Council of Europe and the OSCE. In this context, the EU urges Ukraine to fulfil its commitments and to adapt its legislation to meet the norms and standards of the Council of Europe, in particular the obligations to which Ukraine signed up on its accession to the Council of Europe in 1995. The EU takes note of the findings of the OSCE/Office for Democratic Institutions and Human Rights (ODIHR) election monitoring mission on the conduct of the 1999 presidential elections in Ukraine, to the effect that the conduct of these elections failed to meet a number of OSCE commitments and calls on Ukraine to heed the recommendations made by the OSCE monitoring mission in its report with a view to future elections.

I(ii) Support for the economic transition process in Ukraine

13. The EU is committed to supporting Ukraine's efforts in establishing an environment that is conducive to economic activity and will support Ukraine in its economic and social reforms.

14. The EU encourages Ukraine to establish macro-economic policies aiming at price stability, sound public finances and a sustainable current account position. In order to proceed further to price stability it is important that the central bank is allowed to operate independently of political interference. Existing prudential regulations for financial sector supervision need to be strengthened. Tax collection must be improved, and ad hoc tax amnesties and tax exemptions for specific sectors of the economy should be avoided.

15. The EU strongly encourages Ukraine to intensify its efforts to build a functioning market economy through greater structural, economic and administrative reforms in the context of a comprehensive reform programme agreed with the International Monetary Fund. This should include establishing and enforcing clear property rights, further privatisation, further liberalisation of prices, the raising of communal tariffs for energy, water and rents to full cost recovery levels, restructuring of business, and encouraging the growth of small and medium size enterprises. The overall pace of these reforms needs to be accelerated. As far as sectoral reform is concerned, the agriculture, energy and transport sectors deserve particular attention.

16. The introduction of a land reform process is required to facilitate, inter alia the long term lease of land as collateral for loans, paving the way for more investment in the agriculture sector.

17. Attracting and protecting domestic and foreign investment also plays a key role in Ukraine's development. In this context, the EU notes that allegations of corruption and

poor governance are damaging to Ukraine's economic reputation. The Union will support Ukraine in developing and adopting the economic policies needed to increase domestic and foreign investment and to meet the requirements of international lenders.

18. In view of Ukraine's heavy debt service obligations, Ukraine's economic recovery will require the continued involvement of private creditors. Collaborative solutions to Ukraine's debt service problems must be found.

19. The EU is fully aware of the fact that Ukraine's economic reforms sometimes have to be pursued in a difficult external environment. EU macro-financial assistance would be pursued as appropriate, in accordance with established criteria and procedures, aiming at supporting macro-economic stabilisation and comprehensive structural reform, consistent with programmes of the International Monetary Fund and the World Bank. The EU will continue to stand ready to support economic reforms in Ukraine in those circumstances. EU macro-financial assistance helps Ukraine to open up its economy, improve economic adjustment, enhance competition, and further integrate the Ukrainian economy into the European and global economy.

20. The EU will support Ukraine through the promotion of progressive approximation of legislation towards that of the EU, especially in such areas as competition policy, standards and certification, intellectual property rights, data protection, customs procedures and environment.

21. In implementing a programme that establishes a functioning market economy, a well targeted social security system must be put in place, so that the social aspects of the transition to a market economy are taken into account.

II. Ensuring stability and security and meeting common challenges on the European continent

The EU and Ukraine have a common interest in the maintenance of stability and security in a free and democratic Europe. The geopolitical situation of Ukraine, situated along the North-South and East-West axes gives Ukraine a unique position in Europe. The EU recognises Ukraine's regional importance. In this context, the EU proposes to strengthen co-operation with Ukraine paying particular attention to nuclear safety and to the strengthening of political dialogue, as provided for in the framework of the PCA, with a view of making it more coherent and operational.

The EU wishes to deepen co-operation with Ukraine in order to find effective responses to common challenges facing the continent on the following issues:

II(i) Co-operation to strengthen stability and security in Europe

22. The EU supports Ukraine's efforts to promote co-operation and stability in its region, including in the context of the Black Sea Economic Co-operation Organisation, the

Council of Baltic Sea States and Georgia, Ukraine, Uzbekistan, Azerbaijan and Moldovo. The EU welcomes the positive development of Ukraine's relationship with all its neighbours and believes it has an interest in those relationships remaining strong and stable. The EU also notes Ukraine's contribution to European stability through its role as an observer to the Stability Pact for South-East Europe.

23. The EU and Ukraine share a common interest in the maintenance of stability and security in a free and democratic Europe. Strengthened mechanisms for consultations between the EU and Ukraine in the framework of the PCA, Council of Europe and United Nations, and strong co-operation between the OSCE and Ukraine, are needed to respond jointly and effectively to European and global security challenges.

24. The EU congratulates Ukraine on its election to the United Nations Security Council (2000-2002). This fact reinforces the need for the EU further to deepen and broaden its political dialogue with Ukraine at official and ministerial level, bilaterally and through EU mechanisms. The adoption of the European Security Charter will enhance the co-operation between the Member States of the OSCE.

25. The EU promotes and supports the dialogue on general and specific issues relating to crisis management and security building as developed over the past years between the Western European Union and Ukraine as well as the intensification of practical co-operation in this field, in particular through the implementation of the action plan recently drawn up between the Western European Union and Ukraine.

26. The EU is also interested in strengthening co-operation with Ukraine in the field of export controls and non-proliferation of weapons of mass destruction and their delivery vehicles, and encourages Ukraine to fulfil its obligations under the Chemical Weapons Convention.

27. Moreover, the EU encourages Ukraine to achieve the goals of the Convention on the Prohibition of the Use, Stockpiling, Production and Transfer of Anti-Personnel Mines and on their Destruction. The EU also encourages Ukraine to develop a strategy to combat the destabilising accumulation and the spread of small arms and light weapons.

II(ii) Co-operation in the field of environment, energy and nuclear safety

28. The EU will seek to enhance European stability and work with Ukraine in the fields of energy and nuclear safety, by supporting a comprehensive energy sector reform, inter alia, by continued co-operation with Ukraine on the implementation of the financial Recovery Plan for the energy sector, including price liberalisation, improved cash collection and privatisation of distribution companies. In this context, the EU will promote the efficient and environmentally responsible use of energy in Ukraine and the strengthening of new energy institutions and authorities and their policy-making capacity.

29. Nuclear safety and the decommissioning of the Chernobyl Nuclear Power Plant are a priority in EU-Ukraine relations. The EU encourages the development of an independent nuclear regulatory authority in Ukraine and urges Ukraine to stand by its commitment to implement the G7/Ukraine Memorandum of Understanding of 1995 on the closure of Chernobyl. In return, the EU will support Ukraine in financing replacement energy generating capacity in Ukraine.

30. The EU is also interested in enhancing co-operation with Ukraine on such issues as radiation protection, waste management, decontamination and dismantling of nuclear installations, and studies in the field of fusion technology. The recently signed co-operation agreements in the fields of nuclear safety and thermonuclear fusion between Euratom and Ukraine will facilitate this co-operation.

31. Moreover, the EU encourages Ukraine to take resolute measures in the field of environmental protection. The protection of public health against pollution of drinking water, air and soil, and the sustainable and responsible use of natural resources as well as the limitation of transboundary pollution of air and water are priorities in this area.

III. Support for strengthened co-operation between the EU and Ukraine within the context of EU enlargement

Following the current enlargement process, some future EU Member States will share an external border with Ukraine. The EU wishes to contribute to the mutual benefit of the Union and Ukraine in this process. In this context, the EU proposes strengthened co-operation with Ukraine, paying particular attention to co-operation in the field of justice and home affairs. The EU also encourages Ukraine's participation in regional, European and world structures.

The EU could strengthen co-operation with Ukraine in the following fields:

III(i) Support for Ukraine's integration into European and world economy

32. The Union supports Ukraine and urges it to redouble its efforts to meet the requirements of World Trade Organisation membership. The Union encourages Ukraine to take full advantage of the possibilities offered by the PCA to facilitate two-way trade and investment. The Union will also examine the circumstances which might, in addition to the World Trade Organisation (WTO) accession, allow for the future establishment of an EU-Ukraine Free Trade Area, as foreseen in the PCA.

33. In order to facilitate a favourable investment climate in Ukraine, the EU encourages Ukraine to negotiate and ratify further bilateral investment protection agreements with EU Member States so as to stimulate foreign direct investment. The EU also encourages local, regional and national Ukrainian authorities to avail themselves of the opportunities of the new law on public concession to attract investment in public infrastructure and services.

III(ii) Co-operation in the field of justice and home affairs

34. The EU and Ukraine have a common interest in developing co-operation to combat illegal immigration and trafficking in human beings. The EU and Ukraine also have a common interest in developing their co-operation in the area of border security and the fight against the common scourges of organised crime, including money laundering and illegal trafficking in weapons and drugs.

35. In view of the current EU enlargement process, the EU will seek to intensify dialogue with Ukraine on the adjustment of Ukraine's visa policy with the EU through the introduction of visa requirements in accordance with EC provisions and introduction of travel documents which are sufficiently non-forgeable.

III(iii) Regional and cross-border co-operation with neighbouring countries

36. The EU encourages the development and strengthening of regional and cross-border co-operation initiatives involving Ukraine and its neighbouring countries. In this context, the EU will put increased emphasis on border management issues.

37. As to the development of infrastructure networks, especially in the fields of transport, telecommunications, electricity and energy-pipelines, the EU, through Tacis, pays particular attention to regional initiatives, such as Inogate (Interstate Oil and Gas Transport to Europe) and Traceca (Transport Corridor Europe Caucasus Central Asia), with the aim of improving economic co-operation in the region. The EU will explore the scope for working towards linking the Ukrainian transportation systems (road and rail) with the Trans-European networks. and will seek mutually satisfactory ways to address transport issues. In doing so, special care will be taken to reinforce co-ordination with other donors and with international financial institutions, as well as to stimulate the involvement of the private sector, which will be crucial to the success of this endeavour.

Instruments and means

General provisions

38. This Common Strategy shall be implemented in accordance with the applicable procedures of the Treaties. The Council and the Commission shall in accordance with Articles 3 and 13 of the Treaty on European Union ensure the unity, consistency and effectiveness of the Union's actions in implementing this Common Strategy.

39. The EU will contribute to the cited objectives of this Common Strategy by making appropriate use of all relevant instruments and means available to the Union, the Community and to the Member States.

40. In accordance with Articles 18 and 26 of the Treaty on European Union, the Secretary-General of the Council, High Representative for the Common Foreign and Security Policy (CFSP), in the framework of his obligations under the Treaties, shall assist the Council and the Presidency in implementing this Common Strategy with regard to those objectives and initiatives falling under the CFSP. The Commission shall be fully associated in accordance with Articles 18 and 27 of the Treaty on European Union.

The Council, the Commission and Member States

41. The Council, the Commission and Member States shall:

- review, according to their powers and capacities, existing actions, programmes, instruments, and policies to ensure their consistency with this Common Strategy, based on the principle objectives in Part II and taking due account of the specific initiatives in Part III;
- make full and appropriate use of existing instruments and means, in particular the PCA, as well as all relevant EU and Member States programmes, and to develop and maintain to this end an indicative inventory of the resources of the Union, the Community and Member States through which the Common Strategy will be implemented.

Co-ordination

42. Member States shall make additional efforts to co-ordinate their actions vis-à-vis Ukraine, including in regional and international organisations such as the Council of Europe, the UN, the OSCE, the DECD and the International Financial Institutions (IFIs), and including co-ordination with the Community where it has competencies.

43. Co-ordination between the Member States and the Commission shall also be consolidated, including through regular consultations between their respective representatives in Ukraine.

44. The Council, the Commission and Member States shall work towards more effective co-operation with regional and international organisations, and will seek with other like-minded countries to achieve the objectives of the Strategy.

45. The European Union will invite the candidate countries in the accession process launched in the Luxembourg European Council in December 1997 to associate themselves within the framework of this Common Strategy.

Implementation and review

46. The Council shall:

- ensure that each incoming Presidency presents to the Council, in the framework of its general programme, a work plan for the implementation of this Common Strategy, based on the principle objectives in Part II and taking due account of the specific initiatives in Part III,

• review and evaluate the EU's action under this Strategy and report to the European Council on progress towards its objectives not less than annually,

• review the situation in Ukraine and the state of Ukraine's co-operation in the implementation of this Strategy, including through periodic reports by the Heads of Mission, and make an assessment in its report to the European Council,

• where necessary, submit recommendations for amendments to Part II and III of this Strategy to the European Council.

47. The Commission will contribute to the above within its powers.

Co-operation with Ukraine

48. The EU and its Member States will work closely together with Ukraine to implement this Common Strategy, in particular through the PCA and its institutions.

Specific initiatives

49. The EU shall pursue the specific initiatives set out in Part III of this Common Strategy which are based on the principal objectives identified in Part II. These initiatives shall be adapted when necessary and do not preclude possible new initiatives during the duration of this Common Strategy. The Council, the Commission and the Member States shall, in accordance with their respective powers and capacities, support and work towards the achievement of these specific initiatives.

Part III: Specific initiatives

The following specific initiatives shall be pursued not precluding possible new initiatives:

The consolidation of democracy, the rule of law and public institutions in Ukraine

50. The EU will undertake efforts to foster democracy, good governance, human rights and the rule of law in Ukraine, by:

• supporting Ukraine's efforts to observe its international democratic and human rights obligations in accordance with the Dublin conclusions, in particular with regard to the abolition of death penalty, the promotion of good governance, and an effective and transparent legal system as well as democratic local self government, inter alia, in co-operation with the Council of Europe and the OSCE,

• establishing a regular dialogue between the ombudsman-institutions of the EU Member States and Ukraine in order to strengthen the role of this institution in Ukraine,

• encouraging Ukraine to sign, ratify and implement the relevant international instruments in the field of Human Rights, especially the second Optional Protocol of the United Nations Convention on Civil and Political Rights and the Sixth Additional Protocol of the European Convention on Human Rights and Fundamental Freedoms as well as the United Nations Convention on the Status of Refugees,

• increasing co-operation among journalists and relevant authorities in order to contribute to the development of free media. The Commission in co-operation with the Member States will investigate the possibility of assisting in the transmission of a programme, such as Euronews, on Ukrainian television. Work will begin by June 2000.

Support of the economic transition process in Ukraine

51. The EU will help Ukraine advance the process of economic reform by enhancing the impact of economic policy advice, including through appropriate high-level dialogue, in the framework of the PCA, so as to promote the development of a modern, liberal market economy.

52. The EU stands ready to provide technical assistance in support of Ukraine's economic and social reform process provided that Ukraine takes steps designed to establish the necessary conditions to make reform possible. The EU will examine the possibility of providing technical assistance to Ukraine with a view of:

• supporting the development of a transparent and stable legal, regulator and institutional framework in Ukraine designed to promote increased economic activity and domestic and foreign investment. The Commission in co-operation with Member States and other competent bodies will prepare a report with regard to this initiative by December 2000,

• promoting the progressive approximation of Ukrainian legislation to that of the EU and its implementation, in particular in the areas of competition policy, financial services, standards and certification, fiscal policy as well as employment and intellectual property rights. The Commission is invited to make adequate proposals to this end by June 2000,

• supporting the development of the health system, in particular public health awareness and education with a view to restricting the spread of communicable diseases. The Commission in co-operation with the Member States and other competent bodies will prepare a report with regard to this initiative by June 2001.

53. The Member States will consider means to assist Ukraine in:

• supporting the development of a well-targeted social security system, in particular addressing the social assistance and pension systems,

• supporting social dialogue and the adherence to and implementation of the International Labour Organisation Labour Standards, in particular the seven core Labour Standards. As far as ratification and implementation of legislation in the employment field is concerned, particular attention will be paid to gender equality.

Co-operation to strengthen stability and security in Europe

54. The EU will consider ways to give more continuity, flexibility and substance to the co-operation with Ukraine on stability and security in Europe and to render it more operational and effective, within the framework of the existing political dialogue, as instituted under the PCA, by:

• exploring the possibilities of establishing regular expert level Troika dialogue meetings with Ukraine in the margins of CFSP working groups on disarmament, non-proliferation, export of conventional arms with a view to organising the first meetings during the year 2000/first semester 2000. The dialogue within these groups will aim to set up co-operation between the EU and Ukraine in the following fields: non-proliferation of weapons of mass destruction, including chemical weapons and small arms and light weapons on the basis of the joint action on small arms (1999/34/CFSP),

• considering the possibility of intensifying the dialogue between the EU and Ukraine to promote responsibility and transparency in transfers of conventional arms, making full use of the EU Code of Conduct where appropriate,

• exploring the possibilities for closer co-operation in conflict prevention and crisis management, inter alia, in the framework of relevant international organisations, such as the United Nations and the OSCE, and in seeking a political settlement to conflicts in the region. Periodic meetings between Ukraine and the Troika of the OSCE Working Group would help achieve this. One of the aims would be to work with Ukraine to develop joint foreign policy initiatives in the area of conflict prevention and crisis management with regard to specific third countries and regions, especially in areas adjacent to Ukraine.

55. The EU will, as soon as the year 2000, take up the following specific initiatives concerning the strengthening of security and stability in Europe:

• consider facilitating the participation of Ukraine when the EU avails itself of the Western European Union for missions within the range of the Petersburg tasks,

• consider means to assist Ukraine in fulfilling the obligations of the Convention on the Prohibition of the Use, Stockpiling, Production and Transfer of Anti-Personnel Mines and on their Destruction,

• consider means to initiate co-operation between the EU and Ukraine on prevention of trafficking of small arms, which is a source of instability for Ukraine and other States of the region. The EU could after identification and analysis of the situation and needs in the region, draw up a Joint Action on this subject with a view to:

1. reinforce control capacities of police and/or local custom services;

2. tackle this specific type of criminality in training courses;

3. develop exchange of information between the EU and Europol Member States in order to improve the analysis on criminal activity concerning small arms.

Co-operation in the field of environment, energy and nuclear safety

56. The Community stands ready to support the efforts of the special Task Force established to support the Ukrainian authorities in their effort to reform the energy sector.

57. The Community support to the G7 Action Plan includes a contribution to financing the short term safety improvements of Chernobyl via the Nuclear Safety Account managed by the European Bank for Reconstruction and Development before closure, decommissioning, addressing the social consequences of closure, contributing to the Shelter Implementation Plan and participating in the financing of substitution facilities in line with previous commitments compensating for Ukraine's energy losses, provided that all necessary due diligence procedures can be concluded satisfactorily, including the

establishment of an agreed position regarding the loan conditionality and the wording of the loan and guarantee agreement and provided that Ukraine stands by its commitment to implement the 1995 Memorandum of Understanding.

58. The EU will seek to support Ukraine in its effort to reduce the negative impact on public health of the environmental situation in Ukraine - notably as regards the quality of drinking water, waste water treatment, waste collection and disposal as well as air pollution. The EU will support institutional reform in the public utilities responsible for environmental services, other technical assistance projects and environmental investments.

59. The next 'Environment for Europe' conference will be held in September 2002 in Kiev and will provide the opportunity to increase awareness in Ukraine of environmental issues. Member States and the Commission will consider the possibility of offering technical assistance/support to the Ministry of Environmental Protection and Nuclear Safety with the preparation and planning of the conference.

Support for Ukraine's integration into European and world economy

60. The EU remains ready to maintain and, if appropriate, to enhance its support for Ukraine's efforts to meet the requirements of WTO accession. Special attention will be given to removing obstacles to trade and investment in Ukraine, starting with the elimination of trade measures incompatible with PCA and WTO.

61. The EU will examine the circumstances which might, in addition to WTO accession, allow for the future establishment of an EU-Ukraine Free Trade Area as provided for in Article 4 of the PCA. The on-going joint economic feasibility study of the Free Trade Area will provide important input to evaluate the situation.

62. The Commission will examine ways to deepen the investment dialogue with Ukraine in the framework of the PCA Sub-Committee on trade and investment and will report to the Council by June 2000.

Co-operation in the field of justice and home affairs

63. In view of the EU's current enlargement process, also taking into account Ukraine's position as an important transit country providing a conduit for the cross-border flow of a wide range of non-legal activities, the EU and Ukraine have a particular interest in stepping up co-operation in the field of justice and home affairs. The EU proposes to concentrate its efforts with a view to:

- assessing the scale of illegal immigration via Ukraine. The Member States in association with the Commission will produce a strengths/weaknesses/opportunities/threats ('SWOT') analysis of the existing mechanisms to combat these problems by the end of 2000; where weaknesses are identified, the EU will consider remedial action,

- improving co-operation regarding the readmission of own nationals, persons without nationality and third country nationals, including the conclusion of a readmission agreement,
- supporting a full application of the Geneva Convention, including the right to seek asylum and respect for the principles of non-refoulement,
- establishing a regular dialogue between the judicial authorities of the Member States and Ukraine in civil and criminal matters, including by encouraging Ukraine to sign, ratify and implement key conventions, such as the United Nations Convention on Transnational Organised Crime,
- offering to provide practical help to Ukraine in implementing its legislation on money laundering as soon as it is enacted,
- establishing co-operation between EU Member States' law enforcement agencies, Europol and Ukrainian law enforcement authorities.

64. An informal network will be established in Kiev consisting of EU Member States Embassies, Commission and relevant international organisation representatives in order to improve the exchange and analysis of information in justice and home affairs. A dialogue, within the framework of the PCA, between the Member States, the Commission, including the liaison officers in Kiev and competent Ukrainian bodies will make it possible to analyse Ukraine's requirements in this area more precisely. A report will be submitted to the Council by the end of 2000.

Regional and cross-border co-operation with neighbouring countries

65. The EU will seek to encourage the development and strengthening of regional and cross-border co-operation initiatives involving Ukraine and its neighbouring countries, by:

- making targeted use of existing cross-border co-operation, regional and inter-State programmes. In this context, special attention will be devoted to border management issues, including the technical modernisation of border crossing points on Ukraine's borders with Hungary, Poland, Romania and Slovakia,
- further developing Tacis programmes aimed at improving the development of infrastructure networks, such as Inogate and Traceca in order to improve economic co-operation in the region.

Co-operation in the fields of culture, twinning and exchange programmes

66. The EU will support the fostering of closer links between public institutions, civil society and non-governmental organisations of the Union and Ukraine, by:

- promoting educational and scientific exchange programmes between schools, universities and research institutes, also paying due attention to the Science and Technology Centre in Ukraine,
- promoting twinning programmes between national, regional and local administrations as well as professional associations, trade unions, non-governmental organisations and the media.

The Commission and the Member States will co-ordinate their programmes. The Commission will study the possibility of bringing Community programmes into play for this purpose (Tacis, Tempus and Democracy). The Member States' bilateral instruments will also be used.

On the basis of an inventory of existing instruments (to be drawn up by the Commission in co-operation with the General Secretariat of the Council) and an identification mission to Ukraine, the Commission will report to the Council by June 2000 and will thereafter submit proposals for action as appropriate.

Part IV

Duration

67. This Common Strategy shall apply from the date of its publication for an initial period of four years. It may be prolonged, reviewed and, if necessary, adapted by the European Council on the recommendation of the Council.

Publication

68. This Common Strategy shall be published in the Official Journal.

Done at Helsinki, 11 December 1999.

For the European Council

The President

P. LIPPONEN

ABBREVIATIONS

ASEAN	Association of South East Asian Nations
CEE	Central and Eastern Europe
CFSP	Common Foreign and Security Policy
CIDA	Canadian International Development Agency
CIS	Commonwealth of Independent States
CLRAE	Congress of Local and Regional Authorities of Europe
CoE	Council of Europe
CPU	Communist Party of Ukraine
CS	Common Strategy
CSO	Civil Society Organisation
EBA	European Business Association
EBRD	European Bank for Reconstruction and Development
EC	European Commission
ECHO	European Community Humanitarian Organisation
ECSC	European Coal and Steel Community
EEA	European Economic Area
EEC	European Economic Community
EP	European Parliament
EIB	European Investment Bank
ESDP	European Security and Defence Policy
EU	European Union
FBI	Federal Bureau of Investigation
FDI	Foreign Direct Investment
FSU	Former Soviet Union
G7	Group of 7
GDP	Gross Domestic Product

GDR	German Democratic Republic
GNP	Gross National Product
GSP	Generalised Scheme of Preferences
GUUAM	Georgia, Ukraine, Uzbekistan, Armenia, Moldova
HQ	Headquarters
ICPS	International Centre for Policy Studies
IFI	International Financial Institution
IGC	Inter Governmental Conference
IMF	International Monetary Fund
IPCTF	International Private Capital Task Force
JHA	Justice and Home Affairs
KGB	Committee for State Security (of the USSR)
KFOR	Kosovo Force
MFA	Ministry of Foreign Affairs
MI5	UK counter-intelligence service
MOD	Ministry of Defence
MOU	Memorandum of Understanding
MVD	Ministry of Internal Affairs (of the USSR)
MVS	Ministry of the Interior (of Ukraine)
NAK	Naftogaz of Ukraine
Nato	North Atlantic Treaty Organisation
NBU	National Bank of Ukraine
NGO	Non-governmental Organisation
NIS	Newly Independent States (formerly part of the USSR)
NPP	Nuclear Power Plant
NSDC	National Security and Defence Council
OSCE	Organisation for Security and Co-operation in Europe
PCA	Partnership and Co-operation Agreement
PfP	Partnership for Peace
Phare	Technical assistance for CEE countries (originally PHARE: Poland and Hungary: Action for Restructuring the Economy)
POLUKRBAT	Polish-Ukrainian Battalion
QMV	Qualified Majority Voting
RSFSR	Russian Soviet Federal Socialist Republic
SBU	Security Service of Ukraine

SVR	Foreign Intelligence Service (of Ukraine)
Tacis	Technical assistance to the NIS and Mongolia (originally TACIS: Technical Assistance for the CIS)
TEPSA	Trans European Policy Studies Association
TEU	Treaty on the European Union (the Maastricht Treaty)
UAH	Ukrainian Hryvnia
UCEPS	Ukrainian Centre for Economic and Political Studies
UN	United Nations
USSR	Union of Soviet Socialist Republics
WBI	World Bank Institute
WEU	Western European Union
WTO	World Trade Organisation

NOTES ON CONTRIBUTORS

Christopher Beazley

Mr Beazley was elected Member of the European Parliament (MEP) for the United Kingdom's Eastern Region in 1999. He was previously MEP for Cornwall for 10 years. He is Vice-Chairman of the Constitutional Affairs Committee and a member of the Industry Committee and the Estonia-EU Joint Parliamentary Committee.

Bill Bowring

Professor Bowring is a barrister, and Professor in Human Rights and International Law at the University of North London. He advises the UK's Department for International Development on access to justice and rights issues in Russia and Ukraine, and has accompanied and advised the OSCE's High Commissioner on National Minorities on missions to Ukraine and Russia.

Igor V. Burakovsky

Professor Burakovsky is Senior Economist at the East-West Institute Kiev Centre and Professor of Economics at the Kiev-Mohyla Academy of Ukraine's National University.

Richard Creagh

Mr Creagh is Deputy President of Ukrainian International Airlines. He previously spent almost 30 years in the airline business with AerLingus, including as Vice-President with responsibility for strategy, business development, international relations and alliances, and has held a number of Board appointments in aviation-related businesses in Ireland.

Frank Duffield

Mr Duffield has been Vice President for Central and Eastern Europe, Russia and Central Asia at Shell Gas and Power since 1998. Born and educated in New Zealand, he practiced as a lawyer before joining Shell in 1974. He was inter alia President of the Sakhalin Energy Investment Company Ltd responsible for the Sakhalin II project, which came on stream in 1999.

Ann Lewis

Ms Lewis is a free-lance consultant. She recently retired from the British Diplomatic Service, where she spent most of her career dealing with the Soviet Union and Central and Eastern Europe.

Roger Liddle

Mr Liddle has been Political Adviser on Europe to the British Prime Minister since May 1997. He has spent most of his career in the political world: as local councillor, in party offices, and in think-tanks.

Serhiy Maksymenko

Mr Maksymenko is Deputy Programme Director for Local Government at the East-West Institute Kiev Centre. He is an expert on European and Ukrainian regional policies, trans-frontier co-operation, community governance and urban and regional development.

Michael McCulloch

Mr McCulloch was UK representative on the Board of the EBRD 1997-2001. His previous career was spent in the UK government's overseas development agencies, latterly as Head of the Know How Fund for the former Soviet Union, developing its support for economic and political reform in the region.

Vira Nanivska

Dr Nanivska has been Director since 1997 of the International Centre for Policy Studies in Kiev, the first think-tank in Ukraine to establish a fully-fledged policy process comprising policy research, policy dialogue and public education. After her dissertation on Japanese modernisation, she worked for the World Bank Resident Mission in Ukraine 1992-97.

Anatoliy Orel

Ambassador Orel has been Foreign Policy Adviser to the Ukrainian President and Deputy Head of the Presidential Administration since August 1999. He is a long-standing specialist in international affairs, including in the Communist Party Central Committee in Moscow, as Ambassador to Italy 1992-98 and Deputy Foreign Minister 1998-99.

Yuriy Petrus

Dr Petrus has been Executive Director of the European Business Association since autumn 2000. Before joining EBA he worked for a number of multinational companies in Ukraine including Monsanto and British Petroleum.

Inna Pidluska

Ms Pidluska is President and co-founder of the Europe XXI Foundation and chairperson of the board of the Ukrainian Center for Independent Political Research, both non-governmental think-tanks. Her research interests include various aspects of European integration and EU enlargement.

Robert Pszczel

Mr Pszczel works in the Press and Information Office at Nato Headquarters, acting both as a press officer and as Information Officer (Poland) responsible for Nato's information policy vis-a-vis Poland. He is a career diplomat on unpaid leave from the Polish Foreign Ministry, where he has worked mainly on multilateral issues.

Volodymyr Saprykin

Dr Saprykin is Director for Energy Programmes at the Ukrainian Centre for Economic and Political Studies named after Olexander Razumkov. He has a Doctorate in Chemical Engineering from the Gas Institute of the National Academy of Sciences of Ukraine in Kiev.

Gwendolyn Sasse

Dr Sasse is Lecturer in East European Politics at the London School of Economics and Political Sciences. Her research focuses on post-communist transitions, with particular emphasis on Ukraine and on EU enlargement issues. She is co-editor of "Ethnicity and Territory in the Former Soviet Union: Regions in Conflict" (London: Frank Cass, 2001).

Edilberto L. Segura

Dr Segura has been Director of the SigmaBleyzer Office in Kiev and Fellow and Visiting Professor at the Said Business School, Oxford University, since 1999. He worked for the World Bank 1973-1998, including as Chief of the World Bank Mission in Ukraine 1996-1998.

James Sherr

Mr Sherr has been a Fellow of the Conflict Studies Research Centre at the Royal Military Academy Sandhurst since 1995 and Lecturer at Lincoln College Oxford since 1986. He is a Specialist Adviser to the House of Commons Defence Committee, and a former Director of Services at the Royal United Services Institute.

Javier Solana Madariaga

Dr Solana has been Secretary-General of the Council of the European Union and High Representative for the Common Foreign and Security Policy since October 1999. He has also been Secretary-General of the Western European Union since November 1999, and was Secretary-General of Nato 1995-1999.

He was a Member of the Spanish Cabinet from 1982 to 1995, including Minister of Foreign Affairs 1992-1995.

Olexiy Solohubenko

Mr Solohubenko is Head of the BBC Ukrainian Service. Born and educated in Ukraine, he took a Masters degree in media studies at Manchester University, returned to Kiev to work for Ukrainian Radio, and in 1992 joined the BBC World Service as Deputy Head of the Ukrainian Service which was then being set up.

Elizabeth Teague

Dr Teague has been a member of Eastern Research Group, Research Analysts, Foreign and Commonwealth Office, London, since 1998. Previously she worked as an analyst of Soviet politics for Radio Free Europe/Radio Liberty, as an Adviser to the OSCE High Commissioner on National Minorities, and as an analyst of Russian politics for the Jamestown Foundation.

John Tedstrom

Dr Tedstrom is Vice-President for Policy Studies at the East-West Institute in New York. He worked for RAND 1992-2001, with leave of absence to act as Director for Russia, Ukraine and Eurasian Affairs at the National Security Council 1999-2000.

Andre Vanhaeverbeke

Dr Vanhaeverbeke, a Belgian, has recently retired as Head of the European Commission Delegation in Kiev. He has worked for the Commission since 1970, including as Head of the EC Delegations in Guinea, Zimbabwe, Mali and Senegal.

Andrew Wilson

Dr Wilson is Senior Lecturer in Ukrainian Studies at the School of Slavonic and East European Studies, University College London. His most recent book is "The Ukrainians. Unexpected Nation" (Yale University Press, 2000).

Roman Wolczuk

Mr Wolczuk is a researcher at the University of Wolverhampton. He has written extensively on Ukrainian foreign policy, especially relations with Poland and Romania, and has a book coming out in 2002 entitled "Ukrainian Foreign and Security Policy: The Regional Dimension".

Anatoliy Zlenko

Mr Zlenko has been Minister for Foreign Affairs of Ukraine since October 2000. He is a career diplomat whose earlier posts have included Ambassador to France and Portugal and Permanent Representative of Ukraine to the UN. He also served as Foreign Minister 1990-94.

Notes on TEPSA and the British Embassy Seminar Series

TEPSA

TEPSA (Trans European Policy Studies Association) was established in 1974. It is an independent, non-profit making research and academic network aiming at the promotion of international research on European integration in order to stimulate discussion on policies and political options for Europe. TEPSA links affiliated national research institutes from all European Union Member States and from the candidate countries. TEPSA projects include research, studies and conference series commissioned by the European institutions, foundations and national public and private authorities.

British Embassy Seminar Series

The British Embassy Seminar Series is organised by the British Embassy, Brussels. It aims to address a wide range of contemporary European policy themes through seminars, round table discussions, debates and talks. In the near future, it also hopes to host a series of internet debates on Europe.